# The New Carry-Out Cuisine

ALSO BY PHYLLIS MÉRAS

*First Spring: A Martha's Vineyard Journal*
*A Yankee Way with Wood*
*Miniatures: How to Make Them, Use Them, Sell Them*
*Vacation Crafts*
*Christmas Angels* (with Juliana Turkevich)
*The Mermaids of Chenonceaux and 828 Other Tales:*
    *An Anecdotal Guide to Europe*
*Carry-Out Cuisine* (with Frances Tenenbaum)

# The New Carry-Out Cuisine

by PHYLLIS MÉRAS

with LINDA GLICK CONWAY

HOUGHTON
MIFFLIN
COMPANY
BOSTON

For information about permission to reproduce selections
from this book, write to Permissions, Houghton Mifflin
Company, 2 Park Street, Boston, Massachusetts 02108.

*Library of Congress Cataloging-in-Publication Data*

Méras, Phyllis.
  The new carry-out cuisine.

  Sequel to: Carry-out cuisine / Phyllis Méras with Frances
Tenenbaum.
  Includes index.
  1. Cookery.  2. Grocery trade—United States.  I. Conway,
Linda Glick.  II. Title.  III. Title: New carryout cuisine.
T X652.M453     1986        641.5        86-10668
ISBN 0-395-40427-4
ISBN 0-395-42504-2 (pbk.)

Printed in the United States of America

CRW  13  12  11  10  9  8  7  6  5

The decorations in this book, taken from stencils used in the
interiors of Pennsylvania Railroad coaches in the 1920s and 1930s,
come from the collection of Edward H. Bowers, a designer and
painter for the railroad. These designs and more can be found in
*A Treasury of Stencil Designs for Artists and Craftsmen*, edited and
with an introduction by Martin J. Isaacson and Dorothy A. Rennie
(New York: Dover Publications, 1976).

*To Frances Tenenbaum,*
*patient editor and friend*

## ACKNOWLEDGMENTS

For their assistance in gathering material for this book, we are grateful to Susan Anderson, Beatrice Bentz, Helena Bentz, Stephanie Bruno, Eileen Chambers, Deborah Christiansen, Jeanne L. Conway, Beth Wickenberg Ely, Beatrice Freeman, Yvonne S. Hacker, Barbara Hess, Henrietta Humphreys, Kay Kahle, Norene K. Lahr, Beatrice MacDonald, Carol Mattson, Leslie Méras, Ida Millman, Joan Noone, Georgia O'Connor, Erma Perry, Virginia Poole, Patricia Rich, Prue Salasky, Margaret Sheridan, Regina W. Skaggs, Marilyn Doorn Staats, Janet Steinberg, Judy Thorne, Robert Tolf, Juliana Turkevich, and Katherine Williams.

# CONTENTS

# INTRODUCTION

In 1982, when we published the first *Carry-Out Cuisine*, the gourmet take-out food business was not yet a phenomenon. To many, it seemed like another trendy development that some social arbiter declares "out" just as the rest of us discover that it's "in." As we collected recipes from friendly and generous shop owners, we worried that they might not be in business by the time the book came out.

Four years later, gourmet take-out has become a way of life for people who love good food but who haven't the time to sit over lengthy restaurant lunches or the energy to cook dinner after work. As they eliminate the drudgery of daily meal preparation, these same people like to cook for fun—and friends—over the weekend (although few of them go as far as the Washington businessman who, faced with the typical fast-food alternative to the two-hour restaurant lunch, opened his own gourmet shop).

In 1982, we thought 67 shops was a lot to include in our book. In *The New Carry-Out Cuisine*, it has not been easy limiting the number to 113. About one third are old friends (with all new recipes, of course); the rest are new acquaintances. Earlier the take-out food counters were located in specialty food shops, like The Silver Palate, or groceries, like Balducci's, but today they are also to be found in cafés and restaurants. As this trend increases the variety of take-out foods available to shoppers, happily it has also expanded the repertoire of recipes in *The New Carry-Out Cuisine*.

The 330 recipes you'll find here reflect the latest trends in good eating. Because regional American cooking remains highly popular, we have New Orleans Cajun Gumbo, Maryland Back-fin Crab Imperial, Georgia Pecan Peach Tart, Conch Fritters from the Florida Keys, Green Chili Beef Soup from Santa Fe. Throughout the book you will find recipes calling for interesting new ingredients that have become widely available—wild mushrooms, cilantro, peppers of all kinds, miniature vegetables, Vidalia onions, sun-dried tomatoes, and still more pasta, as fusilli begins to overtake tortellini.

There is a move back to home cooking but with a twist, to please educated palates, so we offer Not Your Mother's Macaroni and Cheese, Arborio Rice Pudding, Amaretto Bread Pudding, and muffins and scones galore. A number of new, unfailingly popular pasta and chicken salads and brownies are also included. International cuisine is still a favorite, and we recommend Oriental Duck Salad, Chicken Empanadas, Afghani Lamb with Spinach, Moroccan Lamb Kebabs, Potato Salad Madagascar, and that delectable Italian dessert, Tiramisu. For the calorie-conscious there are several "enlightened" recipes and a wealth of salads.

Once again it has been a pleasure to meet the owners, managers, and chefs of these shops and restaurants—sophisticated people whose training most often has been outside the food field but whose love of good eating has lured them away from teaching, social work, banking, architecture, and government work, into the kitchen, where their creativity bears immediate and satisfying results.

All of the recipes have been tested and edited for style and consistency, but we have let the recommendations of the individual chefs stand, which means there are several methods for making pie crust or handling phyllo, for example—all workable. Although most of the recipes serve from six to eight people, several are suitable for a crowd. And since the shops prepare most of these dishes in advance, you too will find them perfect to make ahead for entertaining.

Whether your goal is to feed yourself and your family well, to have fun in the kitchen, or to entertain your friends in the manner to which they have become accustomed, *bon appétit!*

PHYLLIS MÉRAS
LINDA GLICK CONWAY

# A REGIONAL LISTING OF SHOPS AND RECIPES

A Regional Listing of Shops and Recipes

A Regional Listing of Shops and Recipes

A Regional Listing of Shops and Recipes

A Regional Listing of Shops and Recipes

A Regional Listing of Shops and Recipes

# PART 1

—

# STARTERS
# AND LUNCHES

—

### APPETIZERS

### SOUPS

### LIGHT FARE

Antipasto Verde

Guacamole

Salsa

Eggplant Appetizer

Bacon Dill Dip

Spinach Crab Spread

Baba Ghanooj

Red Pepper Spread

Mushroom Pâté

Spinach and Artichoke Dip

Spicy Peanut Sauce

Pan-Fried Onion Dip

Cocktail Shrimp

Shrimp Grilled with Mustard Dill Sauce

Glazed Brie

Cheese Madeleines

Mango Chutney Pinwheels

Artichoke Squares

Caviar Éclairs

Gougères

Hot Hot Jalapeño Mustard Cheese Puffs

Porcini Puffs

Mozzarella Cheese Puffs

Sun-Dried Tomato and Cheese Strudel Logs

Buttermilk Biscuits with Virginia Ham and
    Fresh Figs

Conch Fritters

Pickled Fish

Smoked Salmon and Endive

Champagne Seafood-Stuffed Artichokes

Smoked Trout Mousse

Mussels Dijon

Baked Stuffed Quahaugs

Smoked Trout and Cucumbers

Sun-Dried Tomatoes with Basil and Mozzarella
    di Bufala

Goat Cheese Cheesecake

Amaretto Apricots with Walnuts Teriyaki

## ANTIPASTO VERDE

*Makes 2 cups*

2 large bunches parsley, trimmed of stems
2 large cloves garlic
2 tablespoons capers, drained and rinsed
½ medium onion, quartered
2 ounces anchovy fillets
1 teaspoon pepper
¾ cup olive oil
2 tablespoons balsamic vinegar
2 tablespoons red wine vinegar
2 hard-boiled eggs, coarsely chopped

Finely chop the parsley in a food processor. Add the garlic, capers, onion, anchovies, and pepper, and pulse until everything is finely chopped. With the processor running, slowly add the oil and vinegars and process until the mixture is smooth. Transfer the mixture to a bowl and fold in the egg.

NOTE: This dip may be prepared a day in advance (though the chopped egg should not be added until serving time). All manner of crudités may be used, but some suggested ones are strips of sweet red pepper, cauliflower flowerets, bread sticks, and steamed new potatoes with the skins left on.

## FETTUCCINE BROS.

—

### SAN FRANCISCO

*The Fettuccine "brothers" are really partners Bob Battaglia and Don Woodall, owners of 3 take-out shops, one of which, atop Russian Hill, includes a small café. Homemade pasta, needless to say, is the house specialty. They also sell all the trimmings for an Italian meal, including this dip for crudités.*

FISHER
& LEVY
—
NEW YORK CITY

*It was serendipitous, the encounter of Chip Fisher, Harvard '79, with Doug Levy, Pratt Institute '74. When Chip was at Harvard, the bland food that the university served had driven him out to explore the restaurants of Cambridge and Boston. Doug worked part-time in a restaurant while he studied, and that had whetted his appetite, so to speak, for preparing good food. When the pair met in New York through a mutual friend, a joint food venture was the natural outcome.*

## GUACAMOLE

*Serves 4 to 6*

2 to 3 Haas avocados (or other large California avocados)
1 beefsteak tomato (about 1 pound), diced
1 small red onion, diced
¼ to ½ cup diced scallions
2 teaspoons minced garlic
2 teaspoons minced cilantro (fresh coriander)
2 teaspoons ground cumin
¼ to ½ cup lemon juice
1 ounce canned jalapeño or hot cherry peppers, minced
1 teaspoon salt
¼ teaspoon pepper

Peel the avocados, remove the pits, and mash the avocado flesh. (If the avocados are small, use 3; if large, 2.) Add all the other ingredients and mix thoroughly. Chill well and serve as a dip with taco chips. Refrigerated, this guacamole should last 2 to 3 days.

## SALSA

*Makes 1½ cups*

1 14-ounce can tomatoes
¼ medium onion, coarsely chopped
1 clove garlic
½ teaspoon oregano
⅛ teaspoon ground cumin
⅛ teaspoon ground coriander
1 teaspoon red pepper flakes
½ pod small, whole dried chili pepper
1 whole canned jalapeño pepper

Put all the ingredients in a food processor and pulse until the mixture is homogenized but not yet a juice.

## EGGPLANT APPETIZER

*Serves 25 as part of an antipasto*

4 pounds eggplant, peeled
4 tablespoons salt
2 cups white vinegar
2 cups water
Half of a 16-ounce jar of hot cherry peppers, finely
    chopped
1 4-ounce can mushroom stems and pieces
1 6-ounce can pitted black olives, sliced
¼ teaspoon oregano
2 cloves garlic, chopped
1 2-ounce jar pimientos, chopped
¾ to 1 cup olive oil

Cut the eggplant into matchstick-size pieces about 3 inches long. Sprinkle the salt over the slivers and let them sit for 1 hour. Drain them and gently squeeze some of the moisture out.

### THE WINERY
—
SANTA FE

*Though salsa and tortilla-style corn chips are the natural prelude to any Mexican meal, the sauce also makes a wonderful addition to a cheese omelet and, thinned with oil, can be used as a salad dressing.*

### CAMPBELL AND CO.
—
BOCA RATON, FLORIDA

*Campbell and Co. are Faun Campbell and her son Gregory, whose catering and carry-out shop makes a specialty of appetizers. There's hardly a party in Boca Raton where you don't have a chance to sample a Campbell and Co. hors d'oeuvre.*

Bring the vinegar and water to a boil and add the eggplant. Remove the pan from the heat and let it stand for 3 minutes, then drain the eggplant and spread it on dry dishtowels to cool.

Combine the eggplant with the cherry peppers, mushrooms, black olives, oregano, garlic, and pimientos in a bowl. Toss until they are well mixed. Add the olive oil and cover. Refrigerate for at least 24 hours. Serve the appetizer on slices of Italian bread or as part of an antipasto tray.

## BACON DILL DIP

*Makes 4 cups*

¼ pound sliced Black Forest bacon
3 8-ounce packages cream cheese, softened
1 cup sour cream
¼ cup chopped fresh chives
¼ cup snipped fresh dill
Salt and pepper to taste

Sauté the bacon until crisp, drain it, and crumble it into fine pieces. In a food processor, whip the cream cheese until it is smooth. Add the sour cream, chives, dill, and bacon. Process for a few seconds. (Do not overwork or the mixture will be too thin.) Add salt and pepper to taste. Serve with chips or crackers or use in place of mayonnaise as a sandwich spread.

## SAMMY'S TENTH STREET MARKET

—

CLEVELAND

*Sammy's Restaurant and Tenth Street Market are a joint operation housed in a renovated warehouse in an area of downtown Cleveland known as the Flats. Sammy's Restaurant overlooks the Cuyahoga River, with a panoramic view of boats and bridges.*

## SPINACH CRAB SPREAD

*Makes 3 cups*

2 8-ounce packages cream cheese
1 10-ounce package frozen spinach, thawed and
    drained
2 tablespoons dried dill, or 4 tablespoons fresh dill
2 large shallots, finely chopped
1 bouillon cube, crushed
1 teaspoon cayenne pepper
½ pound fresh or frozen crabmeat (thawed if
    frozen)

Soften the cheese and add all the ingredients except the crabmeat. Mix well. Fold in the crabmeat. Serve on a bed of lettuce leaves with crisp
toast.

NOTE: To transform this spread into a dip, add
¼ cup sour cream.

## BABA GHANOOJ

*Makes 5 cups*

2 large eggplants
4 cloves garlic, minced
¼ cup fresh lemon juice
½ cup tahini
1 tablespoon mayonnaise
2 tablespoons chopped fresh parsley
1 tablespoon olive oil
Pinch each of ground cumin and cayenne pepper
Salt and pepper to taste
1 tomato, diced
Chopped parsley and chopped tomato for garnish

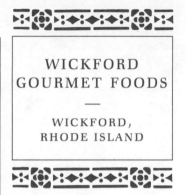

## WICKFORD GOURMET FOODS

—

WICKFORD,
RHODE ISLAND

*Wickford, on Narragansett
Bay, is a charming colonial
town—just the place to
attract two former Rhode
Islanders, Joe and Donna
Dubé, when they got home-
sick after years spent in
other parts of the country.
They also liked the idea of
working together on their
own enterprise.*

## POULET

—

BERKELEY

*Poulet is located in a
section of Berkeley
affectionately known as
"Gourmet Gulch." Chez
Panisse is two blocks away,
and right down the street is
Cocolat, chocolatier par
excellence.*

Prick the eggplants all over with a fork and roast them in a 400° oven for about 40 minutes. When the eggplants are cool enough to handle, peel them and let them drain. Chop the eggplants until almost a purée and add all the remaining ingredients except the diced tomato. Add the tomato just before serving. Top with a garnish of chopped parsley and tomato. Serve the *baba ghanooj* with pita bread as an hors d'oeuvre or on a bed of lettuce as a first course. It will keep for a week in the refrigerator.

## MITCHELL COBEY CUISINE

—

### CHICAGO

RED PEPPER PASTE

To make the Red Pepper Paste called for in the recipe, purée 3 chopped sweet red peppers in a food processor. If the mixture seems too watery, cook it down to a paste over low heat.

## *RED PEPPER SPREAD*

*Makes 2¾ cups*

⅓ cup finely chopped walnuts
½ cup fine fresh breadcrumbs
1 cup olive oil
Juice of 2 lemons
1 tablespoon concentrated pomegranate juice
    (available at Middle Eastern markets), optional
1 teaspoon ground cumin
1 teaspoon cinnamon
1 teaspoon sugar
⅓ cup Red Pepper Paste (see recipe)
1 tablespoon paprika mixed with ¼ cup water
Salt and pepper to taste

In a medium-size bowl, mix together all the ingredients, blending until smooth. Chill for 3 to 4 hours. Taste, and adjust the seasonings. Serve as a dip with pita bread or lavosh (Armenian cracker bread), or as a condiment with cold meat. The dip may also be used as a sandwich spread.

## MUSHROOM PÂTÉ

*Serves 6*

1 shallot, minced
½ pound mushrooms, finely chopped
4½ tablespoons unsalted butter, softened
½ teaspoon lemon juice
¼ cup chopped walnuts
½ teaspoon Tabasco
Salt to taste
Chopped fresh parsley for garnish

Sauté the minced shallot and chopped mushrooms in 2 tablespoons of the butter. Cook over low heat for 30 minutes or until all the liquid is absorbed. Chill. Add the lemon juice, walnuts, Tabasco, and the remaining 2½ tablespoons of butter. Add salt to taste. Transfer the mixture to a small crock, let it come to room temperature, smooth the surface, top with chopped parsley, and serve.

NOTE: This piquant pâté also makes an unusual stuffing for boneless chicken breasts.

### ADELAIDE'S CARRY-OUT CUISINE
—
ATLANTA

*John Wilson opened Adelaide's Carry-Out Cuisine in 1985 after searching for the right location for more than a year. The one he found was in the heart of Atlanta's Buckhead area in an elite shopping mall with cobblestone streets, wrought iron streetlamps, and a European air. His neighbors include an Emilio Pucci boutique, and some of his customers carry home their carry-out in their Rolls-Royces.*

## CULINARY CAPERS

—

PROVIDENCE

*When Rosalind Rustigian isn't busy running Culinary Capers, she's up the street a few blocks selling Oriental rugs at the shop that she inherited from her father. This spinach and artichoke dip is popular at faculty cocktail parties at nearby Brown University and the Rhode Island School of Design.*

## SPINACH AND ARTICHOKE DIP

*Makes 3 cups*

1 10-ounce package frozen chopped spinach,
    thawed and squeezed dry
1 14-ounce can artichoke hearts
1 cup good-quality or homemade mayonnaise
1 teaspoon chopped fresh dill
1 clove garlic, chopped
Juice of 1 lemon
Salt and pepper to taste

Process the spinach and the artichokes in a food processor until they are coarsely chopped. Add the remaining ingredients and process the mixture until it is smooth. Adjust the seasonings to taste. Use as a dip for raw vegetables or as a spread for sandwiches. It is also excellent as a sauce for cold fish or seafood.

## SPICY PEANUT SAUCE

*Makes 2½ cups*

¼ cup tea, cooled
¼ cup red wine vinegar
¼ cup soy sauce
1 cup smooth peanut butter
2 tablespoons sesame oil
1 cup mayonnaise
2 teaspoons Dijon mustard
¼ teaspoon cayenne pepper
1 tablespoon chili paste with garlic (available in
    Oriental markets)

Combine the tea, vinegar, and soy sauce. Slowly mix them with the peanut butter until smooth. Drizzle the sesame oil into the peanut butter mixture. Add the mayonnaise, mustard, and cayenne. Blend in the chili paste slowly. Refrigerate until ready to use. (Tightly covered, the sauce will keep for up to two weeks.)

## PAN-FRIED ONION DIP

*Makes 2 cups*

1 large Spanish onion
1 tablespoon butter
1 tablespoon peanut oil
Pinch of cayenne pepper
¾ cup sour cream
¾ cup mayonnaise
Salt and pepper to taste

Peel and quarter the onion with one vertical cut and one horizontal cut, and slice each quarter

INDIANA
MARKET
& CATERING

—

NEW YORK CITY

*Here is an unusual dip for raw vegetables that may also be used as a sauce for Oriental noodles or a dressing for chicken salad.*

BAREFOOT
CONTESSA

—

EAST HAMPTON,
LONG ISLAND

*The caramelized onions in this dip give it a rich, slightly sweet flavor. Be*

*prepared to wait 20 minutes or more for the onions to turn brown and syrupy. Stir them frequently while they cook.*

MATTERS
OF TASTE
—
ATLANTA

*Matters of Taste is one of the smallest carry-out shops in Atlanta and one of the most popular. Pamela Peterson gave up teach-ing school six years ago to open her own food shop. Her devoted customers say she does home cooking with just the right touch of the gourmet.*

into thin strips. Sauté the onion in the butter and oil until caramelized, about 20 minutes. Cool. Add the remaining ingredients and mix well. Chill for 1 hour. Serve the dip with crudités, crackers, or tortilla chips.

## COCKTAIL SHRIMP

*Makes 2 cups (serves 4 to 6)*

½ pound medium shrimp, peeled and deveined
1 cup cocktail sauce
⅓ cup minced scallions
½ cup grated Parmesan cheese
⅓ cup minced green pepper
1 pound cream cheese, softened

Drop the shrimp into boiling salted water and cook for 1 to 2 minutes, or until they turn bright pink. Drain and roughly chop the shrimp.

Combine the remaining ingredients. Fold in the chopped shrimp and refrigerate. Serve with crackers, celery sticks, or cucumber rounds.

## SHRIMP GRILLED WITH MUSTARD DILL SAUCE

*Serves 6 to 8*

2 egg yolks
¼ cup Dijon mustard
4½ teaspoons red wine vinegar
1½ cups safflower oil
¼ cup fresh dill (do *not* substitute dried)
Salt and pepper to taste
2 pounds large shrimp (10 to 14 to the pound)

Place the egg yolks, mustard, and vinegar in a food processor and process for 30 seconds. Slowly dribble in the oil through the feed tube. When the oil is incorporated, add the dill and process for another 30 seconds. Add salt and pepper to taste.

Peel and devein the shrimp, leaving the tails intact. Thread the shrimp on cocktail skewers and brush with some of the mustard sauce. Let the shrimp sit at room temperature for 1 hour. Brush again with the sauce.

Grill the shrimp over white-hot coals for about 7 minutes, or until they are firm. Do not let the shrimp curl or they will be overdone and tough. Serve immediately on a tray garnished with sprigs of dill. Pass additional sauce for dipping.

## FROM GRAPES TO NUTS

—

### BAINBRIDGE, OHIO

Grapes *to nuts? That's because Karen and Michael Small started out with a wine and liquor business, now expanded to include a thriving carry-out and small restaurant operation. Their shop is in a rambling old house in the small town of Bainbridge, east of Cleveland.*

## CULINARY
## CAPERS

—

### PROVIDENCE

*Paisley and hanging baskets
give this shop on Provi-
dence's fashionable East
Side a country kitchen air.
Chef Laurence Srebrenick
garnishes this Brie ap-
petizer according to the
season.*

## GLAZED BRIE

*Serves 20 to 25*

½ cup almonds
¼ cup pecans
¼ cup walnuts
½ teaspoon cinnamon
¼ teaspoon ginger
Pinch each of nutmeg and allspice
¾ cup light brown sugar
1 to 3 tablespoons water
1 12-inch round Brie
Dried apricots and figs for garnish

Put the nuts, spices, and sugar into a food processor and process the combination until the
nuts are finely ground. Add 1 tablespoon of water
and process. If the mixture does not hold together, add another tablespoon of water. The
mixture should be moist but not runny. Spread
it on the Brie.

Place the Brie under the broiler, but watch it
constantly. Broil until the topping is slightly
browned, then remove the wheel from the broiler
and decorate it with the apricots and figs. Serve
with crackers and fruit.

## CHEESE MADELEINES

*Serves 8 to 10*

4 tablespoons unsalted butter
2 ounces blue cheese
2 8-ounce packages cream cheese
⅔ cup sour cream
3 eggs
1 teaspoon Herbes de Provence
2 teaspoons minced fresh dill
1 teaspoon salt
½ teaspoon pepper
½ cup melted butter
1 cup fine browned breadcrumbs

In a food processor, process the butter, blue cheese, and cream cheese until smooth. Add the sour cream, eggs, herbs, salt, and pepper, and process.

Brush the madeleine pans with the melted butter. Shake the finely ground breadcrumbs into them; then shake out any excess. Refrigerate the pans for 5 minutes before filling them. Fill the molds two-thirds full and bake in a 425° oven until puffed and brown on the top, about 10 minutes. Allow the madeleines to cool in the molds for 5 minutes before turning them out. Serve warm or at room temperature.

### TAKE ME HOME
### —
### WASHINGTON, D.C.

*Many herb and spice racks are graced with those little terra cotta jars of Herbes de Provence, mementos of trips to southern France. The fragrant mixture is a blend of thyme, basil, savory, fennel, and lavender flowers. This elegant hors d'oeuvre, flavored with Herbes de Provence, is especially nice served with champagne or a fine white wine. Surely Proust would approve!*

GERARD'S

—

PHILADELPHIA

*Gerard Greway got his start back in 1973 with a little meat market he opened in Huntington Valley, a residential suburb of Philadelphia. Now he has four shops, including one on South Street in the restored section of Philadelphia. He carries everything one could want for sophisticated, no-work dining at home.*

## MANGO CHUTNEY PINWHEELS

*Serves 6*

4 ounces Montrachet cheese
⅓ cup mango chutney
12 slices prosciutto, turkey, or ham (or 4 slices of
   each)

Combine the cheese and the chutney in a food processor, and process them for about half a minute or until the mixture is fairly smooth.

Lay out each piece of meat and spread the cheese mixture thinly on one side. With the short end toward you, roll the meat tightly. Cut each roll into three pieces crosswise and arrange them attractively on a serving platter.

## ARTICHOKE SQUARES

*Serves 20*

2 6-ounce jars marinated artichokes
1 small onion, finely chopped
1 clove garlic, minced
4 eggs
¼ cup dry breadcrumbs
⅛ teaspoon pepper
⅛ teaspoon oregano
⅛ teaspoon Tabasco
2 tablespoons chopped fresh parsley
½ pound Cheddar cheese, grated

Drain the oil from one jar of the artichokes into a frying pan. Discard the oil from the other jar. Chop the artichokes and set them aside. Sauté the onions and garlic in the oil.

Beat the eggs in a small bowl until they are frothy. Add the breadcrumbs and seasonings. Stir in the cheese, artichokes, and sautéed onion. Turn the mixture into a buttered 7-by-11-inch pan and bake at 350° for 30 minutes. Cut into 1-inch squares and serve warm or at room temperature.

## CAVIAR ÉCLAIRS

*Serves 6*

PÂTE À CHOUX (ÉCLAIR BATTER)

3 tablespoons lightly salted butter
⅛ teaspoon salt
¼ cup water
¼ cup all-purpose flour
3 eggs

WICKFORD
GOURMET FOODS

—

WICKFORD,
RHODE ISLAND

LEONARDI'S
INTERNATIONAL,
INC.

—

FORT LAUDERDALE

Robert Leonardi has a
triple treat of a place in the
heart of Fort Lauderdale.
He offers carry-out cuisine,
has an extensive catering
operation, and runs a small
restaurant where patrons
feast on fresh pasta, fresh
fish, and sandwiches that
are real mouth-benders.
Among his appetizers are
these elegant caviar éclairs.

Put the butter, salt, and water in a 3-quart pan, and bring the mixture to a boil. Add the flour all at once, reduce the heat to medium, and stir the mixture constantly until the flour mixture becomes a ball with nothing sticking to the sides of the pan. Cool the mixture slightly. Add two of the eggs, one at a time, making sure that the first is well blended in before adding the second.

Remove the mixture from the pan. Using either a spoon or a pastry bag with a medium or large tip, spread or pipe the batter into 1½-inch-long strips onto a greased baking sheet. Top each with another strip of the same length to give each éclair its normal height. Repeat the process until all the *pâte* has been used up.

Brush the éclairs with the remaining egg, lightly beaten, and bake them at 375° for approximately 20 minutes, or until they are golden brown. Cool them on a rack.

FILLING

4 ounces whipped cream cheese
2 ounces sliced smoked salmon
⅜ cup sour cream
2 ounces black caviar
½ teaspoon chopped fresh dill
Black pepper to taste
½ teaspoon chopped fresh chives

Cut the puffs in half lengthwise. Arrange the filling on the bottom half of each éclair in exactly this order: cream cheese, strip of salmon, dab of sour cream, sprinkle of caviar, sprinkle of dill, black pepper, and chives. Cap the filling with the top part of the éclair. Serve immediately.

# GOUGÈRES

*Serves 8*

4 tablespoons unsalted butter
¼ teaspoon salt
¾ cup water
⅔ cup all-purpose flour
3 eggs
⅔ cup grated Gruyère (or other medium-flavored)
  cheese
¼ cup Gruyère (or other medium-flavored) cheese
  cut into ¼-inch cubes

Heat the butter, salt, and water in a saucepan.
When the butter is melted, remove the pan from
the heat and add the flour all at once. Heat the
mixture again, stirring it constantly with a
wooden spoon until the paste separates from the
pan. Remove the mixture from the stove and add
the eggs one at a time, mixing well after each
addition. Add the grated cheese.

Using a teaspoon, place the paste in little
piles on a buttered baking tin. (A pastry bag with
a plain tip may also be used.) The puffs should
be placed ½ inch apart.

Put several pieces of the little cheese cubes
on each pile of paste and bake in a 400° oven for
15 minutes. Reduce the oven to 350° and continue the baking for 15 minutes more, watching
carefully. Serve the puffs hot or cold.

## LE PETIT CHEF
—
### MINNEAPOLIS

*There's a European touch
to virtually all of the dishes
that French-born Jean-
Claude Tindillier prepares
in the kitchen of Le Petit
Chef. Easy to make, freeze,
and reheat, these bite-size
Gruyère puffs are ideal to
keep on hand in the
freezer.*

GERARD'S

—

PHILADELPHIA

*Cheeses from virtually everywhere in the world are a major attraction at Gerard's markets, and mustards from around the world are ranged on his display shelves, too. This appetizer, which Gerard praises as "a perfect one," combines mustard and two cheeses with juicy cherry tomatoes and crunchy alfalfa sprouts.*

## HOT HOT JALAPEÑO MUSTARD CHEESE PUFFS

*Serves 4*

1 thin medium-length baguette
⅓ cup Hot Hot Jalapeño Mustard or any jalapeño
  mustard
¼ cup grated Cheddar cheese
¼ cup grated Monterey Jack cheese
6 cherry tomatoes, halved
½ cup alfalfa sprouts

Cut the ends off the baguette and slice the rest of it into twelve ¾-inch slices. Spread mustard evenly on the slices. Then sprinkle each slice with Cheddar and Jack cheese, and top with half of a cherry tomato.

Lay the slices on tin foil, and put them under the broiler until the cheese is just melted. Sprinkle each slice with a few alfalfa sprouts.

## PORCINI PUFFS

*Makes 48 puffs*

½ cup dried porcini mushrooms, soaked in warm
    water for ½ hour and squeezed dry
2 scallions, including green tops, cut into 2-inch
    pieces
4 ounces Gruyère cheese, grated
⅔ cup water
⅓ cup plus 2 tablespoons milk
½ cup (1 stick) unsalted butter
1¼ teaspoons salt
Freshly ground pepper
½ teaspoon freshly ground nutmeg
1 cup all-purpose flour
4 large eggs
Glaze (1 large egg beaten with ½ teaspoon salt)

Mince the porcini and scallions in a food processor. Add the grated cheese; incorporate it by
turning the machine on and off about four times.
Set the mixture aside in another bowl and wipe
out the food processor bowl.

In a saucepan, bring the water, ⅓ cup of the
milk, butter, and seasonings to a boil, stirring to
melt the butter. Remove the pan from the heat.
Beat in the flour with a wooden spoon until the
mixture is well combined and leaves the sides of
the pan. Cook over moderate heat for 2 minutes,
stirring occasionally. Put the mixture in the bowl
of the food processor and add the 4 eggs. Process
for 30 seconds or until the eggs are incorporated
and the mixture is very thick and smooth. Add
the remaining 2 tablespoons of cold milk and
process for 7 seconds. Add the cheese and porcini mixture and process for 5 seconds.

Lightly butter two baking sheets and sprinkle
them with water, shaking off the excess. Spoon
the mixture into a 16-inch pastry bag fitted with

TASTE
UNLIMITED
—
NORFOLK, VIRGINIA

*Peter and Susan Coe were
pioneers in the specialty
food business in their area,
opening their first shop in
1973. They now have five
stores in Norfolk and
Virginia Beach, all slightly
different in emphasis but
offering similar take-out
menus. The Coes travel
extensively in the United
States and Europe and
make a broad selection of
American and European
ingredients available to
their customers.*

a ¾-inch tube. Pipe the pastry onto baking sheets in 1¼-inch rounds, cutting the pastry from the tube if necessary.

Make the glaze and brush it on the puffs, smoothing the tops. Bake the puffs in the lower half of the oven at 400° for 20 to 25 minutes, or until they are well browned. Transfer to racks to cool. The puffs are excellent plain, or they may be stuffed with chicken salad, ratatouille, chèvre and sun-dried tomatoes, mozzarella and green chilies, or a filling of your choice.

## MOZZARELLA CHEESE PUFFS

*Makes about 3 dozen*

1 cup all-purpose flour, sifted
¼ teaspoon salt
¼ teaspoon paprika
½ cup (1 stick) butter
6 ounces mozzarella, shredded

Sift the dry ingredients together. Cream the butter and cheese. Add the dry ingredients and mix well. Shape the mixture into small balls about 1 inch in diameter. Place them on a lightly greased baking sheet and bake them for 15 to 20 minutes at 350°. Serve hot.

---

### SI BON
—
SANIBEL,
FLORIDA

*When you want something special for a cocktail party but haven't much time to fuss, these cheese puffs are perfect.*

## SUN-DRIED TOMATO AND CHEESE STRUDEL LOGS

*Serves 6 to 8*

½ cup grated Parmesan cheese
½ pound mozzarella, chopped into small pieces
1 pound cream cheese
2 eggs
1 cup chopped sun-dried tomatoes
1 cup fresh basil leaves, cut into small pieces and
    loosely packed
2 cloves garlic, crushed
Salt and pepper to taste
2 sticks unsalted butter
1 1-pound box strudel (phyllo) leaves

Mix cheeses, eggs, sun-dried tomatoes, basil, garlic, salt, and pepper in a bowl. Melt the butter, and butter one side of a strudel leaf with a pastry brush. Put a second leaf on top of the first and brush it with melted butter. Continue until you have used four leaves.

Spread about 1 cup of the filling along the lower edge of the strudel leaves, ½ inch in from the edge, and roll up the leaves in jelly-roll fashion. Place on an ungreased baking sheet and butter the top. Repeat the process until all of the leaves have been used up.

Bake in a 350° oven for about 20 minutes or until brown. Slice and serve warm.

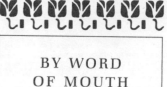

BY WORD
OF MOUTH
—
FORT LAUDERDALE

*Sun-dried tomatoes, packed in olive oil, are an expensive ingredient when bought by the jar, usually imported from Italy. But now you can buy the tomatoes dried, from California, Ohio, and other places in this country, at no more than you would pay for any dried fruit. Add your own olive oil to soften them.*

## AN APPLE
## A DAY

—

### GLENCOE, ILLINOIS

*In Glencoe, An Apple a Day is the place to go for all those foods you wish your mother really had made—crisp doughnuts, buttermilk biscuits, apple pie, rhubarb cobbler—homespun but truly delicious American foods.*

## BUTTERMILK BISCUITS WITH VIRGINIA HAM AND FRESH FIGS

*Makes 16 biscuits*

2 cups all-purpose flour
½ teaspoon salt
2 teaspoons baking powder
½ teaspoon baking soda
1 tablespoon sugar
½ cup vegetable shortening
⅔ cup buttermilk
Fresh figs
Smithfield or other country ham
Dijon or Dusseldorf mustard

Mix the first 5 ingredients together. With a pastry blender or 2 knives, cut in the shortening until it is pea-shaped. Add the buttermilk all at once and mix until it is just blended. Roll the dough to a thickness of ½ inch and cut the biscuits with a cutter or floured glass. Place the biscuits close together on an ungreased baking sheet and bake at 425° for 15 to 20 minutes.

Peel and slice enough fresh figs to cover the tops of the split biscuits. Slice the cooked ham very thin. Assemble by spreading the opened biscuits lightly with the mustard and topping the mustard with the fig slices and the ham.

## CONCH FRITTERS

*Makes 40 fritters*

1 pound conch meat
1 egg
½ cup milk
¾ teaspoon celery seed
½ teaspoon Tabasco
¼ teaspoon sage
½ cup minced onion
1⅓ cups all-purpose flour
2 teaspoons baking powder
1 teaspoon salt
Oil for frying

Coarsely grind the conch meat in a food processor and set it aside. In a bowl, beat together the egg and milk. Add the ground conch, celery seed, Tabasco, sage, and onion to the egg and milk mixture and combine well. Sift the flour, baking powder, and salt together and add to the conch mixture. Fold until the ingredients are combined; do not overbeat or the fritters will be tough.

Heat the oil to 350° and drop rounded tablespoonfuls of the batter into the oil. Fry the fritters until they are golden brown on all sides. Serve them with tartar sauce.

CAMPBELL
AND CO.

—

BOCA RATON,
FLORIDA

*In southern Florida, you never know what sort of party may be in prospect. Campbell and Co. once was asked to cater for a party dedicating a highway ramp —on the ramp. One of the appetizers they offered was this regional specialty.*

*When South African–born
Allan Sheer moved to
Atlanta and opened Sheer's
Simply Delicious in 1984, he
brought with him a num-
ber of recipes from his
birthplace. Among them is
this pickled fish that burns
the roof of your mouth a
little—but not too much.
Stored in the refrigerator
in a dish with a tight-fitting
lid, it will keep for about
two weeks.*

## PICKLED FISH

*Serves 12 to 16*

3 cups chicken stock
1 cup unsweetened coconut
4 tablespoons salad oil
2 medium onions, finely chopped
2 2-inch pieces fresh ginger root, peeled and
    finely chopped
1 clove garlic, finely chopped
2 red chili peppers, finely chopped
2 tablespoons smooth apricot jam
1 tablespoon flour
2 teaspoons turmeric
Salt to taste
2½ pounds fillet of snapper or grouper, cut in
    chunks and dipped in flour

Bring the stock to a boil. Put the coconut in a
bowl and pour the hot stock over it. Let it stand
for 30 minutes, then drain off the liquid and reserve it.

Heat half the oil in a frying pan and sauté the
onions, ginger, garlic, and chilies about 5 minutes, until they are lightly browned. Add the jam,
flour, turmeric, and liquid from the coconut. Season well with salt and simmer over low heat for
20 minutes.

Heat the remaining oil in another frying pan
and fry the chunks of fish on all sides until they
are lightly browned. Transfer them to a deep
dish. Pour the hot curry mixture over the fish and
let the dish stand at room temperature overnight.
Refrigerate in the morning.

## SMOKED SALMON AND ENDIVE

*Serves 6 to 8*

1 pound smoked salmon, diced
2 pounds fresh Belgian endives, cut into small pieces
¼ cup green peppercorns
¼ cup diced pimientos
2 tablespoons virgin olive oil
Bibb lettuce

Combine all the ingredients except the olive oil and lettuce in a large bowl and toss lightly. Sprinkle the olive oil on and mix again. Serve on a bed of Bibb lettuce.

## THE WATERGATE CHEFS
—
WASHINGTON, D.C.

*This is as pretty an appetizer as you could ask for—rosy with salmon, white with endive, and served on a bed of light green Bibb lettuce. It is the creation of Watergate chef Tim Wood and goes particularly well before a light fish or veal entrée.*

*Remember when carry-out meant fried chicken in a bucket? This dish, which combines champagne, artichokes, shrimp, scallops, and crabmeat, shows what a long way we've come. It makes an elegant first course for a special meal.*

## CHAMPAGNE SEAFOOD-STUFFED ARTICHOKES

*Serves 6*

2 tablespoons finely chopped shallots
½ cup champagne
½ pound medium shrimp, peeled and deveined
½ pound bay scallops
½ pound crabmeat
Salt and white pepper to taste
2 egg yolks
1½ cups olive oil
¼ cup champagne vinegar
¼ cup champagne mustard
6 artichokes, steamed, chokes removed, and chilled

Cook the shallots in a sauté pan in enough champagne to cover. When they are soft and translucent, add the shrimp, scallops, and the rest of the champagne. Cover the pan and cook for 4 to 5 minutes over medium heat until the shellfish are just cooked through. Remove from the heat and stir in the crabmeat. Add salt and white pepper to taste. Drain off any remaining liquid and chill the seafood mixture.

Prepare the dressing as you would mayonnaise: whisk the egg yolks until they are thick and lemon-colored, then slowly drizzle in the olive oil while you continue whisking. Slowly drizzle in the vinegar and mix in the mustard.

Combine the chilled seafood mixture with enough of the dressing to hold it together. Stuff the artichokes with the seafood. Serve the remaining dressing on the side.

## SMOKED TROUT MOUSSE

*Serves 8 to 10*

2 tablespoons lemon juice
1 small slice Spanish onion
1 envelope unflavored gelatin
½ cup boiling water
½ cup mayonnaise
10 ounces smoked trout or other white fish
1 tablespoon Dijon mustard
Tabasco to taste
1 cup heavy cream

Put the lemon juice in the blender with the onion. Empty the envelope of gelatin on top. Add the boiling water and blend the mixture for 40 seconds. Turn off the motor. Add the mayonnaise, trout, mustard, and Tabasco. Cover and blend. Add the cream, a third at a time, blending a few seconds after each addition. Pour the mousse into a 4-cup mold and chill. Unmold onto a bed of greens or watercress and serve with small rounds of rye bread or crackers.

## MUSSELS DIJON

*Serves 6*

4 cups water
2 cups white wine
1 cup combined coarsely chopped celery, carrots,
   and onions

### BON APPÉTIT

—

ATLANTA

*Bon Appétit owner Janice Shackelford likes to use Georgia products in her menus and on her shelves. Peaches, peanuts, pecans, poultry, Vidalia onions, Golden Isles shrimp from the islands around Savannah, mountain trout, and country ham are almost sure to be daily offerings. And Bon Appétit is one of the few shops in the state where you can order mayhaw jelly, made from a bright red berry (a little larger than a cranberry) that grows in wetlands along the Flint River in South Georgia.*

### NEUMAN & BOGDONOFF

—

NEW YORK CITY

6 pounds mussels, well scrubbed
6 large, firm sweet red peppers
½ cup cooking oil
2 cups sour cream
1 cup mayonnaise
½ cup Dijon mustard
Juice of 2 lemons
1 bunch Italian (flat) parsley, coarsely chopped
6 small heads Bibb lettuce

Put the water, wine, and coarsely chopped vegetables in a 6-quart pot with a tight-fitting lid and bring it to a rapid boil. Add the scrubbed mussels. Cover the pot and cook for 3 to 5 minutes, until the mussels are open. Take them out of the pot to drain and cool. When the mussels are cool enough to handle, remove the meat from the shells. Save a few of the shells, rinsing them well under running water if they are sandy.

Split the peppers in half lengthwise and remove the seeds. Rub the pepper halves inside and out with the cooking oil until they are lightly coated. Place them skin side up on a lightly oiled baking sheet. Roast them in a 475° oven until the meat is tender and the skin peels from the flesh easily, 15 to 30 minutes. Remove the peppers from the oven and cool them. Peel them and slice the meat into strips ¼ inch wide by 2 inches long.

Mix the sour cream, mayonnaise, mustard, lemon juice, and parsley. Add the mussels and peppers, reserving a quarter of the pepper strips to use as a garnish. Put a head of Bibb lettuce on each plate and make a place in the center for the mussels. Spoon the mussel mixture into the lettuce and decorate the plate with the reserved strips of pepper and mussel shells.

## BAKED STUFFED QUAHAUGS

*Serves 8*

1 quart shucked quahaugs and their liquid
2 slices bacon, cooked and crumbled
2½ cups breadcrumbs
3 tablespoons melted unsalted butter
¾ cup minced green pepper
¼ cup minced onion
¼ teaspoon white pepper
1 tablespoon fresh lemon juice
¼ cup minced celery

Finely chop or grind the quahaug meats, reserving their liquid. Combine the quahaugs with the other ingredients, using a little of the reserved liquid to moisten the mixture, but be sparing—a runny mixture will require a long period of cooking.

Into each quahaug shell or ramekin, spoon enough of the mixture to make a generous rounded portion. Put the filled shells on a baking tray. Cover them lightly with tin foil and bake them for 40 minutes in a 350° oven.

## POOLE'S
## FISH MARKET
—
MENEMSHA,
MASSACHUSETTS

*New Englanders call hard-shell clams quahaugs (pronounced quohogs). The smallest, delicious eaten raw on the half shell, are the littlenecks. Next come the cherrystones, and the largest are the chowder clams, often simply called quahaugs. According to Everett Poole, "The real reason Roger Williams was driven out of the Massachusetts Bay Colony was not religion but the fact that he couldn't spell quahaug correctly. Hence the Rhode Island version of the spelling (quahog), which reminds one of swine, when the name is actually of Indian origin."*

*The Epicure Shop at Neiman-Marcus in Dallas has been preeminent in the specialty food business for decades. Today Neiman-Marcus stores all over the country are bringing their customers both packaged gourmet foods and prepared dishes to take away. In Palo Alto and San Francisco the appetizers and salads are supplied by the team of Martha Perry and George Dolese, outside contractors whose Neiman-Marcus dishes are sold nowhere else.*

## SMOKED TROUT AND CUCUMBERS

*Serves 4*

5 medium smoked trout
2 or 3 English cucumbers
Lettuce
Lemon slices and fresh dill for garnish

DRESSING

½ cup virgin olive oil
½ cup peanut oil
¼ cup cider vinegar
¼ cup Dijon mustard
4 tablespoons chopped fresh dill, or 2 tablespoons
    dried dill
2 tablespoons honey
4½ teaspoons sugar
Salt and white pepper to taste

Remove the skin and bones from the trout, and break the meat into bite-size pieces. Place it in a bowl. Cut the tips off the cucumbers, then score the skins in vertical lines drawn every ¼ inch. Cut the cucumbers in half lengthwise, spoon out the seeds, and slice the cucumbers into thin half circles. Add them to the bowl with the trout.

Mix the dressing ingredients in a blender or food processor. Add the dressing gradually to the bowl with the trout and cucumber, tossing lightly to coat. As a first course, serve the salad on a leaf of lettuce and garnish with the lemon and fresh dill. The salad can be augmented with sliced fresh fruit to make a more substantial luncheon dish.

## SUN-DRIED TOMATOES WITH BASIL AND MOZZARELLA DI BUFALA

*Serves 6*

18 perfect leaves of fresh basil
1½ pounds Mozzarella di Bufala
18 pieces sun-dried tomato, packed in oil
Extra-virgin olive oil
Freshly ground black pepper
A fresh baguette

Wash the basil leaves carefully and drain them on paper towels. Place the leaves on a platter or on individual salad plates. Top each one with a slice of mozzarella and a piece of tomato. Sprinkle each with olive oil and pepper. Serve with slices of the baguette.

REX'S

—

SEATTLE

*A semisoft Italian cheese, mozzarella is more likely to come from a cow than a buffalo these days, though the genuine article, Mozzarella di Bufala, is still produced under stringent standards. If your grocer sells fresh basil leaves, this classic combination can be made at any time of the year, not just when the summer tomato crop has ripened on the vine.*

*Goat's milk cheeses are made in many parts of the world, and the flavors and consistency vary greatly from country to country— from the salty feta of Greece to the sweet gjetost of Norway. Recipes calling for "goat cheese" invariably mean the smooth and rich French chèvre or its increasingly available American counterpart. Chèvre comes in a variety of shapes (logs, pyramids, ovals) and with several different coatings (chestnut or grape leaves, oil marinade, ash, pepper, fragrant herbs).*

## GOAT CHEESE CHEESECAKE

*Serves 30 for cocktails, 15 to 16 as a first course*

CRUST

1½ cups fresh breadcrumbs
½ cup (1 stick) melted butter
3 tablespoons grated Parmesan cheese

Combine the breadcrumbs, melted butter, and Parmesan, and pat the mixture into the bottom of a 10-inch springform pan. Refrigerate it while you prepare the rest of the cheesecake.

FILLING

1¾ pounds cream cheese
4 eggs
⅓ cup half-and-half
1 cup sour cream
½ teaspoon salt
7 ounces uncoated goat cheese

Beat the cream cheese with a spoon until smooth. Add the eggs, followed by the half-and-half, sour cream, salt, and goat cheese. Beat well after each addition. Pour the mixture into the chilled crust and place the springform pan on a jelly-roll pan. Bake in a 325° oven for 1 hour. Turn off the oven, but let the cake remain in the oven for 30 minutes. Cool, remove from the pan, and then refrigerate.

## AMARETTO APRICOTS
## WITH WALNUTS TERIYAKI

*Makes approximately 50*

WALNUTS TERIYAKI

2 cups walnut halves
¼ cup soy sauce
3 tablespoons dark rum or *sake*
2 tablespoons sesame oil
1 clove garlic, crushed
1 teaspoon ground ginger
Tabasco to taste
1 tablespoon dark brown sugar
Kosher salt to taste

Spread the nuts on a jelly-roll pan. Combine the remaining ingredients, except the kosher salt, in a saucepan and heat until the sugar is dissolved. Pour the sauce over the nuts, making sure to coat them well. Bake at 350° for 20 minutes. Place the toasted nuts on lightly oiled foil and sprinkle with the salt.

ASSEMBLY

1 tablespoon Amaretto, or to taste
1 8-ounce package cream cheese, softened
1 pound dried apricot halves

Add the Amaretto to the cream cheese and mix well. Place a teaspoon of the cheese on each apricot and top with a walnut.

GOOD TASTE
—
BROOKLYN HEIGHTS,
NEW YORK

*This sweet and savory combination makes a nice change at cocktail time and works equally well on a dessert tray.*

## SOUPS

Harvest Pumpkin Soup
Red Pepper Soup
Double Mushroom Soup
Leek and Tomato Soup
Tomato Bisque
Roasted Eggplant Soup
Cheese Soup
Carrot Soup with Roquefort Cream
Sopa de Salsa
Broccoli Cheese Soup
Green Chili Beef Soup
Beth's Tortilla Soup
Red Bean and Lentil Soup
Black Bean Soup
Karen's Corn Chowder
Italian Sausage Soup
Sausage Cabbage Soup
Cabbage and Beef Borscht
New Orleans Cajun Gumbo
Bouillabaisse
Shellfish Stew with Ouzo
Bayou Fisherman's Soup
Crab Vegetable Soup
Curried Crab Bisque
Curried Apple Soup
Minted Pea Soup
Spinach Vichyssoise
Cold Tomato Soup
Senegalese Soup
Cold Cantaloupe Soup
Brandied Peach Soup

## HARVEST PUMPKIN SOUP

*Serves 8*

2 tablespoons minced shallots
1 medium onion, chopped
7 tablespoons unsalted butter
2½ pounds pumpkin, peeled and diced (or 3 cups
    pumpkin purée)
6 cups chicken stock
3 tablespoons flour
½ teaspoon salt or to taste
2 cups heavy cream
Freshly ground nutmeg
Sherry or port (optional)

In a heavy soup pot, sauté the shallots and onion in 4 tablespoons of the butter until they are transparent. Add the pumpkin and chicken stock. Bring to a boil, then lower to simmer and cook until the pumpkin is soft. (If you are using purée, simmer the mixture for 10 minutes.) Sieve the soup to remove any lumps of pumpkin and the bits of onion. Return the soup to the pot and set it over low heat.

Make a roux by melting the remaining 3 tablespoons of butter, adding the flour, and cooking, stirring constantly, for 3 or 4 minutes. When the soup is hot, whisk in the roux. Stirring constantly, bring the soup to a boil. The soup will thicken. Add salt to taste. Just before serving, add 1 cup of the cream; for a richer soup, add 4 tablespoons of butter.

For a garnish, whip the remaining cream in a chilled bowl and salt it lightly. Serve the soup in warm bowls or in a medium-size pumpkin shell that has been scraped clean. Top with a dollop of the salted cream and a dash of nutmeg.

NOTE: The soup may be partially prepared the

### THE ELEGANT PICNIC

—

LENOX,
MASSACHUSETTS

*Although Ted Weiant's busiest season is summer, when the Boston Symphony Orchestra is in residence at its Tanglewood performance center, autumn in Berkshire County is also a very special time. This soup is marvelous for a leaf-watching picnic. When there is a nip in the air, or even when there isn't, you might want to add a shot of shooting sherry or aged port. If you like the idea of "putting foods by," get several fresh pumpkins in the fall and freeze or can the purée for use throughout the winter.*

day before. Refrigerate the sieved pumpkin-stock mixture and do the thickening and finishing the next day.

*These days, much of the green pepper crop is being left on the vine to turn red and sweet. No longer just used as a spot of color on an antipasto tray, red peppers are turning up in dips, soups, salads, and vegetable side dishes.*

## RED PEPPER SOUP

*Serves 10 to 12*

1 small potato, peeled and cut into ½-inch pieces
2 stalks celery, chopped
1 carrot, chopped
1 small onion, chopped
1 clove garlic, minced
4 tablespoons butter
6 sweet red peppers, seeded and cut into 1-inch chunks
1½ teaspoons green peppercorns
6 cups chicken stock
1 bay leaf
4 cups heavy cream
Salt and pepper to taste

Sauté the potato, celery, carrot, onion, and garlic in the butter over low heat for 5 minutes, or until the vegetables are tender. Add the peppers, green peppercorns, chicken stock, and bay leaf and boil until reduced by approximately one third. Purée the mixture in batches in a blender or food processor. Strain the mixture and add the cream. Bring to a boil, remove from the heat, and add salt and pepper to taste.

## DOUBLE MUSHROOM SOUP

*Serves 6*

1 cup boiling water
½ to 1 ounce dried mushrooms (cèpes, porcini, or morels)
4 tablespoons butter
2 cloves garlic, minced
1 onion, minced
1 sweet red pepper, in ¼-inch dice
2 stalks celery, in ¼-inch dice
2 carrots, in ¼-inch dice
1 pound mushrooms, stems chopped and caps sliced
½ cup flour
8 cups hot chicken or beef stock (preferably homemade)
1 bay leaf
1 teaspoon salt
1 teaspoon freshly ground pepper
1 teaspoon dried chervil

Pour boiling water over the dried mushrooms and soak for 30 minutes. Drain off and reserve the liquid, and chop the mushrooms. Set the liquid and mushrooms aside.

Melt the butter in a heavy soup pot and sauté the garlic and onion for 10 minutes. Add the red pepper, celery, carrots, and mushrooms and cook for 15 minutes. Sprinkle the flour over the vegetable mixture and mix until it is absorbed. Gradually add the hot stock, stirring constantly. Add the remaining ingredients and the reserved dried mushrooms and their liquid, and simmer the soup for 30 minutes. Serve it piping hot.

LET'S EAT

—

TIBURON,
CALIFORNIA

Boletus edulis *is the mushroom species that goes by several popular names—porcini, cèpes, king bolete, or Steinpilz. These mushrooms are usually found dried. Since they grow in warm, wet weather, it's not easy to get them to the market in good condition. Morels are available fresh in early spring, dried the rest of the year.*

## REX'S
—
SEATTLE

*Seattle's Pike Place Public Market is a bustling mix of local residents who come to buy their fresh fruits and vegetables and straight-from-the-Pacific fish and of tourists entranced with the market's picturesque quality. Built at Pike and Virginia streets in 1907, the market is now a historic site.*

## *LEEK AND TOMATO SOUP*

*Serves 6 to 8*

6 leeks, white part only
3 medium onions, thinly sliced
5 cloves garlic, finely minced
½ cup (1 stick) butter
½ cup all-purpose flour
4 cups half-and-half
32 ounces canned tomatoes, drained and diced
    (reserve juice to thin soup if necessary)
½ cup white wine
4 tablespoons chopped fresh basil
2 tablespoons chopped fresh parsley
2 tablespoons grated Parmesan cheese
2 tablespoons grated Romano cheese
Salt and pepper to taste

Cut the leeks in half lengthwise and rinse them well, then slice them thinly crosswise. Sauté them with the onions and garlic in the butter. Add the flour and stir 3 minutes. Gradually whisk in the half-and-half. Continue to whisk until the mixture thickens and comes to a boil.

Meanwhile, heat the tomatoes with the white wine. When the mixture simmers, add it to the leek-onion mixture. Add the basil and parsley, the two cheeses, and salt and pepper to taste. Serve hot with a little cheese sprinkled on top.

## TOMATO BISQUE

*Serves 6*

2 medium onions, chopped
2 large cloves garlic, minced
4 tablespoons butter
1 28-ounce can whole tomatoes
1 46-ounce can tomato juice
2 bay leaves
1 8-ounce package cream cheese
1 pint light cream
Salt and pepper
Lemon juice

Sauté the onions and garlic in the butter until soft. Add the tomatoes, tomato juice, and bay leaves. Simmer for 20 minutes. Remove from heat and let cool. Drain the tomatoes, reserving the juice, and purée them in a blender or food processor with the cream cheese. Mix the purée with the reserved juice. Add the light cream and season to taste with salt, pepper, and lemon juice.

This soup may be served hot or cold, according to the season, and garnished with fresh herbs (chopped fresh dill or basil). Goodies' Croutons with Chèvre and Red Peppers (see recipe) are a marvelous accompaniment.

## GOODIES TO GO

—

LEXINGTON, MASSACHUSETTS

CROUTONS WITH CHÈVRE AND RED PEPPERS

Cut a baguette into ¼-inch slices. Brush the slices lightly with olive oil and bake at 350° for 10 minutes, or until they are light brown. Work 4 ounces of marinated chèvre with its marinade until the mixture is creamy. Spread a thin layer of cheese on each crouton and top with a strip of roasted and peeled sweet red pepper (use a total of 2 peppers). Place the croutons under the broiler until bubbly. Serve at once.

*When you're roasting the eggplants for this cold-weather soup, don't be afraid to see the skin burn and split, curl up, and drop off. That's just what you want to impart the proper roasted flavor to the eggplant meat itself. A filling soup, this is better served by the cup than the bowl. Chef Robert Shumaker thinks it goes exceptionally well as a first course for a vegetable or seafood lasagna dinner or before pasta with cream sauce.*

## ROASTED EGGPLANT SOUP

*Serves 6 to 8*

2 medium eggplants
Olive oil
3 quarts chicken stock
4 cloves (or more) fresh garlic, peeled and chopped
2 medium onions, chopped
1 6-ounce can tomato paste
1 cup fresh basil leaves or ¼ cup dried basil
Salt and pepper to taste

Rub the eggplants with olive oil and place them directly on the open flame of a gas stove. Use a fork to position and turn them. Roast them as long as necessary to char the skin completely. (If you do not have a gas stove, halve the eggplants, place them skin side up on greased baking sheets, and broil them.) Cool the eggplants.

Heat the chicken stock. Peel and cut up the cooled eggplant and sauté it for about 15 minutes with the garlic and onion in a small amount of olive oil. Add the mixture to the heated chicken stock along with the tomato paste and basil. Purée the mixture in a food processor or blender.

Pour the soup into a pan, adjust the seasonings, and heat the soup before serving it. You may wish to top it with grated Parmesan cheese, and French bread is a perfect accompaniment.

NOTE: For an excellent cold soup, thin the mixture with additional chicken stock.

## CHEESE SOUP

*Serves 7 or 8*

1 large onion, chopped
3 tablespoons unsalted butter
⅓ cup all-purpose flour
¼ teaspoon salt, or to taste
Freshly ground black pepper to taste
4 cups milk, scalded
2 cups grated sharp Cheddar cheese
2 tablespoons tomato sauce
1 tablespoon Worcestershire sauce
Dash of Tabasco

In a large saucepan, sauté the onion in the butter until it is golden. Sprinkle it with the flour, add the salt and pepper, stir, and cook for about 3 minutes. Add the hot milk slowly, stirring all the while. Add the cheese and stir while it melts. Simmer, covered, about 15 minutes. Add the tomato sauce, Worcestershire, and Tabasco and simmer 10 minutes longer. Serve immediately.

## CARROT SOUP WITH ROQUEFORT CREAM

*Serves 8 to 10*

2 large onions, chopped
4 tablespoons clarified butter (see recipe, page 136)
3 pounds carrots, peeled and cut into 2-inch pieces
2 shallots, chopped
2 green apples, peeled, quartered, and cored
½ teaspoon cayenne pepper, or to taste
Chicken stock (about 2 quarts)
3 cups heavy cream
Salt and pepper

ZABAR'S

—

NEW YORK CITY

*Zabar's started out as a kosher-style Jewish deli, and its smoked fish department is still a drawing card, although today you'll find caviar and Scotch salmon along with the lox and whitefish. You'll also find soups and other hot and cold foods to carry home.*

RYAN'S

—

SAN FRANCISCO

*Here is a soup that is delicious hot or cold. The creation of Ryan's sous-chef, John Mitzewich, the combination of an unusually tasty carrot soup with a garnish of Roquefort cream is unbeatable.*

About ⅓ cup each crumbled Roquefort, *crème fraîche,* and whipped cream
Chopped fresh chives for garnish

Sauté the onions in the butter until they are caramelized (this may take 20 or 30 minutes). Add the carrots, shallots, apples, cayenne, and enough chicken stock to cover the mixture by 2 inches. Simmer until the carrots are tender. Purée and bring back to a simmer. Add the cream, and salt and pepper to taste.

Blend the Roquefort and *crème fraîche* until smooth, then add the whipped cream. Ladle the soup into bowls and top with a dollop of the Roquefort cream. Sprinkle with chopped chives.

## PROVENDER

—

TIVERTON,
RHODE ISLAND

*Salsa, a mixture of tomatoes, onions, garlic, spices, and chili peppers, comes in varying strengths. One manufacturer labels its salsas "mild," "medium," "hot," and "ay-yi-yi!"*

### SOPA DE SALSA

*Serves 8*

1 large Spanish onion, chopped
4 teaspoons unsalted butter
2 28-ounce cans Italian plum tomatoes
3 ounces hot salsa
1 pound cream cheese
3 cups chicken or beef broth
2 cups light cream
Juice of ½ lemon
1 teaspoon African Bird Pepper or Tabasco
4 teaspoons chopped cilantro (fresh coriander)
Lemon slices and cilantro leaves for garnish

Sauté the onion in the butter. Add the tomatoes and salsa. Simmer until the liquid is almost gone. Add the cream cheese slowly in small amounts so that it melts into the tomato-salsa mixture. When all the cheese is melted, add the remaining ingredients except the garnish. Serve hot. Top each bowl with a paper-thin lemon slice and a cilantro leaf.

## BROCCOLI CHEESE SOUP

*Serves 6 to 8*

1 head broccoli
6½ cups water
1 cup diced celery
1 cup diced onions
8 ounces cream cheese
½ cup cornstarch
2 pounds Cheddar cheese, grated
2 cups half-and-half
1 teaspoon parsley flakes
Salt and pepper to taste

Trim the broccoli into flowerets. Save the trim-mings. Heat 6 cups of the water to boiling and blanch the flowerets in it, then remove the flow-erets from the water with a slotted spoon. Chop the trimmed-off broccoli ends into small pieces, add them to the boiling water, and simmer them for 30 minutes to 1 hour, until tender. Remove the ends from the water with a slotted spoon.

Keeping the water at a gentle boil, add the celery, onions, and cream cheese, stirring until the cheese dissolves and is smooth. Simmer this "stock" until the celery is tender. Add the broc-coli flowerets.

Dissolve the cornstarch in the remaining ½ cup of water and add it to the soup, stirring con-stantly, until the desired thickness is reached. Fold in the Cheddar cheese and stir. Add the half-and-half, parsley, and salt and pepper. Sim-mer the soup for 10 minutes. Serve it with a green salad and warm hard rolls.

## WOLFERMAN'S GOOD THINGS TO EAT

—

### FAIRWAY, KANSAS

*Since 1888, when Wolfer-man's was established by the present owner's great-grandfather, it has had a tradition of of-fering fine groceries. Its English muffins are mail-ordered by devotees across the nation. Its shelves fairly burst with imported and domestic jams and jellies and mustards and sauces. Wolferman's newest addition to its own butcher shop, bakery, fish counter, delicatessen, and fresh produce counter is a carry-out food department that creates such good things to eat as this popular and hearty soup. It may be prepared ahead, refrig-erated, and reheated.*

## THE WINERY

—

SANTA FE

*As its name indicates, this shop began as a wine store, with a special emphasis on small California wineries and the burgeoning vineyards of the Southwest. Today the store has grown to include a full range of gourmet foods, featuring products made in New Mexico, such as salsas, red chili jam, and blue corn tortilla chips.*

## GREEN CHILI BEEF SOUP

*Serves 6*

½ pound lean stew meat, cut into ¾-inch cubes
¼ cup all-purpose flour
3 tablespoons vegetable oil
2 cups chicken broth
1 carrot, peeled and diced
1 stalk celery, diced
1 medium onion, chopped
1 4-ounce can chopped green chilies
1 clove garlic, minced
1½ teaspoons oregano
1½ cups diced peeled potatoes
2½ cups beef broth
1¼ cups drained canned tomatoes, chopped
Salt and pepper

Roll the meat in the flour and brown it in half the vegetable oil. Add the chicken broth, bring to a boil, and simmer for 1 to 1½ hours, stirring occasionally to prevent the meat from sticking to the bottom of the pan. Brown the carrot, celery, onion, green chilies, garlic, and oregano in the remaining oil.

When the meat is tender, add the vegetable-herb mixture, the diced potatoes, beef broth, and chopped tomatoes. Bring to a boil and simmer for 20 to 30 minutes, until the potatoes are done. Add salt and pepper to taste.

## BETH'S TORTILLA SOUP

*Serves 8*

2 large tomatoes, quartered and seeded
1 small onion, coarsely chopped
1 large clove garlic, finely minced
½ cup (1 stick) butter
8 cups chicken broth or stock
1 teaspoon marjoram
2 tablespoons cayenne seasoning juice (optional)
Tortilla chips
Sour cream, chopped avocado, and grated Cheddar
    cheese for garnish

Chop the tomatoes and onion together and cook them with the garlic in the butter in a soup pot over high heat, stirring until the mixture comes to a boil.

Stir in the stock and marjoram and (if desired) cayenne, and bring the soup to a boil again, stirring constantly. Put a handful of chips in each bowl, and add the soup. Garnish with sour cream topped with the chopped avocado and the grated cheese.

## RED BEAN AND LENTIL SOUP

*Serves 8*

1 pound dried small red beans
1 or 2 ham hocks, cut in half
1 large onion, chopped
1 large leek, or 2 small leeks, well cleaned and finely
    sliced

After nearly twenty years as
film and theater critic for
the San Francisco Exam-
iner, Stanley Eichelbaum
traded late-night dead-
lines for predawn
preparations at a restaurant
carry-out catering oper-
ation. His tiny storefront
features a take-out counter
and a handful of tables
squeezed together,
resulting in a warm,
neighborly atmosphere.
This hearty soup is a
favorite on those gray days
that do indeed happen in
San Francisco.

2 medium carrots, peeled and sliced
2 stalks celery, finely sliced
2 cloves garlic, minced
Bouquet garni consisting of a pinch of thyme, 2 bay
    leaves, 4 parsley stems, a pinch of rosemary, 3
    cloves, and 6 white peppercorns, crushed
Salt and pepper
6 ounces lentils
1 quart fresh chicken stock (or canned chicken
    broth)
¼ cup sherry wine vinegar or red wine vinegar
Dash of balsamic vinegar (optional)
¼ cup good sherry or brandy
Sour cream and snipped fresh chives for garnish

Soak the red beans in salted water overnight (or
fast-soak, covered, for 1 hour in salted water
brought to a boil). Drain well. Put the ham hocks
and beans into a large pot with water to cover.
Bring to a boil and simmer for 45 minutes to 1
hour, until beans are tender. Halfway through
cooking add the onion, leeks, carrots, celery,
garlic, bouquet garni, and salt and pepper.

While the beans are cooking, cook the lentils
in salted water for 20 minutes, or until tender.
Drain and set aside.

Remove the ham hocks from the soup pot.
Take off the meat (discarding fat and gristle), and
mince it finely. Purée the red beans, vegetables,
and cooking liquid in small batches in a blender
or food processor, making sure to remove the
bouquet garni before puréeing.

Return the puréed mixture to the soup pot
and add the chicken stock. Add the vinegar and
sherry. Add the lentils and ham. Simmer for 20
minutes, correct the seasonings, and serve the
soup garnished with a dollop of sour cream and
some snipped fresh chives.

## BLACK BEAN SOUP

*Serves 8 to 10*

1 pound black beans
3 tablespoons olive oil
1 tablespoon minced garlic
¾ pound Spanish onions, diced
4 stalks celery, diced
6½ cups chicken stock or water
1 ham bone
1 bay leaf
½ sweet red pepper, diced
1 tablespoon ground cumin
½ teaspoon cayenne pepper
Salt and pepper to taste
1 tablespoon brown sugar
1 tablespoon lemon juice
⅓ cup sherry
4 tablespoons chopped fresh parsley
½ cup sour cream, ¼ cup chopped scallions, and 1
    hard-boiled egg, chopped, for garnish

Soak the beans overnight and drain. In a soup pot heat the olive oil and sauté the garlic, onions, and celery until the vegetables are transparent. Add the stock or water, the ham bone, the beans, and the bay leaf and simmer for 1 hour. Add the red pepper, cumin, cayenne, salt, pepper, brown sugar, lemon juice, and sherry and simmer for 20 minutes. Remove the ham bone. Purée about a quarter of the soup and mix it back in. If desired, chop the meat from the ham bone and add it to the soup. Add the chopped parsley.

Serve the soup hot, garnished with a dollop of sour cream and a sprinkling of chopped scallions and chopped egg.

## INDIANA MARKET & CATERING

—

### NEW YORK CITY

*Families of both Elizabeth Schaible and her partner David Turk hail from Indiana, so the choice of a name with a "down-home" ring to it for their East Village establishment was easy. Happily, the name is also memorable and makes one think of hearty fare.*

## TRUFFLES

—

MARBLEHEAD,
MASSACHUSETTS

*Being part of a sailing community adds a special dimension to Mary Ellen Falck's carry-out business, since she is often asked to provision boats for cruising trips and races. Her biggest challenge was to provide three meals a day for ten days at sea for the crew of a 75-foot contender in the Bermuda Race. Karen Brook's chowder is perfect for blustery days at sea as well as chilly days ashore.*

## KAREN'S CORN CHOWDER

*Serves 8 to 10*

6 tablespoons unsalted butter
½ pound kielbasa sausage, diced
1 medium onion, chopped
4 stalks celery, including the leaves, diced
1 pound red new potatoes, unpeeled, diced
2 12-ounce cans corn niblets, or kernels from 3 ears fresh corn
4 cups half-and-half
4 tablespoons all-purpose flour
Salt and pepper to taste
½ cup chopped fresh parsley

Melt 2 tablespoons of the butter in a Dutch oven. Add the kielbasa, onion, and celery, and sauté until the vegetables are tender. Add the potatoes and the juice from the canned corn. (If there is not enough corn juice to cover the potatoes or if you are using fresh corn, add ½ cup water.) Cover the pot and simmer for 8 to 10 minutes. Add the corn and stir; then cover and simmer for an additional 10 minutes. Add the half-and-half and simmer until the chowder is almost at the boiling point.

Meanwhile, prepare a roux by melting the remaining 4 tablespoons of butter in a small pan. Add the flour to the butter and stir until the mixture is smooth. Whisk the roux into the chowder and cook over medium high heat until the soup has thickened. Add salt and pepper to taste. Serve the chowder in individual bowls or a tureen and sprinkle with the parsley.

## ITALIAN SAUSAGE SOUP

*Serves 8 to 10*

1½ cups coarsely chopped celery
1½ cups coarsely chopped onions
1 clove garlic, minced
3 tablespoons olive oil
2 cups canned Italian tomatoes, coarsely chopped
 (reserve the liquid)
1 cup tomato purée
1¼ pounds Italian sausage, sautéed and drained
6 cups chicken broth
½ teaspoon oregano
2 bay leaves
½ teaspoon thyme
½ cup chopped parsley
3 tablespoons sugar
1 cup orzo or other small pasta
Grated Parmesan cheese for garnish

Sauté the celery, onions, and garlic in the olive oil until barely tender. Add the tomatoes, purée, and sautéed sausage. Cook for 10 minutes over medium heat. Add the broth, herbs, and sugar, and simmer for 30 minutes. Add the pasta and continue cooking until it is just done. Serve with Parmesan cheese.

NOTE: The amount of sausage and pasta may be varied according to taste and thickness desired. If you wish a thinner soup, use the reserved juice from the tomatoes as additional liquid.

## PASTA PRESTO

—

### KANSAS CITY, MISSOURI

*At Westport, the oldest section of Kansas City, the pioneers used to stop for supplies before heading west along the Santa Fe and Oregon trails. Today, Westport Square has been restored and renovated, and Pasta Presto, shiny white and inviting inside, is one of its highlights, located next door to its sister restaurant, the Prospect of Westport.*

*This hearty soup, in which the shop uses its own homemade pasta and sausage, is best when made a day or two in advance and allowed to ripen in the refrigerator; it can also be frozen.*

## WICKFORD GOURMET FOODS

—

### WICKFORD, RHODE ISLAND

*On a cold winter's night, with the wind blowing off Narragansett Bay, this soup, served with chunks of crusty bread, really warms the cockles of a New England heart. It's a cinch for the cook, too.*

## SAUSAGE CABBAGE SOUP

*Serves 10*

3 tablespoons olive oil
1 large onion, chopped
2 cloves garlic, minced
1 pound sweet Italian sausage meat, broken up
1 small head cabbage, chopped
4 28-ounce cans whole tomatoes and liquid
1 bay leaf
1 tablespoon basil
1 teaspoon oregano
Pinch of rosemary
Salt and pepper to taste

Pour the olive oil into the bottom of a soup pot, and sauté the onion and garlic until they are golden. Add the sausage and brown it. Drain off the extra fat. Add the cabbage and cook slightly. Add the tomatoes and seasonings, and simmer slowly until the cabbage is tender. Serve the soup piping hot with crusty Italian bread.

## CABBAGE AND BEEF BORSCHT

*Serves 6 to 8*

⅓ cup peanut oil
1¼ pounds lean brisket of beef
2½ quarts rich brown veal or beef stock
¾ pound onions, chopped
1 tablespoon minced garlic
1¼ pounds cabbage, cut in 1-inch cubes
¾ cup wine vinegar
1½ tablespoons brown sugar
3 bay leaves
2 teaspoons chopped fresh thyme
3 6-ounce cans julienne-cut beets, drained
6 tablespoons lemon juice
Salt and pepper to taste

Heat the oil in a heavy soup pot and sear the brisket until it is brown. Add enough stock to cover the beef, and simmer, partially covered, for about 2 hours or until the meat is very tender. In a separate pan, sauté the onions and garlic in a little oil until they are soft but not brown. Add them, along with the cabbage, vinegar, brown sugar, bay leaves, and thyme, to the soup pot, and reduce a little. Remove the meat, cool it, and cut it into cubes. Add whatever stock remains and simmer for 30 to 40 minutes. Add the beets and return the meat to the pot. Add the lemon juice and salt and pepper. Add boiled potatoes if you wish, and adjust the sweet-sour flavor with additional lemon juice and brown sugar to suit your taste.

SOMEPLACE
SPECIAL
—
MCLEAN, VIRGINIA

*This Eastern European soup should be topped with dollops of sour cream or served with sour cream on the side. The addition of small boiled potatoes makes the borscht a meal in itself.*

Bond & Burkhart calls
itself an American
charcuterie. In addition to
standard specialty food
favorites, the take-out menu
features food indigenous to
specific parts of the United
States—not only New
Orleans gumbo, but
Maryland fried chicken,
Chesapeake crab cakes,
and Tex-Mex barbecued
ribs.

## NEW ORLEANS CAJUN GUMBO

*Serves 6*

½ cup diced sweet red pepper
½ cup diced green pepper
½ cup diced white onion
½ cup diced celery
1 tablespoon minced garlic
6 cups chicken stock
1 tablespoon gumbo filé
2 bay leaves
1 teaspoon thyme
1 tablespoon Tabasco
2 cups canned tomatoes
1 cup cooked white rice
6 cooked shrimp, sliced in half horizontally
1 cooked chicken breast, boned, skinned, and diced
1 spicy sausage (preferably andouille), blanched in
    boiling water for 10 minutes and diced

In a soup pot, cover the first five ingredients with
the chicken stock, bring to a boil, and simmer
until the vegetables are tender (about 8 minutes).
Add the seasonings and the tomatoes and simmer for 10 minutes. Add the remaining ingredients and simmer for another 10 minutes. Serve
hot with crusty French bread.

NOTE: Filé, ground young sassafras leaves, is a
crucial ingredient for gumbos and is available in
most specialty food shops.

# BOUILLABAISSE

*Serves 6 to 8*

### BOUILLABAISSE BASE

½ cup olive oil
2 cups sliced leeks, white part only
1 cup grated onion
3 cloves garlic, crushed
1 pound fresh tomatoes, peeled and cut in pieces
2 stalks celery
1 bay leaf
4 tablespoons chopped fresh parsley
½ teaspoon thyme
2 teaspoons fennel seed
6 threads saffron
Grated rind from 1 orange
4 tablespoons tomato paste
12 cups fish stock (see recipe, page 57)

Heat the oil in a large pot and sauté the leeks and onions until they are soft. Add the garlic, tomatoes, celery, herbs, orange rind, and tomato paste, and cook for 3 or 4 minutes. Add the fish stock and simmer for 45 minutes to 1 hour. Strain the liquid into a bowl. If you wish, you may grind the solids in a food mill or food processor and add them to the base liquid.

### FINAL PREPARATION

Claws and tails of 3 1-pound lobsters, cut through
    the shell into bite-size pieces
1 dozen littleneck clams
2 pounds monkfish (or cusk or wolf fish), in large
    bite-size pieces
2 pounds cod (or haddock or pollock), in large bite-
    size pieces
1 dozen medium shrimp

## THE FISHMONGER

—

### CAMBRIDGE

*Bouillabaisse is becoming an unaffordable delicacy in restaurants, even in the South of France. Making your own is a slightly more affordable proposition.*

2 dozen mussels
1½ pounds scallops

In a large pot, bring the bouillabaisse base to a simmer. Add the lobster, clams, and monkfish and cook for 10 minutes. Then add the remaining ingredients one at a time, starting with the cod. Bring to a simmer and cook until the mussel shells have opened. To serve, remove the fish to a tureen or individual bowls with a slotted spoon, then pour in the broth.

NOTE: The lobsters, clams, shrimp, and mussels are to have their shells left on. Before cutting the lobsters into pieces, kill them by turning them on their backs and making a slit down the center with a sharp knife.

### Fish Stock

*Makes about 12 cups*

6 pounds bones and heads of white, nonoily fish,
    with some meat attached
3 onions, each stuck with 2 cloves
3 leeks, white part only, cut up
3 stalks celery, cut up
¼ teaspoon thyme
2 cups dry white wine
10 cups water

Combine all ingredients and bring them to a boil. Skim off scum as it rises to the surface. Reduce the heat and simmer for 20 minutes. Strain the stock through cheesecloth or a fine sieve. Unused fish stock may be frozen.

## SHELLFISH STEW WITH OUZO

*Serves 6*

½ cup chopped onion
3 cloves garlic, finely minced
Chopped rind of 1 lemon
4 tablespoons olive oil
4 tablespoons chopped fresh oregano, or 2
    tablespoons dried oregano
1 cup white wine
1 pound littleneck clams, scrubbed
½ cup lemon juice
¼ cup ouzo
½ pound shrimp, shelled and deveined
½ pound scallops, washed and muscle removed
Meat of 1 medium lobster
½ cup heavy cream
½ sweet red pepper, minced

Sauté the onion, garlic, and lemon rind in the olive oil until translucent. Add 1 tablespoon of the oregano and the wine and bring to a boil. Add the clams and cover the pot, steaming the clams until they just begin to open. Add the lemon juice, ouzo, shrimp, and scallops, and cover. Cook until the shrimp are pink, about 1 minute. Remove the clams, scallops, and shrimp from the pan. To the broth left in the pan, add the lobster, the cream, the red pepper, and the remaining oregano, and heat through. Return the shellfish to the pan and mix thoroughly, off the heat. Serve the stew in shallow soup plates as a first course or for lunch or supper with a salad.

NOTE: If you are using very small bay scallops, they should not be added until the shellfish is returned to the pan at the end, as they will cook in the heat of the liquid. If you use large sea scallops, slice them in half crosswise.

## THE KITCHEN DOOR AT ABIGAIL'S

—

WEST FALMOUTH, MASSACHUSETTS

*The Kitchen Door at Abigail's is open only during the summer months, when the population of West Falmouth stretches to include numbers of vacationers. Many of them rent houses in the area, and part of the vacation is not always having to cook. Happily, this typical seaside dish can be recreated inland, thanks to the speed with which fish and seafood are now transported all over the country.*

*Dutch-born Ype Hengst studied cooking in Germany, the Netherlands, and Switzerland before coming to the United States and now finds himself enamored of regional American cuisine. He suggests that this Louisiana fish soup be served with French bread toasted with garlic.*

## BAYOU FISHERMAN'S SOUP

*Serves 6 to 8*

2 cups canned tomatoes in purée
2 bay leaves
1 cup uncooked brown rice
5 cups fish stock (see recipe, page 57)
3 tablespoons olive oil
1½ cups carrots, julienne-cut
4 cups okra, cut in small pieces
½ teaspoon dried thyme
¼ teaspoon cayenne pepper
1 heaping teaspoon minced garlic
2⅓ cups chopped celery
⅔ cup chopped onion
Corn cut from 3 ears fresh corn (or 1 12-ounce can corn niblets)
1 tablespoon Worcestershire sauce
2 anchovy fillets
1 teaspoon kosher salt
1 pound monkfish, cleaned and membrane discarded
1 pound redfish, deboned

Chop the tomatoes in large chunks and combine them with the bay leaf, rice, and stock. Bring the mixture to a boil. Meanwhile, heat the olive oil and sauté the carrots, okra, thyme, cayenne, garlic, celery, onion, and corn together for 5 minutes. Add the sautéed vegetables, the Worcestershire sauce, the anchovies, and the salt to the stock and again bring to a boil. Cut the monkfish and redfish into ¾-inch cubes and add them to the soup. Cook until the fish is just tender.

## CRAB VEGETABLE SOUP

*Serves 6 to 8*

2 slices bacon, chopped
1 clove garlic, minced
1 small onion, minced
2 tablespoons butter
1 cup coarsely chopped celery
1 cup sliced carrots
3 cups peeled, seeded, and chopped tomatoes
2 teaspoons thyme
1 teaspoon celery seed
1 tablespoon Worcestershire sauce
¾ teaspoon Tabasco
1 teaspoon paprika
2 quarts crab stock (see recipe)
1 cup cut green beans
1 cup corn (frozen will do)
½ cup sliced okra (optional)
¼ cup sherry
1 cup lump crabmeat

In a Dutch oven or large casserole cook the bacon pieces until crisp. Remove them with a slotted spoon. Sauté the garlic and onion in the bacon fat until the onion is transparent but not brown. Add the butter, celery, and carrots, and cook, stirring often, for 10 minutes. Add the tomatoes and all of the seasonings to the pot, along with the crab stock. Simmer for 15 minutes. Add the green beans and cook for 15 minutes. Add the corn and okra (if desired) and simmer for 5 minutes. Add the sherry and correct the seasonings. With the soup at a simmer, gently stir in the crabmeat and serve.

*Specialty food shops like to make the most of local ingredients, and the Green Grocer is no exception. Crabmeat is practically a staple in coastal Virginia, and this hearty soup is a nice change from bisques and other rich concoctions.*

CRAB STOCK

4 whole crabs, or ½ pound crab roe
2 quarts water
1 teaspoon salt
Freshly ground pepper
1 large bay leaf
1 small dried hot pepper
½ cup white wine

Rinse the crabs. In a stockpot bring all other ingredients to a boil. Add the crabs (or roe), cover, and cook for 15 minutes. Strain.

*Having grown from a one-shop operation in Boston's Back Bay to a six-store sweep of the city in just three years, Rudi's, like its customers, is upwardly mobile. A classic line of French pastry and a wide selection of breads are complemented by take-out foods that combine "new American cuisine" with a touch of old-world exotica.*

## CURRIED CRAB BISQUE

*Serves 12*

⅓ cup minced Spanish onion
⅓ cup minced celery
½ cup (1 stick) butter
2 tablespoons all-purpose flour
1 red Delicious apple, peeled, cored, and minced
½ cup puréed banana
1½ tablespoons curry powder
1 bay leaf
1¼ cups tomato paste
3 cubes chicken bouillon
2 tablespoons shrimp paste (available at Oriental grocery stores)
1 cup clam juice
1 cup water
Pinch of nutmeg
1 clove garlic, minced
Salt and white pepper to taste
1 pound crabmeat, with its juice
6 cups heavy cream
6 cups milk

Sauté the onion and celery in the butter until the vegetables are tender. Add the flour, apple, and banana and cook for 5 minutes. Add the remaining ingredients, except the crabmeat, cream, and milk, and simmer for ½ hour. Purée the mixture in batches in a food processor or blender. Add the crabmeat and its juice. Refrigerate the mixture until ready to use (for 1 or 2 days). When ready to serve, add the cream and milk, heat, and adjust seasonings to taste.

## CURRIED APPLE SOUP

*Serves 6*

2 large apples, unpeeled but cored and chopped
2 medium red onions, chopped
3 10½-ounce cans beef or chicken broth
Salt to taste
Pinch of paprika
1 tablespoon curry powder (or more, to taste)
1½ cups heavy cream

Purée the apples and onions with a small amount of the broth in a blender or food processor. In a saucepan, combine the purée, the remainder of the broth, and the spices. Simmer for 15 minutes. Add the cream and reheat, but do not boil. Serve the soup hot or very cold, decorated with apple peel.

## MINTED PEA SOUP

*Serves 6 to 8*

5 cups chicken broth
2 cups diced onions
3 10-ounce packages frozen peas
1 teaspoon salt
Dash of nutmeg
½ bunch fresh mint, washed and patted dry
3 cups heavy cream
Mint leaves for garnish

Simmer together the first five ingredients, until the onions are soft, about 20 minutes. Reserve six or eight small leaves of the mint for garnish and roughly chop the rest, discarding the stems. Add

## MONTICELLO GOURMET

—

WASHINGTON, D.C.

*At Washington's Monticello Gourmet, this curried apple soup, made festive with a sliver of bright apple peel as decoration, is an all-time favorite. For the do-it-at-home cook, it's even easier than apple pie.*

## FORMAGGIO KITCHEN

—

CAMBRIDGE

*Norma Wasserman, owner of Formaggio Kitchen, was introduced to specialty food shopping when she was studying painting in London and became accustomed to making*

*daily stops at the fish-monger, the greengrocer, the butcher, and the baker. Her shop in Cambridge recreates that European shopping experience and, not so coincidentally, is located among a cluster of stores that includes The Fishmonger and Le Jardin, a greengrocer and flower shop.*

## MONTICELLO GOURMET

—

WASHINGTON, D.C.

the chopped mint and the heavy cream to the chicken broth—pea mixture. Purée the mixture in batches in a blender or food processor. Serve the soup chilled, garnishing each bowl with a mint leaf.

### *SPINACH VICHYSSOISE*

*Serves 6*

7 leeks, white part only
4 tablespoons butter
8 medium potatoes, peeled and sliced
1 tablespoon salt
5 cups rich chicken stock
2 cups half-and-half
1 cup heavy cream
1 pound spinach, cooked, squeezed dry, and
    chopped
Fresh chives for garnish

Sauté the leeks in the butter. Add the potatoes, salt, and stock and simmer until the potatoes are soft. Add the spinach. Purée while pouring in the half-and-half and the cream. Chill. Top with fresh chives and serve. This soup is also good served hot.

## COLD TOMATO SOUP

*Serves 6*

8 large ripe tomatoes, peeled
2 ounces ham, julienne-cut
1 cucumber, seeded and finely diced
3 shallots or green onions, finely chopped
Grated rind of 1 lemon
Salt and pepper to taste
½ teaspoon sugar
1 cup heavy cream
½ cup chopped fresh parsley or basil

Blend the tomatoes in a blender or food processor until they are finely chopped but not completely liquid. Combine them with all the other ingredients. Chill thoroughly and serve.

## SENEGALESE SOUP

*Serves 6*

½ cup (1 stick) butter
¾ pound celery, chopped
¾ pound carrots, chopped
¾ pound onions, chopped
3 tablespoons curry powder
2 Granny Smith apples, cored and coarsely chopped
4 cups chicken stock
2 cups heavy cream
Salt and pepper to taste
6 ounces skinned, boned chicken, cooked and diced
Chopped fresh parsley and grated coconut for
    garnish

### FÊTE ACCOMPLIE
—
WASHINGTON, D.C.

*On a hot summer day, what could be more refreshing than a chilled tomato soup? Jake Martin and Millie White's customers at Fête Accomplie find it a perfect midsummer luncheon soup or a delicious starter for a summer dinner.*

### NEUMAN & BOGDONOFF
—
NEW YORK CITY

*This rich and creamy cold soup with a dash of curry in it is a favorite of Paul Neuman's and Tracy Bogdonoff's. Although it's not available every day, it*

*can always be ordered—or made at home according to these directions.*

## THE GROANING BOARD

—

WASHINGTON, D.C.

*"Not unlike a daiquiri without liquor" is the way Mitch Kernuf, owner of The Groaning Board, describes this smooth spring-summer soup. Because it is slightly sweet, it goes best before a lunch of light wine and cheese or French bread and pâté.*

Melt the butter in a heavy-bottomed pan. Add the celery, carrots and onions and cook them over medium heat for 15 to 20 minutes, until the onions are translucent. Add the curry powder and cook 5 minutes more. Add the apples and chicken stock and cook 20 minutes over medium heat. Remove the soup from the heat and strain it through a colander, reserving the liquid. Pass the solids through the medium blade of a food mill. Pour the liquid back in with the solids and allow the soup to cool. Add the cream and salt and pepper. Add the cooked diced chicken, reserving a small amount with which to garnish the bowls. Chopped parsley and a little grated coconut make a nice additional garnish. Serve the soup cold.

## COLD CANTALOUPE SOUP

*Serves 6 to 8*

3 cantaloupes
2 cups pear nectar
2 cups papaya juice
Pinch each of ginger, allspice, and cinnamon
1 cup heavy cream

Peel and halve the melons and remove the seeds. Cut the melon meat into 1-inch cubes. Place it and all other ingredients except the cream in a pan and bring it to a simmer. Cook until the fruit is soft. Let the mixture cool and purée it until it is smooth.

Refrigerate the soup for at least 1 hour, then add the cream and whisk it in thoroughly. Serve cold.

## BRANDIED PEACH SOUP

*Serves 4*

4 large ripe peaches, peeled, pitted, and quartered
⅓ cup sugar
⅛ teaspoon cinnamon
Juice of 1 lemon
¾ cup sour cream
1 cup white wine
1½ cups water
Fresh mint for garnish

Purée the peaches, sugar, cinnamon, and lemon juice in a blender or food processor. Add the sour cream and blend until well mixed. Pour the mixture into a large bowl and add the wine and water, blending well. Chill and serve, garnishing each cup or bowl with fresh mint.

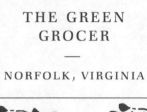

## THE GREEN GROCER

—

NORFOLK, VIRGINIA

*Having owned a gourmet supermarket in Philadelphia, Herschel and Helene Blum moved to Norfolk to be near their children and grandchildren and enjoy the more leisurely pace of a Southern port. In March 1983 they opened The Green Grocer, a combined specialty food store and café. So much for the leisurely life.*

## LIGHT FARE

Three-Vegetable Mousse
Broccoli Cheese Soufflé
Potato Torte
Lavosh Sandwich
Eggplant "Sandwiches"
Mama Mia's Mozzarella in Carrozza
Tortilla Turnovers
Marty's Layered Tortilla Flats
Gâteau of Basil Crêpes with Wild Mushrooms
    and Goat Cheese
Crêpe Sandwich Loaf
Corn Puffs with Maple Sauce
Stuffed Vidalia Onions
Polpettini de Spinache
Spanakopita
Chicken Empanadas
Cheese and Ham Pie
Annette Gall's Meat Pies
Mediterranean Tart
Onion Tart
Victoria's Fish Tart
Broccoli and Cheese Quiche
Porcini Pine Nut Frittata
Creole Sausage Frittata
Piedmontese Spinach and Cheese Sausages
Enlightened Pizza
Italian Sausages

## THREE-VEGETABLE MOUSSE

*Serves 10*

½ yellow onion, chopped
2 tablespoons butter
1 10-ounce package frozen chopped spinach,
    thawed
4½ tablespoons unflavored gelatin
1 cup chicken broth
3 cups heavy cream
Salt and pepper to taste
1 small head cauliflower
3 cups diced carrots

Sauté the onion in the butter until it is soft. Drain the spinach and squeeze it dry; add it to the onion and sauté 3 to 4 minutes.

Mix 1½ tablespoons of the gelatin with ⅓ cup of the chicken broth. Stir until smooth. Put the spinach mixture into a food processor or blender. Add the gelatin mixture and purée. Slowly add 1 cup of the heavy cream and salt and pepper to taste. Pour into a mold to set. Refrigerate.

Cook the cauliflower until it is tender. Drain. Repeat the preparation of the gelatin mixture, mixing another 1½ tablespoons of gelatin with ⅓ cup of chicken broth and stirring until the mixture is smooth. Combine the cauliflower and the gelatin mixture in the food processor or blender and purée. Slowly add 1 cup of the heavy cream and salt and pepper. Pour on top of the spinach purée to set. Return the mold to the refrigerator.

Cook the carrots until tender. Drain. Repeat preparation of the gelatin mixture, using the last of the gelatin and the last of the broth. Purée the carrots and the gelatin mixture. Slowly add the last of the cream and salt and pepper. Pour the purée into the mold on top of the cauliflower layer, and refrigerate the mousse until well set.

## BON APPÉTIT
—
ATLANTA

TOMATO VINAIGRETTE

1 cup red wine vinegar
3 tablespoons Dijon
    mustard
1 teaspoon thyme
Salt and pepper to taste
3 cups salad oil
2 tomatoes, peeled
Tomato paste for color

Put the vinegar, mustard, thyme, salt, and pepper in a food processor or blender, and process until the mixture is smooth. Add the oil in a steady stream with the motor running. Add the tomatoes and process, then add the tomato paste to color and process again.

Serve with Tomato Vinaigrette (see recipe, page 68).

*Washington Depot is located in the lovely rolling countryside of north-western Connecticut, in an area blessed with antiques shops, the celebrated White Flower Farm nursery and garden center, and the "perfect picnic spot" around every corner. The Pantry is the place to pick up a take-away gourmet feast or to have a proper restaurant lunch.*

## *BROCCOLI CHEESE SOUFFLÉ*

*Serves 8 to 10*

1 bunch broccoli
1 medium onion, chopped
2 tablespoons butter
2 tablespoons oil
2 cups grated cheese (Fontina, Swiss, or Cheddar)
4 ounces cream cheese
1½ cups breadcrumbs
8 eggs, beaten
4 cups heavy cream
Dash of Tabasco
Salt and pepper to taste

Trim and grate the broccoli stems. Separate the flowerets into small pieces. Sweat the broccoli and onion in the butter and oil over low heat for 10 minutes, until the vegetables are slightly cooked. Stir in the grated cheese and cream cheese, breadcrumbs, eggs, and cream. Season the mixture to taste with Tabasco and salt and pepper.

Pour the mixture into a lightly oiled rectangular baking dish and bake at 375° for 45 minutes to 1 hour, until the top is lightly browned and the soufflé has set. Serve hot or at room temperature. This dish may be prepared and baked one or two days in advance and reheated. It also freezes very well. Served with a fresh tomato salad, it makes a lovely lunch.

NOTE: To make a less rich soufflé, substitute 2 cups of milk for 2 cups of the heavy cream.

## POTATO TORTE

*Serves 12*

1 egg
2 egg yolks
4 cups heavy cream
Salt and pepper to taste
4 large baking potatoes, peeled and sliced thin
1 medium onion, minced
1 10-ounce package frozen chopped spinach,
    drained
1 tablespoon Dijon mustard
½ pound Gruyère cheese, grated
1 pound baked ham, sliced very thin
1 large jar sweet roasted peppers, drained, or 3
    sweet red peppers, roasted and peeled

In a large bowl, combine the egg, yolks, cream, salt, and pepper. Rinse the potato slices in cold water and pat dry. Add the potatoes to the cream mixture, stirring until they are well coated. Drain off the cream mixture and reserve. In a small bowl, combine the onion, spinach, and mustard.

Butter a 9-by-13-inch casserole. Place a layer of potatoes and grated cheese and a grinding of black pepper in the bottom of the pan. Drizzle some of the cream mixture over this layer and top it with the ham. Repeat the potato and cheese layer and the cream, this time topping it with the spinach mixture. Do another layer of potatoes and cheese and cream, then add a layer of sweet peppers and a layer of potatoes, cheese, and cream. Top with additional grated cheese.

Bake the torte at 325° for approximately 2 hours. The torte should be quite firm when pressed with a spatula (a skewer may be used to test the potatoes for doneness), and the top should be well browned.

NOTE: This dish is marvelous served hot as a

## RYAN'S
—
### SAN FRANCISCO

*After several years in the catering business, Lenore and Michael Ryan decided to open a restaurant/ charcuterie and took over the former Fanny's restaurant in the Castro District of San Francisco. Feeling that the neighborhood had enough bars but not enough quality food emporiums, they turned the downstairs café into a take-out shop. The restaurant is upstairs in a series of small, cozy rooms. This recipe was concocted for Michael, a potato lover, by the sous-chef at Ryan's, John Mitzewich. It makes a hearty one-dish meal.*

main course or chilled and sliced thin. It is better the second day, reheats perfectly, and freezes well.

## THE GOURMET GROCER

—

PRAIRIE VILLAGE, KANSAS

*This satisfying sandwich made on lavosh—Armenian cracker bread—makes fine picnic fare, though you had better take along knives and forks. One of the secrets of preparing the sandwich is to roll it up as snugly as possible for the overnight refrigeration, twisting the end of the wrap tightly.*

## *LAVOSH SANDWICH*

*Serves 8 to 10*

1 large (12-inch) round unbroken lavosh
Softened butter
8 slices Swiss cheese
8 thin slices smoked ham
Mayonnaise
2 whole pimientos, cut into strips
8 thin slices smoked turkey
6 to 8 lettuce leaves, carefully dried and with the ribs removed
2 tomatoes, thinly sliced
2 hard-boiled eggs, thinly sliced

Soften the lavosh by running it under cold water briefly, placing it on a cookie sheet, and covering it with a damp towel until it is pliable, 30 to 60 minutes. Remove the towel and spread the lavosh with softened butter, leaving 2 inches of lavosh plain at the end nearest you. Add a layer of cheese to cover the butter. Next, add a layer of ham, then a light spreading of mayonnaise. Top with a layer of pimiento and then with the smoked turkey. Add another thin layer of mayonnaise. Top with the lettuce, tomato, and egg slices.

Roll the lavosh in jelly-roll fashion, starting with the plain end. Wrap it tightly in plastic wrap, slipping the wrap under the rolled sandwich and twisting the ends. Refrigerate it for 24 hours, and cut it into 8 or 10 slices.

## EGGPLANT "SANDWICHES"

*Makes 6 or 7*

1 eggplant, approximately 1¼ pounds
Thinly sliced mortadella or salami
Thinly sliced provolone cheese
2 eggs, beaten
⅓ cup fine dry breadcrumbs
⅓ cup grated Parmesan cheese
2 tablespoons minced Italian (flat) parsley
Olive oil

Slice the eggplant into 12 or 14 circles about ½ inch thick. If the flesh is cream-colored and seeds are not easily visible, proceed with the recipe. If the eggplant is more mature, salt the slices lightly, let them drain in a colander under a 2-pound weight for an hour, and pat them dry with paper towels.

Tear the mortadella so that each piece fits in a single layer between two slices of eggplant. Fold the provolone similarly and place it over the mortadella on each of the 6 or 7 sandwiches. Press down on each sandwich so the filling will cling to the eggplant.

Dip the sandwiches first into the beaten egg, coating them evenly and well, and then into a plate containing a mixture of the breadcrumbs, Parmesan cheese, and parsley. (Be sure to coat the edges of the sandwiches as well as the tops and bottoms with the crumb mixture.) Drizzle about ½ teaspoon of best-quality olive oil over each top and bottom. Arrange the sandwiches in a shallow baking dish and place in a 400° oven for about 35 minutes, until golden brown and crisp. Turn the sandwiches once during the cooking process. Serve hot or at room temperature.

## VIVANDE PORTA VIA

—

SAN FRANCISCO

*The tantalizing smell of roasting cheese is irresistible to Vivande's staff and customers each morning when Carlo Middione's eggplant "sandwiches" come out of the oven. Some eat them out of hand, like the Italian street food from which they stem; others eat them as an appetizer.*

*The wise aficionado of Zabar's knows that on the weekend it's essential to get to this Broadway shop early. By midday the aisles are jammed with customers making their selections from among forty breads, hundreds of cheeses and sausages, and prepared carry-out items.*

## MAMA MIA'S MOZZARELLA IN CARROZZA

*Serves 4*

SANDWICHES

4 slices mozzarella
8 slices fresh Italian bread, about ½ inch thick
2 eggs, slightly beaten
4 tablespoons olive oil
4 tablespoons butter

Put each slice of mozzarella between 2 slices of bread. Dip the sandwiches into the beaten egg. In a large skillet, heat about ¼ inch of the olive oil. Melt the butter in the olive oil. Sauté the sandwiches in this mixture until they are golden brown on both sides and the cheese begins to ooze out.

ANCHOVY SAUCE

4 tablespoons olive oil
4 tablespoons unsalted butter
10 cloves garlic, coarsely chopped
2 2-ounce cans anchovies

Make the anchovy sauce by heating the oil and butter in a saucepan, adding the garlic and anchovies and cooking until the anchovies are dissolved and the garlic is light golden.
    Serve the sandwiches hot with the anchovy sauce.

## TORTILLA TURNOVERS

*Serves 6 to 10*

6 links chorizo sausage, thinly sliced
1 onion, chopped
2 cloves garlic, minced
1 tablespoon olive or vegetable oil
1 fresh jalapeño pepper, chopped
1 4-ounce can chopped green chili peppers
1 tablespoon chili powder
1 tablespoon minced cilantro (fresh coriander)
Salt and pepper to taste
2 cups grated Cheddar cheese
12 small flour tortillas, cut in half
Vegetable oil for deep frying

Sauté the chorizos, onion, and garlic in the 1 tablespoon of oil. Add the fresh and canned chilies, chili powder, cilantro, salt, and pepper. Transfer the mixture to a bowl and allow it to cool. Fold in the grated cheese.

Place a spoonful of this mixture on each tortilla half. Fold the tortilla over and secure the open sides with toothpicks.

Heat the oil to 375° in a heavy pot and fry the tortillas in batches until they are lightly browned and crisp. Drain them on paper towels. Remove the toothpicks and serve the tortillas warm. These are particularly good served with salsa, sour cream, or guacamole.

### TAKE ME HOME
### —
### WASHINGTON, D.C.

*Alison Zaremba, co-owner of this Georgetown shop, travels extensively when she isn't cooking and keeps a food journal of her discoveries, including these tortilla turnovers with chorizos and Cheddar, of Mexican origin.*

## MARTY'S
—
### DALLAS

*Though Marty's selection of packaged and prepared foods compares to those of Fauchon in Paris and Harrod's in London and the pâtés are prepared by a resident charcutier, in Dallas one is never very far from Tex-Mex.*

## MARTY'S LAYERED TORTILLA FLATS

*Serves 8 to 10*

2 tablespoons butter
½ pound cooked chicken breast, thinly sliced
2 serrano peppers, minced
2 tablespoons cilantro (fresh coriander)
½ pound cooked flank steak, thinly sliced
14 buttered flour tortillas
1 cup guacamole or puréed avocados
1½ cups refried beans, preferably black beans
1 cup sour cream
⅓ pound Monterey Jack cheese, grated
2 cups shredded lettuce
3 large tomatoes, chopped, black olives, and
    chopped fresh parsley for garnish

Heat 1 tablespoon of the butter in a skillet. Add the sliced chicken, half the peppers, and half the cilantro, and sauté until heated through. Follow the same procedure with the beef and the remaining pepper and cilantro. Set aside the chicken and beef mixtures.

On a large platter, place one of the flour tortillas. Spread on it a portion of the guacamole, then press another tortilla on top of the first. Top with a layer of refried beans, then another tortilla. Lay some chicken slices on this layer. Top the chicken with another tortilla and spread with some of the sour cream and shredded cheese. Continue alternating layers of tortillas, guacamole, beans, chicken, and beef until all the ingredients have been used. Top with the remaining sour cream and shredded cheese. Garnish with chopped tomatoes, black olives, and parsley. To serve, cut into wedges.

## GÂTEAU OF BASIL CRÊPES WITH WILD MUSHROOMS AND GOAT CHEESE

*Serves 12 to 14*

### CRÊPES

1 cup all-purpose flour
3 large eggs
1 cup milk
4 tablespoons chopped fresh basil
½ teaspoon salt
½ teaspoon white pepper
½ teaspoon grated nutmeg

Place the flour in a bowl and make a well in the center. Crack the eggs into the well and beat them slowly, incorporating the flour until it is all absorbed. Slowly pour in the milk, stirring constantly. Add the basil to the batter with the seasonings. Let it rest at least 1 hour; then make the crêpes in a 10-inch buttered skillet. If the batter seems too thick, add more milk.

### FILLING

2 large onions, chopped
4 cloves garlic, chopped
4 tablespoons butter
2 pounds fresh mushrooms (shiitake, oyster, or
    other exotic), thinly sliced
3 large eggs
¾ cup heavy cream
1 pound goat cheese (Montrachet or Boucheron)
1 teaspoon salt
½ teaspoon white pepper
½ teaspoon nutmeg

Sauté the onions and garlic in the butter until they are wilted. Add the mushrooms to the onion

## METROPOLIS
—
CHICAGO

*Shiitake mushrooms, widely available fresh or dried, have a rich, meaty taste. The fanlike oyster mushrooms, if you can find them, have a buttery texture and taste. The goat cheeses called for in this recipe are French chèvres. Boucheron is a white log-shaped cheese with a chalky texture; Montrachet, named for the wine region that produces Montrachet Burgundy, is a moist, mild white chèvre.*

mixture, cooking for 15 to 20 minutes or until all the moisture has been cooked out. Remove the pan from the heat and transfer the mixture to a large bowl, spreading it along the sides of the bowl to speed up the cooling. When the mixture is cool, beat in 3 eggs. Slowly add the heavy cream. Crumble the cheese and add it to the mixture. Add the seasonings and mix well.

Butter a deep 9-inch glass pie plate. Alternate layers of crêpes and filling, beginning and ending with crêpes. Butter a piece of parchment and place it on the top. Cover with foil and bake at 350° for 1 hour. Cool for 2 hours. Loosen the cake with a knife and invert it on a large plate. Slice it into wedges and serve it with strong mustard.

## MIRABELLE
—
DALLAS

*In addition to the carry-out business, Mirabelle does a good deal of catering. One of its most enthusiastic clients is owner Chris Jonsson's father, Philip Jonsson, an active patron of the arts in Dallas.*

## CRÊPE SANDWICH LOAF

*Serves 4 to 6*

CRÊPES

4 eggs
1 cup all-purpose flour
⅛ teaspoon salt
Pinch of sugar
1 cup milk
2 tablespoons melted butter
Vegetable oil for cooking the crêpes

Combine all the ingredients except the vegetable oil in a blender or food processor and process until smooth. Refrigerate the batter for several hours or overnight. To cook the crêpes, heat a small amount of oil in a 7- or 8-inch skillet or crêpe pan. Pour in approximately ¼ cup of batter and tilt the pan so that the bottom is covered with a thin layer of the batter. The crêpe must be very thin, so any excess batter should be poured off before cooking. Cook until the crêpe is browned on the bottom, then turn with a rubber spatula and brown the other side. Repeat the process until all the batter is used; there will be 20 to 24 crêpes. Stack them on a plate. (The crêpe recipe can easily be doubled or tripled. The unused crêpes may be tightly wrapped and frozen for future use.)

FILLING

2 cups milk
5 tablespoons butter
5 tablespoons all-purpose flour
½ teaspoon salt
Dash of white pepper
Freshly grated nutmeg
1 cup heavy cream
¾ cup grated Swiss cheese
3 cups chopped mushrooms
2 tablespoons minced shallots
2 pounds fresh spinach
1½ cups chopped cooked ham

Begin by preparing a béchamel sauce: Heat the milk in a heavy saucepan. In a heavy skillet, melt 4 tablespoons of the butter and whisk in the flour until the mixture is smooth. Cook the mixture for 3 minutes over medium heat, stirring constantly. Remove the pan from the heat, whisk in the hot milk, and add the salt, white pepper, and nutmeg to taste. Place the pan over medium heat and allow the mixture to thicken slightly. Add the cream and cheese and stir until the mixture is smooth and thick.

Melt the remaining 1 tablespoon of butter, add the chopped mushrooms and shallots, and cook until the liquid in the bottom of the pan has evaporated. Set aside.

Wash the spinach carefully to remove all sand and grit. Sauté the spinach in a skillet over medium heat, using the water that adheres to the leaves as the only liquid. When the spinach has wilted, drain it thoroughly and wring it in a dry cloth to remove all liquid, then chop it finely with a knife or in a food processor. Set aside.

Place the mushrooms, spinach, and ham in three separate bowls and add enough béchamel to each to form a thick mixture. Reserve the extra béchamel.

ASSEMBLY

Grated Parmesan cheese
Chopped fresh parsley

Place one crêpe on a heatproof serving dish. Spread with approximately one quarter of one of the fillings. Cover the filling with another crêpe and one third of another filling. Repeat the process, alternating fillings, until all the mixtures and crêpes have been used, ending with a crêpe.

Reheat the remaining béchamel and spread it over the top of the loaf. Sprinkle the top with grated cheese and bake at 375° for 30 minutes or until the loaf is warm throughout. Garnish the top with chopped parsley, slice the loaf into 6 wedges, and serve.

# CORN PUFFS WITH MAPLE SAUCE

*Makes about 3 dozen*

MAPLE SAUCE

1 cup pure maple syrup
6 tablespoons butter
½ teaspoon cinnamon
¼ teaspoon allspice

Place all the ingredients in a saucepan and boil them for 2 to 3 minutes. Remove the sauce from the heat and beat it until it is blended.

PUFFS

1½ cups all-purpose flour
¾ teaspoon salt
2 teaspoons baking powder
2 eggs
½ cup milk
2 cups corn kernels (either frozen or fresh)
½ cup vegetable oil

Sift the flour, salt, and baking powder together. In a large bowl, beat the eggs and add the milk and corn. Fold in the flour mixture, being careful not to overmix. Let the batter sit for a while. Then drop it by tablespoonfuls into the hot oil and fry the puffs until they are golden brown. Drain them and serve with the maple sauce. The sauce can be poured over the puffs or served on the side as a dip.

*These puffs are best served as soon as they are made.*

## J. BILDNER & SONS

—

### BOSTON

*The kitchen that prepares both take-out and catering orders at J. Bildner & Sons is headed by Volker Nagel, a former chef at the Ritz-Carlton in Atlanta. His years in Georgia introduced Nagel to one of that state's best-kept agricultural secrets—the Vidalia onion.*

## STUFFED VIDALIA ONIONS

*Serves 4*

2 large Vidalia onions, or Spanish onions
1 tablespoon olive oil
2 slices white bread
2 eggs
¼ cup milk
⅓ pound cured boiled ham, chopped
3 tablespoons grated Parmesan cheese
2 dashes nutmeg
1 tablespoon chopped fresh parsley
Additional grated Parmesan cheese for garnish

Blanch the onions, with their skins on, for 10 minutes. Drain and let cool. When the onions are cool enough to handle, remove the skins, leaving the ends intact—this will prevent the onions from falling apart. Cut the onions in half, trim the ends, and scoop out the centers, leaving a ¼-inch rim. Mince the scooped-out onion meat and sauté it in the olive oil until it is translucent but not brown.

Lay the slices of bread in a shallow dish. Whip the eggs and milk together and pour the mixture over the bread.

Place the sautéed onions, the chopped ham, the Parmesan cheese, the nutmeg, and the egg-and-milk-soaked bread in the bowl of a food processor. Process until the ingredients are well blended. Add the chopped parsley. Stuff the reserved onion shells with the mixture, sprinkle the tops with the extra Parmesan cheese, and place in a greased shallow baking dish. Bake the onions at 375° for 20 minutes or until the filling is bubbly and the tops begin to brown. Serve hot as a luncheon or supper dish.

# POLPETTINI DE SPINACHE

*Serves 8*

### PATTIES

2 tablespoons butter
¼ cup diced onion
3 cloves garlic, minced
⅛ teaspoon nutmeg
⅛ teaspoon salt
Pinch of white pepper
2 pounds frozen leaf spinach, thawed, chopped, and
    with excess water squeezed out
½ to ¾ cup grated Parmesan cheese
¼ cup ricotta cheese
1 egg
A dusting of flour

Melt the butter in a large sauté pan. Add the onion and sauté it over medium heat until translucent. Add the garlic and sauté it for 3 minutes. Add the nutmeg, salt, white pepper, and spinach, and sauté, stirring constantly, for 5 minutes. Place the spinach mixture in a large bowl; add the Parmesan, ricotta, and egg and mix thoroughly. Let the mixture cool a bit, and then form it into patties. Lay them on a floured cookie sheet, sprinkle some flour on the top of each, and put the sheet in the refrigerator for 30 minutes.

### PREPARATION FOR FRYING

Oil or butter
3 tablespoons grated Parmesan cheese
3 tablespoons all-purpose flour
6 eggs

Heat enough oil or butter to fill a cast-iron skillet to a depth of about ¼ inch. Meanwhile, prepare

## DDL FOODSHOW
—
### LOS ANGELES

*These spinach and cheese patties are a lunchtime and carry-out favorite at film producer Dino De Laurentiis' spectacular DDL Foodshow in Beverly Hills. Though movies are his business, De Laurentiis maintains that food is his passion. He believes it should be presented in a beautiful setting, which is what he has created with Italian-tiled floors, brass-bound double doors, and effective lighting.*

a batter by combining the Parmesan cheese and the flour and then adding the eggs one at a time, beating vigorously after each addition. Dip the patties into the batter; cover both sides well. Fry the patties in the skillet for 1 to 2 minutes on each side, until they are golden brown. Drain the patties on paper towels, patting off any excess grease.

Serve the patties either warm or cold.

## FERNANDO'S INTERNATIONAL FOOD MARKET

—

### FORT LAUDERDALE

*The word "international" is no idle part of the title of Fernando's Fort Lauderdale emporium. There are Scandinavian, South American, Greek, Middle Eastern, and Central American take-out foods and wines and just about every spice and gadget for the gourmet cook.*

*The only delicate part of preparing this spinach pie is working quickly with the tender phyllo dough.*

### SPANAKOPITA

*Serves 12*

¾ pound ricotta cheese
¾ pound feta cheese, crumbled
2 tablespoons grated Romano cheese
4 eggs, beaten
2 pounds fresh spinach, chopped, or 4 packages
    frozen chopped spinach, thawed and with the
    liquid squeezed out
1 large onion or 2 small scallions sautéed in olive oil
2 tablespoons finely chopped fresh dill
¼ teaspoon pepper
28 sheets phyllo dough
1½ cups (3 sticks) butter, melted

Mix together all ingredients except the phyllo dough and the melted butter. Place 14 sheets of the phyllo, brushing the top of each sheet with melted butter, on the bottom of a 12-by-18-inch buttered pan. Spread the filling on top. Cover it with 14 more sheets of buttered phyllo dough. Cut the pastry with a sharp knife into 3-inch squares and bake at 375° for 25 minutes.

## CHICKEN EMPANADAS

*Serves 6*

### FILLING

½ cup minced onion
½ cup minced sweet red pepper
½ cup minced green pepper
2 tablespoons olive oil
3 or 4 fresh tomatoes, seeded and chopped
1 tablespoon chopped garlic
3 large chicken breasts, poached, skinned, boned,
    and minced
Salt to taste
African Bird Pepper to taste
½ cup chopped cilantro (fresh coriander)

Sauté the onions and peppers in olive oil until the onions are translucent. Add the tomatoes and garlic and cook until the mixture begins to become dry. Add the minced chicken and the seasonings, except the cilantro. Continue cooking until the filling is dry, then add the cilantro. Let the filling cool.

### ASSEMBLY

1 17¼-ounce package frozen puff pastry
1 beaten egg yolk

Cut out six 6-inch circles of puff pastry. Place one sixth of the filling in the middle of each circle and fold the circle in half. Seal the edges with beaten egg yolk and press the edges with a fork to secure the closing. Place the empanadas on an ungreased baking sheet and bake at 350° for 20 minutes.

## BOND & BURKHART

—

NEWTON,
MASSACHUSETTS

*When Meri Bond, Harvard MBA, and Lynne Burkhart, with a Ph.D. in anthropology, started their gourmet food business, they ventured far from the halls of academe. Bond quickly realized that MBA skills can be an essential complement to creativity and food savvy. Like all good managers, she gives credit to her talented staff, both in the kitchen and out front.*

*Cranberry Hill is a tiny
shop on Church Street in
downtown Montclair.
During the warm summer
months customers spill out
onto the wide sidewalk, to
eat lunch at tables set up
under the trees.*

## CHEESE AND HAM PIE

*Serves 6 to 8*

2 cups creamed cottage cheese
2 cups ricotta cheese
½ pound smoked ham, diced
¼ pound prosciutto, diced
¼ pound capicola, diced
⅔ cup freshly grated Parmesan cheese
1 teaspoon basil
½ teaspoon oregano
½ teaspoon parsley
¼ teaspoon freshly ground pepper
Pastry for a 2-crust 9-inch pie
1 egg yolk, slightly beaten

Combine all ingredients except the pastry and egg yolk and set aside.

Divide the pastry into 2 parts, one to make a 16-inch circle and one to make a 10-inch circle. Roll the larger portion of pastry into a circle ⅛ inch thick. Carefully lift the dough into a 10-inch springform pan. Press the pastry into the bottom and sides of the pan, and trim the excess pastry from around the rim. Brush the pastry with some of the egg yolk.

Spoon the filling into the bottom crust. Fold the edge of the crust over the filling and brush with more of the egg yolk. Roll the dough for the top crust into a 10-inch circle. Place the pastry over the filling, pressing the edges lightly to seal. Cut a design in the top to allow the steam to escape. Brush the top with the remaining egg yolk. Bake the pie in a 375° oven for 1 hour or until a knife inserted in the center comes out clean. The pie is best served cold or at room temperature.

# ANNETTE GALL'S MEAT PIES

*Serves 6*

FILLING

1 pound ground beef
¾ cup chopped onion
3 tablespoons flour
½ cup chopped celery
¼ teaspoon cinnamon
1 tablespoon lemon juice
1 tablespoon dried parsley flakes
1 teaspoon salt
¼ teaspoon pepper
⅓ cup sour cream
½ cup cooked garbanzo beans

In a large skillet, brown the beef and onions, breaking up the meat with a wooden spoon. Remove the skillet from the heat and drain off and discard the fat. Add the flour to the beef and onion mixture and stir to mix well. Add the remaining filling ingredients and mix again. Return the skillet to low heat and barely heat the mixture through.

ASSEMBLY

1 17¼-ounce package frozen puff pastry
Egg wash (1 egg mixed with 1 tablespoon water)

Cut each pastry sheet into six 3⅓-by-5-inch rectangles. Top six of the rectangles with ½ cup of the meat mixture on each, being careful to keep the edges of the pastry clean. Moisten the edges of the pastry with water and top each with another square of pastry. Press the edges together to seal. Place on a lightly greased baking sheet.
Prepare the egg wash by beating together the

## FIREHOUSE
## NO. 4

—

CHARLESTON,
WEST VIRGINIA

*In this recipe, Firehouse No. 4 manager Annette Gall combines the flavors of her Lebanese heritage with a passion for puff pastry. The meat pies may be frozen before baking or prepared the day before and refrigerated until baking time.*

egg and water. Brush the tops of the pies with the wash and make decorative cuts to allow steam to vent. Bake at 375° for about 30 minutes, until golden brown. Serve hot or warm, with a green salad.

*The gourmet food shop business seems to have a special appeal for the homesick. Tom Anderson was working as a chef in a French restaurant in Spokane, Washington, when he found himself longing for the sweeping skies of his native Kansas. He returned to open the Gourmet Grocer in the Kansas City suburb of Prairie Village, and when that became a success, to open a second shop in the city itself.*

## MEDITERRANEAN TART

*Serves 12*

2 onions, diced
3 cloves garlic, chopped
½ sweet red pepper, julienne-cut
½ green pepper, julienne-cut
Oregano to taste
Salt and pepper to taste
Olive oil for sautéing
2 pounds fresh tomatoes, scalded, peeled, and
    sliced, or 1½ cups drained canned tomatoes,
    diced
1 cup sliced mushrooms
3 whole chicken breasts, split
Chicken stock for poaching
1 pound phyllo dough
Melted butter or oil for moistening phyllo dough
1 cup fine breadcrumbs
½ pound diced ham
1 avocado, mashed
1 cup pitted black olives, sliced
1 teaspoon anchovy paste

Sauté the onions, garlic, and peppers with the seasonings in a small amount of olive oil. When the vegetables are tender, add the tomatoes and cook the mixture for 5 minutes. Set it aside. Sauté the mushrooms in a scant amount of olive oil, then set them aside. Poach the chicken breasts in the stock. Cool, skin, and bone the chicken and tear it into bite-size strips.

Lay two sheets of phyllo on a buttered baking sheet. Spread melted butter or olive oil on them and sprinkle fine breadcrumbs on top. Lay two more sheets on top of the first two and again put on melted butter or oil and breadcrumbs. Continue until 12 sheets of the phyllo dough have been laid on the baking sheet. Spread a layer of the chicken on top. Add a layer of the diced ham, and sprinkle it with the onion-tomato mixture. Next, add a layer of the mushrooms, then the avocado and the black olives. Dab the last layer with anchovy paste in 12 different places, so everyone can have a taste but not too much.

Finish by covering the tart with the remaining sheets of phyllo, using the butter and breadcrumb procedure outlined above. When all the phyllo has been used, slice the tart into 12 pieces but do not separate them. Brush the top with butter or olive oil. Bake the tart, brushing it frequently with oil, in a 375° oven for 20 to 30 minutes, until it is golden brown.

NOTE: Except for the baking, this tart can be made and refrigerated a day in advance. Let the butter or oil brushed on top solidify and then wrap the tart carefully in plastic wrap and refrigerate it.

## MITCHELL COBEY CUISINE

—

### CHICAGO

*Visiting Mitchell Cobey's sleek, bright Chicago food shop is a heady experience —one smells freshly baked croissants, fresh chocolate truffles, a fragrant onion tart by chef Ann Sarrafian baking in the oven. On the walls are framed autographed menus from France's leading restaurants.*

## ONION TART

*Serves 6*

CRUST

½ cup (1 stick) frozen butter, cut into pieces
1⅓ cups all-purpose flour
½ teaspoon salt
4 tablespoons ice water

Process the butter, flour, and salt in a food processor until the mixture resembles coarse meal. Add the water and continue processing until the dough begins to form a ball, 2 to 3 minutes. Roll the dough into a circle 13 inches across. Press the dough into a 9-inch tart pan, prick the bottom, and chill it for 1 hour. Cover the crust with foil and bake it in a 375° oven for 15 minutes. Remove the foil and let the crust cool.

FILLING

½ cup (1 stick) butter
2 large Spanish onions, thinly sliced
1 teaspoon all-purpose flour
1 teaspoon Dijon mustard
1½ cups heavy cream
4 eggs, lightly beaten
1 cup grated Gruyère cheese
Salt and pepper to taste
Pinch of nutmeg

Melt the butter in a large skillet and sauté the onions until they are wilted and translucent. Stir in the flour and sauté for 2 minutes longer. Remove the onions from the heat.

Spread the bottom of the crust with the mustard and then with the onion mixture. Mix together the cream, eggs, cheese, salt, pepper, and nutmeg and pour it over the onions. Bake in a 350° oven for 30 to 35 minutes, or until the top is golden brown. Serve hot.

## VICTORIA'S FISH TART

*Serves 8*

1 pound phyllo dough
2 large onions, sliced thin
1½ tablespoons olive oil
1½ tablespoons butter, melted
1 bunch leeks, cleaned and sliced
2 cloves garlic, finely minced
1 pound spinach, stemmed and washed
3 tablespoons finely chopped fresh dill
Salt and pepper to taste
4 cups ricotta cheese
3 tablespoons finely chopped onion
1 tablespoon chopped fresh parsley
1½ cups grated Swiss cheese
¼ cup grated Parmesan cheese
4 eggs, beaten
1 cup (2 sticks) melted unsalted butter
½ pound fresh halibut or other whitefish, filleted
    and poached in white wine with bay leaf, salt to
    taste, and sliced onion

Remove the phyllo dough from the refrigerator an hour before using it, but leave it in its plastic bag so it won't dry out.

Sauté the onions in the olive oil and butter until they are translucent. Add the leeks and sauté 5 minutes more. Add the garlic and cook 1 minute. Set aside. Steam the spinach for 3 minutes. Squeeze the spinach dry and chop it. Add the spinach and dill to the onion mixture. Season with salt and pepper, mix all the ingredients thoroughly, and set aside.

In a separate bowl, mix the ricotta, finely chopped onion, parsley, Swiss and Parmesan cheeses, and beaten eggs. Season with salt and pepper and set aside.

Unroll the pastry sheets carefully. Use a 2- to

## BRUSSEAU'S

—

### EDMONDS, WASHINGTON

*Jerilyn Brusseau likes promoting the fishermen and farmers of the Pacific Northwest in the café and carry-out kitchen she calls "brusseau's" in the north Seattle suburb of Edmonds. She values fresh fruits and vegetables and local cheese, and she makes frequent trips to the countryside for fresh butter, local mushrooms, wild berries, and edible flowers. Brusseau's talented baker and cook, Victoria John, created this fish tart, combining fresh fish with fresh spinach, leeks, and dill and putting them all into a flaky phyllo crust.*

3-inch pastry brush to brush melted butter on one sheet at a time. Stack four buttered sheets and cut them in half lengthwise. Place the buttered sheets one at a time in a 10-inch glass pie plate, laying them clockwise around the dish with the edges hanging over. Repeat the process to finish lining the plate.

Layer the filling into the pie plate, starting with half the cheese mixture, then adding all the onion-vegetable mixture, then the poached halibut pieces, and finally the remaining cheese mixture. Fold the pastry edges up onto the filling.

Butter four more pastry sheets. Place them on top of the pie and tuck the edges into the sides of the pie. Butter the edges thoroughly. Cut air vents in the top and bake the tart in preheated 350° oven for 1 hour, or until it is golden brown on both top and bottom.

## BROCCOLI AND CHEESE QUICHE

*Makes 1 10-inch deep-dish pie*

A 10-inch pie shell for deep-dish container
Egg wash (1 egg mixed with a little water)
1 cup chopped cooked broccoli, fresh or frozen
¾ cup grated Swiss cheese
¾ cup grated Cheddar cheese
2 tablespoons chopped pimientos
1 tablespoon chopped onion
½ teaspoon salt and pepper, combined

BATTER

6 extra large eggs
1 cup half-and-half
1 cup heavy cream

Coat the unbaked pie shell with the egg wash. Prick the shell and bake it in a 350° oven for 15 minutes. Let the pie shell cool.

Combine all the other ingredients except the batter and place the mixture in the pie shell. Mix together the batter and pour it into the shell until the filling almost overflows. Bake at 275° for 40 to 50 minutes or until the blade of a silver knife inserted into the quiche comes out clean.

LA PRIMA
—
WASHINGTON, D.C.

*Greg Leisch, a business consultant, decided to enter the gourmet carry-out business because he could never get good food fast. "I was sick of eating crummy fast food or spending hours at lunchtime to eat a good meal," he says.*

## FORMAGGIO KITCHEN

—

### CAMBRIDGE

*Not only is there a growing
number of Italian restau-
rants in this country, but
Norma Wasserman finds
that there is a general
trend toward Italian in the
gourmet food business.
Tortas and frittatas are
almost more commonplace
than quiches these days.
This frittata is a favorite
with Formaggio Kitchen's
Cambridge clientele—
especially for picnics of all
kinds, from beach to
tailgate.*

## PORCINI PINE NUT FRITTATA

*Serves 6 to 8*

½ cup white wine
3½ cups chicken broth
1½ ounces dried porcini mushrooms, crumbled
1 cup superfine arborio rice
1 cup heavy cream
1 pound mushrooms, cleaned and sliced
2 cups diced onions
3 cloves garlic, minced
½ cup (1 stick) butter
6 eggs
1 tablespoon salt
Dash of nutmeg
⅔ cup breadcrumbs
1 bunch scallions, chopped
4 ounces grated Parmesan cheese
½ cup pine nuts, toasted

Combine the white wine and ½ cup of the
chicken broth, add the crumbled porcini, and
bring the mixture to a boil. Remove the pan from
the heat immediately and set it aside to soak
while you prepare the other ingredients. Bring
the remaining 3 cups of chicken broth to a boil
and stir in the rice. Reduce the heat and simmer
the rice until all the liquid is absorbed, stirring
frequently. Add the cream and the porcini mixture. Bring the mixture to a boil while stirring,
and then remove it from the heat to cool.

Sauté the mushrooms, onions, and garlic in
the butter until tender. Set aside to cool. Beat the
eggs with the salt and nutmeg. Add the breadcrumbs, scallions, and Parmesan cheese to the
eggs. Fold in the cooled mushroom and rice mixtures and the pine nuts and pour into a greased
9-inch square pan. Bake the frittata at 350° for 45
minutes to 1 hour, until set. Cut in squares and
serve warm or at room temperature.

## CREOLE SAUSAGE FRITTATA

*Serves 5 to 6*

1 pound Creole sausage (andouille preferably, but
   any cooked, smoked sausage will do)
¼ cup vegetable oil
2 cloves garlic, chopped fine
1 green pepper, diced
1 sweet red pepper, diced
2 stalks celery, diced
1 medium onion, diced
6 eggs, beaten
¼ cup chopped fresh basil (or 2 tablespoons dried
   basil)
½ cup freshly grated Parmesan cheese
1 baked potato, peeled and diced
Salt and pepper to taste

Cut the sausage into bite-size pieces. In a sauté
pan, heat the oil and add the garlic, green and
red peppers, celery, and onion and cook them
for about 5 minutes. In a mixing bowl, combine
the sausage with the sautéed vegetables and add
the eggs, basil, Parmesan cheese, potato, and salt
and pepper to taste. Pour into a lightly greased
9-by-12-inch casserole and bake at 375° for 45
minutes to 1 hour, until the top is brown and the
eggs are set all the way through. Cool until just
warm, cut into small portions, and serve. This
frittata reheats well.

## MAGAZINE CUISINE

### NEW ORLEANS

*Chef Robert Shumaker's
customers buy this spicy
dish for breakfast as well as
for a luncheon or dinner
entrée. With Cajun and
Creole cooking taking over
the country, andouille
sausages are becoming
readily available.*

## CONVITO ITALIANO

—

### CHICAGO

Convito, *in Italian, means banquet and everything that goes into a meal, and Convito Italiano has been bringing a veritable banquet of Italian foods and culinary traditions to Illinois. These spinach and cheese sausages from the Piedmont region of Italy make good lunch or brunch fare; they can be almost entirely prepared a day in advance.*

## PIEDMONTESE SPINACH AND CHEESE SAUSAGES

*Serves 12*

1 pound fresh spinach, stemmed
1⅓ cups dry breadcrumbs
1 cup plus 2 tablespoons ricotta cheese
4 eggs
2 medium cloves garlic, finely minced
½ teaspoon salt
5 cups chicken stock
½ cup all-purpose flour
½ cup (1 stick) melted butter
2 teaspoons dried sage, crumbled
Freshly grated Parmesan cheese and parsley sprigs
    for garnish

Wash the spinach thoroughly and shake off the excess water. Cook the spinach in a covered Dutch oven over low heat until wilted (about 5 minutes), stirring frequently. Drain the spinach well and squeeze it dry. Chop it coarsely. Transfer it to a large bowl and blend in the crumbs, cheese, eggs, garlic, and salt until the mixture is very firm. Form it into ½-by-2-inch sausages. Then, if you like, cover and refrigerate them until you are ready to proceed.

Generously butter a large baking dish. Bring the stock to a rapid boil in a large saucepan. Roll the sausages in flour, shaking off all excess. Carefully add the sausages to the stock in batches of 15 to 20 and cook until the sausages float to the top, about 2 minutes. Transfer them to the buttered baking dish, using a large slotted spoon.

Pour the melted butter over the sausages. Sprinkle them with sage and warm them through in a 350° oven. This should take about 10 minutes. Transfer the sausages to individual serving plates and sprinkle with Parmesan cheese. Garnish them with parsley and serve immediately.

## ENLIGHTENED PIZZA

*Serves 8*

SAUCE

⅓ cup chopped onion
4 teaspoons minced garlic
¾ cup chopped mushrooms
⅓ cup finely chopped green peppers
1½ teaspoons oregano
½ teaspoon basil
1 1-pound can ground tomatoes in purée
½ teaspoon salt
½ teaspoon pepper

Combine all the ingredients in a saucepan and bring them to a boil. Cover and simmer over low heat for 20 to 30 minutes, until the vegetables are tender and the sauce somewhat thick. Refrigerate the sauce until you are ready to use it.

PIZZA DOUGH

½ cup warm (110°) water
1½ teaspoons dry yeast
1 teaspoon sugar
1 tablespoon corn oil
1 teaspoon salt
1½ cups flour

Sprinkle the yeast over the water and let it rest for 5 minutes, then stir to dissolve the yeast. Put the remaining ingredients in a food processor or mixing bowl and pour the yeast and water over them. Process or stir and knead the dough until it is smooth. Cover it and let it rise in a warm place until it has doubled in bulk. Punch the dough down and form it into a ball. Let it rest, covered, for 10 minutes. Then form the dough

THE MARKET
OF THE
COMMISSARY

—

PHILADELPHIA

*This vegetarian pizza is appetizing to look at, delicious to eat, and low in calories—only about 250 per slice. The dough can be made in advance and frozen, and the sauce can be prepared three to four days before serving.*

into a circle by putting it on an ungreased baking sheet and pushing it down and out with your hands until you have a 13-inch circle. Make the edges slightly thicker than the center. Cover the dough and let it rise for 30 to 45 minutes, then bake it, uncovered, for 15 to 20 minutes at 325°. Remove it from the oven. Either top it with vegetable topping and sauce or cool it, wrap it in plastic wrap, and freeze it until you are ready to use it.

VEGETABLE TOPPING

3 cups sliced raw mushrooms
2 medium green peppers, seeded and julienne-cut
2 cups thinly sliced onions
8 ounces low-fat mozzarella, shredded

Toss the vegetables with the sauce and pile them onto the baked shell on an ungreased baking sheet. Sprinkle the cheese over the top. Bake the pizza at 350° in the upper third of the oven for about 10 minutes or until the cheese has melted. Score to cut into 8 pieces.

## ITALIAN SAUSAGES

*Serves 6*

2 pounds pork butt, coarsely ground
½ pound pork fat, coarsely ground
1 tablespoon coarsely ground pepper
2 teaspoons salt
1 tablespoon anise seeds
½ cup red wine
Casings, approximately 3 feet

Place the pork and pork fat in a large bowl. Add the remaining ingredients, except casings, and mix well with your hands. Sauté a small amount of the mixture and taste. Correct the seasonings if necessary.

Stuff the mixture into casings or form it into patties. Cook as you would store-bought sausages, but be sure to prick the casings.

NOTE: This recipe is best made a day ahead of cooking so that the flavors can develop.

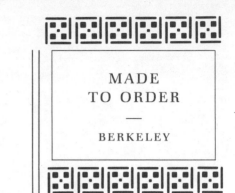

MADE
TO ORDER
—
BERKELEY

*Although sausage making may seem a somewhat formidable operation, the food processor and the option of doing this recipe in patties instead of using casings makes the dish manageable. An added benefit of homemade sausages is being able to control the seasonings to suit your taste.*

# PART 2

—

# ENTRÉES AND ACCOMPANIMENTS

—

POULTRY AND MEAT

SEAFOOD

PASTA

VEGETABLES AND RELISHES

## POULTRY AND MEAT

Chicken Cointreau
Chicken in Watercress Sauce
Chicken Sauté à l'Armoricaine
Pesto Chicken Breasts
Catalonian Chicken and Rice
Parmesan Chicken
Curried Chicken with Papaya and Lime
Chicken Molds with Tomato Cilantro Sauce
Stir-Fried Ginger Chicken
Shai's Stuffed Cantaloupe with Chicken
Stuffed Rock Cornish Game Hens
Smoke-Roasted Quail with Armagnac
Italian Veal-Style Turkey Roast
Veal and Spinach Meatloaf
Stuffed Breast of Veal with Spinach
Stuffed Beef Tenderloin
Beef Bracciole with Pesto and Prosciutto
Orange Cumin Beef Stew
Ruby-Glazed Corned Beef
German Meatloaf
Jalapeño Chili
Baked Kibbe
Moroccan Lamb Kebabs
Afghani Lamb with Spinach
Roast Loin of Pork in Ginger Marinade
Bourbon and Honey Smoke-Roasted
  Pork Tenderloin

## CHICKEN COINTREAU

*Serves 4*

2 large whole chicken breasts, skinned, boned, and
   halved
2 eggs, beaten
Flour for dredging
1 cup cooking oil
¾ cup white wine
¼ cup orange juice concentrate
¼ cup Cointreau
4 tablespoons butter
½ teaspoon all-purpose flour
1 orange, thinly sliced, and chopped fresh parsley
   for garnish

Pound the chicken breasts and dip them first in
the beaten eggs, then in the flour. Heat the oil in
a skillet. Sauté the chicken in the oil until it is
golden and remove it to a baking pan. In a saucepan over high heat, reduce the wine, orange juice
concentrate, and Cointreau by half. Add the butter, stirring until it has melted. Add the ½ teaspoon flour and stir until the mixture reaches a
boil. Pour the sauce over the chicken and place
the baking pan in a 350° oven for 20 minutes.
Place the chicken and sauce on a platter and
garnish with sliced orange and parsley.

## GOURMET PASTA

—

GREAT NECK,
LONG ISLAND

*Chef Kenneth Morakkabi is
following in the footsteps of
his father, who was the
chef at the famous Tour
d'Argent in Paris. He began
his own training in res-
taurants at the age of
fifteen.*

## THE GROANING BOARD

—

### WASHINGTON, D.C.

BEURRE MANIÉ

Knead together 2 table-spoons softened butter and 2 tablespoons flour and roll the mixture into little balls. Add the balls to sauces one by one until the desired consistency is reached.

## CHICKEN IN WATERCRESS SAUCE

*Serves 6*

2 eggs
3 whole chicken breasts, skinned, boned, and halved
1 cup flour
¼ cup oil
Salt and pepper to taste
½ orange, sliced, for garnish

SAUCE

3 cups heavy cream
½ bunch watercress, stems removed
½ bunch parsley, stems removed
4 tablespoons butter
½ clove garlic, minced
1 small onion, finely chopped
*Beurre manié* (see recipe)

To prepare the chicken, first beat the eggs with a whisk until they are well mixed. Dip the chicken breasts in the flour and then in the beaten eggs. Sauté the breasts in the oil for 3 to 4 minutes a side, until they are golden brown. Set aside and keep warm.

Combine all the ingredients for the sauce in a blender or food processor. Blend until smooth but not completely puréed and pour the mixture into a large saucepan. Heat to the boiling point and simmer for 2 to 3 minutes over medium-low heat. While the sauce is simmering, whisk in balls of the *beurre manié* until the desired consistency is reached. Pour the sauce over the chicken breasts, add salt and pepper to taste, and garnish each serving with an orange slice. Serve with rice or pasta.

# CHICKEN SAUTÉ À L'ARMORICAINE

*Serves 8*

2 2-pound frying chickens, quartered
Salt and pepper to taste
¾ cup all-purpose flour
4 tablespoons olive oil
6 tablespoons unsalted butter
1 onion, diced
1 carrot, diced
5 cloves garlic, minced
2 large shallots, chopped
½ cup cognac
2 cups dry white wine
3 tomatoes, peeled, seeded, and chopped
½ cup tomato purée
2 tablespoons chopped fresh parsley
2 teaspoons chopped fresh thyme
2 bay leaves
2 teaspoons chopped fresh tarragon

Season the chicken pieces with salt and pepper and dredge them in flour, shaking off any excess. Heat 2 tablespoons of oil and 2 tablespoons of butter in each of two heavy skillets and sauté the chicken for 10 to 15 minutes, until the pieces are golden brown. Remove the chicken to a heavy casserole or Dutch oven. In one of the skillets, sauté the onion and carrot in the butter and oil for 5 minutes. Add the garlic and shallots and cook for another 5 minutes. Remove the vegetables with a slotted spoon and transfer them to the casserole. Heat the cognac, flambé it, and pour it over the chicken and vegetables. Add the wine, tomatoes, tomato purée, parsley, thyme, bay leaves, half the tarragon, and salt and pepper to taste. Cover the casserole and cook over low heat until the chicken is tender, 20 to 25 minutes. Transfer the chicken to a warmed platter.

## LE MARMITON
—
### LOS ANGELES

*In this dish, chicken replaces lobster in that great French culinary creation,* homard à l'armoricaine. *The origin of the name is a matter of some dispute. According to Julia Child, one faction holds that it refers to the ancient province of Armorique in Brittany, a source of lobsters. Others disagree, contending that the tomato flavor is more typical of Provence and adding that the recipe more likely came from a Parisian chef who named the dish either after an American client or after the country that claims to be home to the tomato. Mrs. Child calls the classic dish* homard à l'americaine, *which seems to indicate her persuasion.*

Put the sauce through a strainer, forcing through as much of the vegetables as possible. Once the sauce is strained, whisk in the remaining 2 tablespoons of butter to make it glossy. Add the rest of the tarragon. Pour the sauce over the chicken and serve. Serve with saffron rice or gnocchi.

NOTE: If you prefer a less full-bodied sauce, substitute 1 cup of chicken stock for 1 cup of the wine.

## GRAPEVINE WINE AND CHEESE
### —
### FORT LAUDERDALE

*Grapevine Wine and Cheese began as just that a decade ago. Today, in tune with the times, they sell croissants and sixty varieties of fancy coffee along with frozen delights like these chicken breasts with pesto.*

## *PESTO CHICKEN BREASTS*

*Serves 6*

3 cups fresh basil leaves, tightly packed
¾ cup olive oil
½ cup pine nuts, toasted and finely chopped
4 cloves garlic, finely chopped
1 cup freshly grated Parmesan cheese
3 large whole chicken breasts, halved and boned but with the skin left on

To make a pesto sauce, process the basil leaves in a food processor and slowly add the olive oil, creating a smooth purée. Add the pine nuts, garlic, and cheese, processing just until the ingredients are combined.

Loosen the skin of each chicken breast just enough to form a pocket. Be sure to leave the skin partially attached. Spoon approximately ¼ cup of pesto sauce under the skin. Tuck the skin and meat around the pesto to make a smooth, even shape. Place the breasts in an oiled baking dish and bake at 350° for 25 to 30 minutes, or until they are golden brown.

## CATALONIAN CHICKEN AND RICE

*Serves 8*

½ cup plus ⅓ cup olive oil
¼ pound bacon, chopped
2 3-pound chickens, cut into serving pieces
½ pound chorizo sausages, skinned and sliced
2 onions, chopped
4 cloves garlic, minced
1 teaspoon fennel seeds
1 sweet red pepper, chopped
1 tablespoon paprika
2 fresh tomatoes, seeded and chopped
4 cups chicken stock
2 cups long-grain rice
Pinch of saffron
½ cup minced fresh parsley
½ teaspoon thyme
1 teaspoon Tabasco
1 cup fresh or frozen peas

In a heavy casserole heat ½ cup of the olive oil and sauté the bacon until it is lightly browned. Remove the bacon from the oil with a slotted spoon and set it aside. In the same oil, sauté the chicken until lightly browned and set it aside; then sauté the chorizo and set it aside. Discard the used oil and add the remaining ⅓ cup oil. Sauté the onions, garlic, fennel seeds, and red pepper. Stir in the paprika and tomatoes. Cook until all the tomato liquid evaporates; then return the chicken, bacon, and sausage to the pan. Bring the chicken stock to a boil. Add the rice, the stock, and all remaining ingredients except half of the parsley to the chicken mixture. Bring it to a boil. Cover and simmer over low heat for 30 minutes. Toss with the remaining parsley and serve.

### TAKE ME HOME
—
WASHINGTON, D.C.

*Olives grow abundantly in Catalonia, a triangle of northeastern Spain near the French Pyrenees, and this chicken and rice recipe makes good use of the mellow oil of good olives.*

**GRETCHEN'S OF COURSE**

—

SEATTLE

*Gretchen Mathers opened her first restaurant/carry-out at Seattle's famed Pike Place Market. By now she has three shops, all strategically placed to serve the city's professionals. She has been repeatedly honored as an entrepreneur and in 1985 won the Washington State Restaurant Woman of the Year award.*

## PARMESAN CHICKEN

*Serves 4 to 6*

½ cup Dijon mustard
2 to 4 tablespoons white wine
1 cup fresh breadcrumbs
1 cup grated Parmesan cheese
3 pounds chicken pieces

Thin the mustard with white wine until a dipping consistency is reached. Set aside.

Combine the breadcrumbs and cheese. Dip the chicken pieces in the mustard mixture and then roll in the crumb mixture. Bake the chicken on a greased baking sheet at 375° for 45 minutes, or until cooked through.

This dish is good served hot or at room temperature and makes a great choice for the picnic basket.

## CURRIED CHICKEN WITH PAPAYA AND LIME

*Serves 4 to 6*

SAUCE

2 tablespoons corn oil (or ½ cup water or
   unseasoned stock)
1 cup diced onions
2 ½-ounce packages Thai green curry paste
2 tablespoons Madras curry powder
½ teaspoon ground cardamom
1 teaspoon minced garlic
2 teaspoons minced ginger root
1 teaspoon salt
2½ cups fresh tomatoes, cut into ½-inch dice
1½ cups ripe fresh papaya, cut into ½-inch dice

Heat the oil and sauté the onions in it over medium heat for about 5 minutes. (Or put the onions and the water or stock in a cold pan; cover it and cook the onions over low heat for about 5 minutes or until they are just tender. Drain.) Add the curry paste and powder, cardamom, garlic, ginger, and salt. Stir to break up the curry paste and cook over medium heat for 2 to 3 minutes. Turn the heat under the sauce to high, add the tomatoes and papaya, and cook for 5 to 7 minutes. Set aside.

CHICKEN

2 tablespoons corn oil (or ¾ cup water or
   unseasoned stock)
1 pound boneless, skinless chicken breast, cut
   across the grain into ½-inch-wide strips
1 large green or sweet red pepper, cut in ¼-inch-
   wide strips

## THE MARKET OF THE COMMISSARY

—

### PHILADELPHIA

*The calorie-conscious chefs at the Market of the Commissary suggest substituting water or stock for the oil in this recipe. They also insist that you not substitute any other curry paste for the Thai green curry, which is available at any Oriental food market.*

1 cup broccoli flowerets, cut into ¾-inch pieces and
    blanched
2 tablespoons fresh lime juice
16 snow peas, steamed
1 cup plain yogurt mixed with 1 tablespoon finely
    chopped fresh mint for garnish

In a separate 10-inch skillet, heat the oil and sauté the chicken over medium heat for 5 minutes. (Or, if you are using the water or stock, put whichever you select in a cold skillet with the chicken.) Add the peppers to the chicken if you have sautéed it and cook 2 minutes more. Add the broccoli and the lime juice to the sauce and keep it warm. Add the snow peas to the chicken and cook them about 30 seconds more. Test the chicken to see if it is done. Pour the sauce over it and mix. Season with salt and pepper to taste. Serve over rice and with the plain yogurt freshened with mint.

## CHICKEN MOLDS WITH TOMATO CILANTRO SAUCE

*Serves 8*

2½ pounds boneless, skinless chicken breasts,
    cut into pieces
10 eggs
4 egg yolks
2 cups heavy cream
Salt and pepper to taste
Nutmeg to taste
20 very thin slices Westphalian ham or prosciutto
Melted butter
Chopped fresh chives and lemon wedges for garnish

TOMATO CILANTRO SAUCE

1½ tablespoons olive oil
4 pounds fresh tomatoes, peeled, seeded, and diced
1 bouquet garni (fresh thyme, bay leaf, parsley)
2 chicken bouillon cubes
2 teaspoons chopped cilantro (fresh coriander)
4 teaspoons butter

Combine the chicken, eggs, egg yolks, cream, salt, pepper, and nutmeg, and blend in batches in a food processor until the mixture is completely smooth. Add 2 of the ham slices, diced, to the chicken mixture. Brush the insides of 8 individual custard cups with melted butter. Line each cup with 2 ham slices and pour in the chicken mousse mixture. Fold the edges of the ham slices over the top to cover. Then cover each filled cup with buttered parchment paper. Place the custard cups in a large, deep baking dish and add water halfway up the depth of the cups. Bake at 220° for 40 to 45 minutes.

    While the molds are baking, prepare the sauce. Place the olive oil, the diced tomatoes, and the remaining ham, diced, in a saucepan. Add

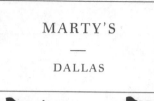

MARTY'S
—
DALLAS

*Marty's is the granddaddy of the Dallas food emporia, having celebrated its fortieth birthday in 1983. The shop claims to carry five thousand gourmet food items as well as a full stock of wines and liquors. Its haute cuisine to take out knows no limits when it comes to service—Marty's will even supply a helicopter to fly its picnicking customers to the site.*

the bouquet garni and the bouillon cubes and simmer for 15 minutes. Remove the bouquet garni and pour the sauce through a strainer into a saucepan. Add salt and pepper to taste and the cilantro, and keep the sauce warm.

Remove the molds from the oven, take off the parchment paper, and unmold onto a platter. Add the 4 teaspoons of butter to the sauce (to provide a glossier finish) and pour the sauce over the molds. Scatter chopped chives on the molds and garnish the platter with lemon wedges.

## STIR-FRIED GINGER CHICKEN

*Serves 8*

4 whole boneless, skinless chicken breasts
1 tablespoon vegetable oil
1 bunch broccoli, separated into flowerets
    and sliced stems
2 cups snow peas
2 cups chicken stock
1 2-inch piece of ginger, peeled and grated
2 cloves garlic
1 tablespoon cornstarch
⅓ cup cold water
⅓ cup soy sauce
⅓ cup dry sherry
1 teaspoon sesame oil

Cut the chicken into 1-inch strips and stir-fry it in the oil over high heat for about 2 minutes, until it has browned and is barely cooked through. Drain the chicken and set it aside. Steam the broccoli flowerets and the sliced stems for 3 minutes, and the snow peas for 1 minute. Set them aside. Boil the chicken stock, ginger, and garlic for 5 minutes and then strain the stock.

Combine the cornstarch with the cold water. Stir it into the chicken stock and boil the mixture until it has thickened. Add the soy sauce, sherry, and sesame oil. Add the chicken and vegetables to the sauce and heat through. Serve with boiled rice.

### FÊTE ACCOMPLIE
—
WASHINGTON, D.C.

*When Jake Martin and Millie White met while looking over storefront property for their separate carry-out shops, the result was fortuitous. They decided to collaborate, and their joint expertise is behind Fête Accomplie.*

## POULET

—

### BERKELEY

*Every Wednesday in July and August, Poulet serves what it calls "garlic lunches." Although not loaded with garlic, this delicious and unusual dish has appeared on those menus. With a green salad and freshly baked bread, it makes a superb lunch or supper.*

## SHAI'S STUFFED CANTALOUPE WITH CHICKEN

*Serves 4*

2 cantaloupes
1 small onion, diced
1 cup cooked rice
1 egg
1 cup diced poached breast of chicken
   (about 1 large breast)
1 tablespoon chopped fresh parsley
1½ teaspoons olive oil
2 cloves garlic, minced
Pinch each of cumin, cayenne pepper, and ginger
Salt and pepper to taste

Cut the cantaloupes in half, peel, seed, rub with salt, and allow to drain upside down for 20 minutes. Combine the remaining ingredients and let stand for 20 minutes. Once the cantaloupes have drained, cut a slice from the bottom of each half so that it will remain upright. Stuff the cantaloupe halves with the chicken mixture and place them on a jelly-roll pan covered with slightly oiled parchment paper. Bake at 350° for 30 minutes, or until the melon begins to brown. Serve hot.

## STUFFED ROCK CORNISH GAME HENS

*Serves 4*

½ cup chopped onion
1 tablespoon olive oil
½ pound ground lamb
1 tablespoon salt
1 teaspoon allspice
1 teaspoon ground cumin
1 teaspoon nutmeg
Pinch of saffron
Pinch of cardamom
1 cup water
½ cup long-grain rice
4 Rock Cornish game hens

Sauté the onions in the oil in a heavy skillet. Add the lamb, 1 teaspoon of the salt, and the spices. Cook the mixture over low heat until the lamb crumbles. Bring the water to a boil. Add the rice, cover, and cook over low heat for 30 minutes or until the rice is tender. Cool and combine with the lamb mixture.

Wash and drain the hens and season them inside and out with the rest of the salt. Stuff the hens with the lamb mixture, truss them, and roast them in a 350° oven for about 1 hour (depending on weight), basting frequently.

## THE WATERGATE CHEFS
—
WASHINGTON, D.C.

*When residents of the Watergate hotel-apartment-office complex don't feel like preparing dinner but do feel like entertaining elegantly, they are likely to stop in at The Watergate Chefs downstairs on their way home and pick up a couple of chef Richard Sultani's Rock Cornish game hens.*

*If possible, get your butcher to prepare the quail for this delectable party dish for you. If you must prepare the quail at home, split them at their backbones, remove the backbones, and flatten the quail to loosen the breastplates. Remove the breastplates carefully with your fingers, being careful not to tear the meat. Cut each quail in half, using the tip of a boning knife. Remove the breastbones of both halves of each quail.*

# SMOKE-ROASTED QUAIL WITH ARMAGNAC

*Serves 4*

1 tablespoon whole black peppercorns
1½ tablespoons chopped fresh tarragon
1½ tablespoons grated lemon peel
2 tablespoons lemon juice
2 tablespoons Armagnac
1 teaspoon kosher salt
1 cup virgin olive oil
6 quail (see instructions for preparing)
Charcoal briquettes
6 to 8 wood chips (preferably fruitwood)

Crack the peppercorns on a cutting board with the bottom of a heavy pan until they are coarse. Mix the peppercorns, tarragon, lemon peel and juice, Armagnac, and salt with the olive oil and blend well.

Place the quail, skin side up, in a ceramic or glass baking dish. Pour the marinade over them, working it in with the fingers to ensure that each quail is well coated. Marinate for no more than 3 hours.

In an outdoor grill, preheat the coals. Soak the wood chips in water for 30 minutes. Pat each quail dry to prevent high flames, add the wood chips to the fire, and barbecue the quail for about 20 minutes on one side, or until crisp, turning and cooking on the other side for an additional 15 minutes.

## ITALIAN VEAL-STYLE TURKEY ROAST

*Serves 6 to 8*

A 5- to 6-pound turkey breast, boned but with the
    skin attached
Salt and pepper to taste
A sprinkling of powdered bay leaf
¼ pound pancetta or prosciutto
6 dried porcini mushrooms, soaked in ½ cup hot
    water to soften
3 tablespoons olive oil
3 tablespoons butter
1 cup chopped onions
2 cloves garlic, mashed
1 cup chopped carrots
Bouquet garni (parsley, thyme, and bay leaf)
2 cups turkey stock

Place the turkey breast, skin side down, on the
counter. Sprinkle the turkey lightly with salt and
pepper and the powdered bay leaf. On one side
of the breast, line up the pancetta or prosciutto,
overlapping the pieces.

Drain the soaked mushrooms, reserving the
liquid, and place the mushrooms along the center of the breast. Roll the breast into a sausage
shape, tucking the ends under to seal in the filling and wrapping the roast securely with the
skin. Tie with cotton twine every 2 inches to help
the roast keep its shape during the cooking.

In a large ovenproof pan, heat the oil and butter and brown the roast on all sides. Add the
onions, garlic, and carrots, and sauté until the
onions begin to brown. Add the bouquet garni,
the reserved mushroom liquid, and 1 cup of the
turkey stock. Place the pan in a 350° oven and
cook, adding more stock as needed and basting
frequently until the roast is cooked through,
about 1½ hours. Remove the turkey from the

### D'ANGELO BROTHERS

—

#### PHILADELPHIA

*The present Santo (Sonny)
D'Angelo's grandfather,
Santo D'Angelo, started this
butcher shop at the time of
the First World War, and it
retains the décor of his day
—glossy tile walls, hanging
wild feathered game and
antlered deer heads. Hostesses all over Philadel-
phia maintain their reputa-
tions by serving Sonny's
stuffed roasts, which
he sells ready to pop into
the oven.*

pan; strain the liquid and discard the solids. Pour off the excess fat and serve the juices as a gravy over slices of roast.

NEUMAN &
BOGDONOFF

—

NEW YORK CITY

*The combination of tomato paste, spinach, and carrot quite transforms this entrée from an ordinary meatloaf to something special. It is spicy, with a somewhat softer consistency than that of other meatloaves.*

## VEAL AND SPINACH MEATLOAF

*Serves 8*

1½ pounds lean ground veal
2 pounds fresh spinach, chopped, or 1 10-ounce
    package frozen chopped spinach, thawed
¾ cup minced carrot
1 cup minced onion
5 eggs
1 cup tomato paste
Salt and pepper to taste
1 cup unseasoned breadcrumbs

Mix all the ingredients except the breadcrumbs, being careful not to force out the air by overmixing. Add the breadcrumbs gradually until the consistency is firm enough that a smooth ball can be formed in the palm of the hand. (To check the seasoning, cook a small patty in a lightly oiled pan over medium heat.)

Line 2 loaf pans or molds with parchment paper and gently spoon the meat into the pans, being careful not to make the mixture too dense. Bake in a 375° oven for 40 to 50 minutes or until the internal temperature reaches 140° on a meat thermometer. If you wish to unmold the loaves, let them cool first. If you are eating the meatloaf hot, slice from the pan.

## STUFFED BREAST OF VEAL
## WITH SPINACH

*Serves 8 to 10*

Approximately 6 pounds boneless breast of veal
Salt and white pepper to taste
2 pounds fresh spinach, or 2 10-ounce packages
    frozen chopped spinach, thawed and with
    liquid squeezed out
½ cup olive oil
1 tablespoon minced garlic
2 15-ounce containers ricotta cheese
1 cup freshly grated Parmesan cheese
1 cup milk
3 eggs
1 tablespoon chopped fresh parsley
1 tablespoon dried basil
1 tablespoon dried rosemary

Lay the boneless breast of veal flat on the table
and cut a 1½-inch pocket the length of the breast
(or ask your butcher to do it). Season the pocket
with salt and white pepper. Pick over and wash
the spinach, pat it dry, and roughly chop it, if
fresh spinach is being used, and lightly sauté it
(or the defrosted, squeezed-dry frozen spinach)
in as much olive oil as is necessary (no more than
4 tablespoons) along with 1 teaspoon of the
garlic. Remove it from the heat and squeeze out
all the excess juice. Put the spinach in a bowl
and add the ricotta and Parmesan cheese, milk,
eggs, and salt and white pepper to taste. Mix to
make a light and creamy stuffing. Then force the
stuffing into the pocket in the breast. Tie the
breast in 4 or 5 places with butcher's string or
skewer it together.

Season the outside of the meat with about 4
tablespoons of the olive oil, the remaining garlic,
and the parsley, basil, and rosemary. Put the
breast in a roasting pan with ⅛ inch of water in

## THE CHEF'S
## MARKET
—
### PHILADELPHIA

*Ed Barranco, George
Georgiou, and Michael
Silverberg are the
triumvirate who opened
The Chef's Market in the
Society Hill section of
Philadelphia in the summer
of 1985. It's modeled after a
combination of Dalmayer's
in Munich and Dean &
DeLuca's, Balducci's, and
Zabar's in New York City.
The thirty-one different
departments of The Chef's
Market include a fish
market that sells more than
thirty kinds of fresh fish
and a meat market where
Black Angus beef is the only
beef sold. This stuffed
breast of veal with spinach
is one of the most popular
of chef Kevin Smith's
prepared entrées.*

the bottom and roast at 350° for 1¾ to 2 hours. When it is done, the veal should have an internal temperature of 150°. Let the veal rest for a few minutes after it is removed from the oven; then slice it and serve.

NOTE: If any spinach stuffing is left over, it makes a fine omelet filling with the addition of a little cheese.

*This stuffed beef tenderloin is delicious served hot but is equally good chilled and then sliced very thin for a cold buffet.*

## STUFFED BEEF TENDERLOIN

*Serves 10 to 12*

1 10-ounce package frozen chopped spinach
2 tablespoons red wine
3 ounces sharp Cheddar cheese, grated
¼ cup black currants
1 egg
1 clove garlic, minced
Salt and black pepper to taste
A 5½ to 6-pound beef tenderloin, trimmed and
    butterflied, at room temperature

Defrost the spinach and squeeze out the extra moisture. Add the wine, cheese, currants, egg, and seasoning. Flatten out the tenderloin and place a 1-inch-wide row of filling down the center of the meat. Bring the long sides of the meat up over the filling and tie the meat at about 1-inch intervals. Sprinkle with salt and pepper.

Roast the meat for 30 minutes, or until a meat thermometer inserted into the thickest part of the tenderloin registers 135°. Remove the meat from the oven and let it rest for 15 minutes before slicing it, or, after it has cooled, refrigerate it and serve it cold another day.

## BEEF BRACCIOLE WITH PESTO AND PROSCIUTTO

*Serves 6*

### STUFFING

2 cups fresh basil leaves
6 cloves garlic
1 cup pine nuts
1 cup extra-virgin olive oil
1 cup grated Parmesan cheese
Black pepper to taste
¼ pound prosciutto, cubed
½ cup breadcrumbs

Process the basil, garlic, pine nuts, and olive oil in a food processor until coarsely chopped. Add the cheese and pepper and process until all the ingredients are combined. Scrape the pesto into a bowl. Add the prosciutto and breadcrumbs and mix together.

### ASSEMBLY

12 slices of beef round, pounded to ¼-inch thickness with a cleaver or mallet
Salt and pepper to taste
¼ cup olive oil
2 cups beef broth
1½ cups dry vermouth or sherry

Spoon the stuffing onto the slices of meat and add salt and pepper to taste. Roll each slice and secure it with toothpicks. Heat the oil in a Dutch oven and brown the beef rolls over medium heat. Add the beef broth and simmer over low heat 1¾ hours, or until tender.

Remove the bracciole from the pot and degrease the gravy. Add the sherry and reduce the

## CHRISTIN'S CHARCUTERIE

—

WELLESLEY, MASSACHUSETTS

*The cheerfully chic pink, white, and gray art deco motif of this gourmet food shop in Wellesley is quite different from the bureaucratic décor at the State Department of Social Services, where George Christin once served as an administrator. A unique style is equally evident in chef Tony Vischer's version of bracciole, in which thin slices of beef are stuffed with a wonderful combination of salt-cured Italian ham and the smooth, nutty taste of pesto.*

gravy by half. Adjust the seasonings. Return the beef rolls to the pot and warm them over low heat. Serve with fresh pasta and tomato salad with balsamic vinaigrette.

*If you look at the mouth-watering take-out menus at the Monticello Gourmet, you don't know where to begin—or end. You can start with a cognac liver mousse appetizer; follow that with crabmeat-stuffed mushrooms or raw sirloin strips in mustard scallion sauce; have a green pea with mint soup or a tomato aspic with blue cheese and avocado salad; or choose a hearty entrée like this cumin beef with pearl onions, which, all by itself, is quite a treat.*

## ORANGE CUMIN BEEF STEW

*Serves 6*

3 pounds chuck for stew, in 1-inch cubes
Cooking oil
½ cup orange juice
Grated rind of 1 orange
½ cup beef broth
1 6-ounce can tomato paste
¼ cup red wine vinegar
2 tablespoons light brown sugar
4½ teaspoons ground cumin
1 tablespoon oregano
3 cloves garlic, minced
1½ teaspoons allspice
1 bay leaf
Half of a 16-ounce bag frozen pearl onions
1 pound small mushrooms
Butter for sautéing
Salt and pepper to taste

Sauté the beef in foaming oil a few pieces at a time. Transfer it to a large pot and add all the other ingredients except the onions, mushrooms, butter, and salt and pepper. Simmer for about 1½ hours, or until the beef is tender. If the sauce is too thin, add 2 tablespoons of *beurre manié* (see page 103) or cornstarch dissolved in water. Sauté the onions and mushrooms briefly in butter and add them to the stew. Simmer briefly again; add salt and pepper to taste and then serve.

## RUBY-GLAZED CORNED BEEF

*Serves 8 to 10*

A 10½-pound fresh corned beef, with water to cover
12 whole black peppercorns
2 large yellow onions (approximately ½ pound each)
8 whole cloves
6 large cloves garlic, peeled
2 large carrots, peeled and cut into 2-inch lengths
2 large stalks celery, cut into 2-inch lengths
½ cup coarse-grain mustard
½ cup dark brown sugar

RUBY CURRANT PORT SAUCE

2 cups red currant jelly
½ cup ruby port wine
1 tablespoon orange zest (removed from 2 oranges
   with zester)
1½ tablespoons lemon zest (removed from 3 lemons
   with zester)
¼ cup orange juice
¼ cup lemon juice
½ cup finely chopped shallots
1 tablespoon dry mustard
1½ teaspoons ginger
1½ teaspoons coarsely ground black pepper
½ teaspoon salt

Place the corned beef in a large heavy casserole on top of the stove. Add water to the casserole to cover the meat, and add the peppercorns. Peel the onions, stud them with the cloves, and add to the casserole. Add the garlic, carrots, and celery, and bring the liquid to a boil over medium heat. Reduce the heat to low, cover the casserole, and cook it for 3¼ hours, or until the corned beef is tender. Turn the beef every hour during the cooking so that it cooks evenly.

While the corned beef is cooking, prepare the

THE SILVER
PALATE
—
NEW YORK CITY

*The fame of their small neighborhood store on Manhattan's Upper West Side has spread far and wide by now, but Sheila Lukins and Julee Rosso continue to turn out exciting recipes while juggling the running of a thriving mail order business, a large catering service, and cooking classes that take note of the many details that add up to pleasurable dining. Enhanced by a sauce of port wine and citrus fruits, this sturdy Irish favorite is excellent hot or cold.*

ruby currant port sauce. In a small saucepan over low-medium heat, combine all the ingredients. Stir the mixture frequently until the jelly has melted. Remove from the heat and let stand for at least 30 minutes.

When the corned beef has finished cooking, remove it from the liquid and place it in a 12-by-17-by-2½-inch roasting pan, fat side up. Remove any excess fat. With a wide pastry brush, evenly spread the mustard over the top of the beef. Pour the currant port sauce over the beef and in the bottom of the pan. Sprinkle the top of the meat with the brown sugar. Place the pan on the middle rack of a 350° oven. Baste the meat every 15 minutes for 45 minutes, or until the corned beef is glazed and has a deep, rich color.

Place the beef on a large oval serving platter and spoon some sauce over the top. Pass the remaining sauce.

## GERMAN MEATLOAF

*Serves 6*

1 large onion, minced
3 tablespoons vegetable oil
2 cups coarse rye breadcrumbs
½ cup milk
1 pound ground chuck
½ pound coarsely ground pork
2 cloves garlic, minced
½ cup grated Parmesan cheese
2 eggs
1 teaspoon fennel seed
1 teaspoon salt
1 teaspoon pepper
½ cup minced fresh parsley

Sauté the onion in the oil until tender, about 10 minutes, and cool. Soak the breadcrumbs in the milk for about 10 minutes, until the milk has been absorbed. Toss the breadcrumbs and onions lightly with the rest of the ingredients. Place the mixture in a 9-by-5-inch loaf pan and bake at 375° for approximately 45 minutes.


## JALAPEÑO CHILI

*Serves 8 to 10*

1 pound hot Italian sausages, cut into 1-inch lengths
1 pound sweet Italian sausages, cut into
    1-inch lengths
4 tablespoons best-quality olive oil
2 cups chopped onion
3 tablespoons minced garlic
2 pounds ground chuck
2 green peppers, coarsely chopped
2 sweet red peppers, coarsely chopped

### LET'S EAT
### —
### TIBURON, CALIFORNIA

*Marsha Workman and Sharon Leach started their take-out shop in 1980, having owned a bakery next door to the premises for several years. They never had time for meal preparation and decided the only way out was to be able to cook during working hours. Since opening they have been joined by a third partner, Cathy Lasky, and by chef Bob Hynes.*

### THE SILVER PALATE
### —
### NEW YORK CITY

*Since the very ingredients can be so fiery, it's not surprising that chili recipes*

*are a frequent subject of heated debate among cooks. Everyone has a favorite. This hearty version from The Silver Palate tones down the bite of jalapeño peppers and hot Italian sausages by including their cooler counterparts as well.*

6 medium green jalapeño peppers, seeded, stemmed, and cut into ⅛-inch dice
5 cups drained canned Italian plum tomatoes
1 cup red wine
1 cup chopped fresh parsley
2 tablespoons tomato paste
6 tablespoons chili powder
3 tablespoons ground cumin
2 tablespoons oregano
1 tablespoon basil
1 tablespoon salt
1½ teaspoons fennel seeds
2 teaspoons freshly ground black pepper
2 pounds fresh Italian plum tomatoes, quartered
Grated Monterey Jack cheese, sour cream, and sliced scallions (greens included) for garnish (optional)

In a large heavy skillet over medium heat, cook the sausage pieces until they are well browned. (You may add ¼ cup water to the skillet during the browning.) Let the sausages drain on paper towels. Set aside.

Place the oil in a deep heavy casserole over low heat and sauté the onions and garlic for 5 minutes, until just wilted. Raise the heat to medium, add the ground chuck, and cook until the meat is browned, stirring frequently. Add the sausages to the casserole. Add the peppers and cook for 10 minutes longer, stirring frequently, until the peppers are slightly wilted. Remove the casserole from the heat and add the drained tomatoes, wine, parsley, tomato paste, and all the herbs and spices. (Do not add the fresh plum tomatoes.) Return the casserole to medium heat and cook the chili slowly, stirring frequently, for 10 minutes. Add the quartered fresh tomatoes and cook for an additional 10 minutes. Serve the chili in bowls and pass bowls of the optional garnishes. Crusty bread and a hearty red wine are good accompaniments.

## BAKED KIBBE

*Serves 12*

KIBBE

1½ cups bulghur
1 pound ground lamb
1 pound ground beef
1 medium onion, finely grated
2 teaspoons salt
¼ teaspoon black pepper
1½ teaspoons allspice
1½ cups ice water

Rinse the bulghur in cold water 3 to 4 times. Drain the water from it by cupping the hands and squeezing out all the moisture. Set it aside for 15 minutes. Place the meat, grated onion, salt, pepper, and allspice in a large bowl. Soften the mixture by kneading with the ice water. Add the bulghur as you knead to give body to the mixture.

Grease a 9-by-13-inch pan with vegetable oil and spread half of the raw kibbe smoothly over the bottom of the pan.

FILLING

1 pound ground lamb
Butter for browning (not more than 2 tablespoons)
1 medium onion, finely chopped
⅓ cup pine nuts
½ teaspoon salt
½ teaspoon allspice
⅛ teaspoon black pepper
3 tablespoons vegetable oil

Sauté the lamb in the butter for 5 minutes. Add the onions, pine nuts, and spices and continue sautéing until the lamb is nicely browned.

Spread the filling evenly over the layer of

*Once a mosquito-infested mangrove swamp and more recently the famous spring-recess rendezvous for 250,000 college students, Fort Lauderdale is now undergoing yet another transformation—into a regional city with a new museum, a renovated downtown area, and that latest symbol of revitalization, a variety of good places to eat and to buy gourmet foods to go. Fernando D'Amico and his niece, Carla Pastura, are part of the new Fort Lauderdale scene.*

kibbe. Then cover the filling with the remaining kibbe. Smooth the surface well and score it into triangles with a knife. Loosen the edges of the pan with a spatula. Pour the oil over the top of the kibbe to keep it from drying out, and bake it at 475° for 40 to 45 minutes. Let the dish sit about 15 minutes after you have removed it from the oven; then pour off the excess oil before serving.

*A cool cucumber, yogurt, and mint salad would make a refreshing accompaniment to this spicy North African lamb dish.*

## MOROCCAN LAMB KEBABS

*Serves 4*

2 pounds lean lamb, cut into 2-inch cubes
3 cloves garlic, peeled
Pinch of saffron
2 teaspoons ground cumin
2 teaspoons turmeric
1 teaspoon cinnamon
1 teaspoon paprika
1 teaspoon minced fresh ginger root
1 teaspoon salt
1 tablespoon *harissa* (Moroccan hot pepper paste)
½ cup olive oil
1 tablespoon sherry wine vinegar
1 sweet red pepper, cut into 1-inch squares
1 sweet yellow pepper, cut into 1-inch squares

Place the lamb in a stainless steel or ceramic mixing bowl. Combine all the other ingredients except the peppers in a blender or food processor. Purée to a smooth paste and pour over the lamb, mixing thoroughly. Allow the lamb to marinate overnight in the refrigerator.

The next day, alternate lamb and pepper pieces on skewers and grill them over a medium-hot fire for 6 to 10 minutes, turning often.

## AFGHANI LAMB WITH SPINACH

*Serves 4 to 6*

2½ pounds lamb stew meat, preferably leg
⅓ cup olive oil
¾ pound onions, diced large
4 teaspoons chopped garlic
2 teaspoons turmeric
¼ teaspoon nutmeg
¼ teaspoon ground cardamom
1 teaspoon crushed red pepper, or to taste
½ teaspoon cinnamon
1 32-ounce can tomatoes, drained and chopped
1 cup rich brown veal or beef stock
⅓ pound fresh spinach, washed and drained
½ cup yogurt
1 tablespoon grated lemon peel
Salt to taste
¼ cup pine nuts, roasted in a 350° oven for about
    3 minutes

Sear the lamb in the olive oil in a cast-iron skillet or Dutch oven. Add the onions and sauté them for 2 minutes; then add the garlic and sauté it for 1 minute. Put in the turmeric, nutmeg, cardamom, crushed red pepper, and cinnamon and sauté the mixture for 1 to 2 minutes more, being careful not to burn the onions or garlic. Add the tomatoes and veal stock and stir.

Cover the dish and bake it in a 350° oven for about 1 hour, until the meat is tender and begins to break up. Remove the dish from the oven and add the spinach, stirring until the spinach is wilted and blended in. Allow the stew to cool slightly. Add the yogurt and lemon peel and salt to taste. Sprinkle with the roasted pine nuts.

### SOMEPLACE SPECIAL
—
MCLEAN,
VIRGINIA

*Executive chef Phil Soroko created this dish that takes its inspiration from the Middle East. Serve it over rice pilaf and top with a sprinkling of pine nuts.*

## CAFFÈ QUADRO

—

### SAN FRANCISCO

*Joyce Goldstein has been a serious food professional since 1965, when she turned from a successful career as a painter to teaching cooking. Since then she founded the first international cooking school in the Bay Area, was a food writer for* Rolling Stone, *wrote a cookbook, and taught kitchen design, and she now runs two highly successful restaurants, Caffè Quadro and Square One. She has traveled a great deal and her menus often include dishes from the Mediterranean, the Orient, and Latin America.*

## *ROAST LOIN OF PORK IN GINGER MARINADE*

*Serves 4 or 5*

A 2- to 2½-pound boneless pork loin, trimmed of all
    fat and sinew
1 clove garlic, minced
1 3-inch piece of fresh ginger root, peeled and
    roughly chopped
2 tablespoons soy sauce
2 tablespoons tomato purée
1 tablespoon wine vinegar
4 tablespoons brown sugar
½ cup chicken or beef stock

Place the pork loin in a glass or ceramic dish, and blend the remaining ingredients in a food processor or blender. Cover the pork with the marinade and refrigerate overnight.

Bring the pork to room temperature and roast in a baking pan in a 350° oven for approximately 1 hour, basting occasionally with the marinade. The pork may be served warm or at room temperature, sliced thin and accompanied by chutney or mustard. Caffè Quadro serves the pork with Curried Rice Salad, page 234.

## BOURBON AND HONEY SMOKE-ROASTED PORK TENDERLOIN

*Serves 6*

1 cup olive oil
½ cup bourbon
3 tablespoons honey
½ cup lemon juice
1 tablespoon minced garlic
1½ tablespoons peeled and grated fresh ginger root
¼ cup soy sauce
½ cup thinly sliced onion
2 tablespoons fresh sage, coarsely chopped
2 teaspoons black pepper
1 teaspoon salt
3 pork tenderloins
Charcoal briquettes
6 to 8 wood chips (preferably fruitwood)

Combine all ingredients except the last three to make the marinade, and blend well. Lay the pork tenderloins in a ceramic or glass dish and pour the marinade over them. Turn the tenderloins several times during the 24 hours that they are marinating in the refrigerator. When ready to cook, pat the pork dry.

Preheat the charcoal in an outdoor grill and soak the wood chips in water for 30 minutes. Add the chips to the hot coals. Roast the pork evenly about 40 minutes or until its internal temperature is 165°. If the pork is to be eaten hot, allow it to sit on the edge of the grill for 10 minutes or so after it is cooked so that the juices can be drawn back into the meat.

SOMEPLACE
SPECIAL
—
MCLEAN,
VIRGINIA

*The marinade for this dish can be prepared a day in advance, and the marinating should go on for 24 hours. The pork is good either hot or cold, accompanied by a green tomato chutney.*

## SEAFOOD

Fillet of Sole Pré-Catalan
Fillet of Sole with Creamed Spinach and Pears
Grey Sole in Carrot and Sherry Sauce
Snapper Orphie
Calamari Sesame
Codfish Cakes with Ginger
Redfish Milford
Hot Peppered Shrimp
Shrimp and Artichoke Hearts in Phyllo
Shrimp and Rice Arabella
Soft-Shell Crabs Dijon
Maryland Backfin Crab Imperial
Regina's Crab Cakes
Oysters in Fresh Tarragon Cream
Key West Lobster

## FILLET OF SOLE PRÉ-CATALAN

*Serves 8*

4 pounds fillet of sole
4 tablespoons unsalted butter
3 shallots, chopped
Salt and pepper to taste
3 tomatoes, peeled, seeded, and diced
1 pound mushrooms, sliced
Juice of 2 lemons
Dry white wine almost to cover
3 cups heavy cream
¼ cup chopped fresh parsley

Flatten the fillets and fold them in half, skin side in. Butter the bottom of a heavy skillet, and sprinkle it with the shallots. Lay the folded fillets on top, and cover them with the tomatoes and mushrooms. Season with salt and pepper and pour the lemon juice on, reserving a few drops for the sauce. Add enough wine almost to cover the fish. Lay buttered parchment paper over the fish and put a lid on the skillet.

Bring the fish to a simmer on top of the stove over medium heat, then move it to a 425° oven for 8 to 10 minutes. When the fillets flake easily when touched with a fork, remove them to a serving platter, along with the mushrooms, tomatoes, and shallots, and cover with parchment paper to keep warm.

Reduce the cooking juices in the skillet almost completely by cooking over high heat. Add the cream and reduce it until the sauce is the consistency of heavy cream. Whisk the sauce occasionally to prevent sticking. (The reduction process may take some time, so be patient.) When the sauce has thickened, correct the seasoning if necessary, add the reserved lemon juice, some small pieces of butter, and the

## LE MARMITON

—

### SANTA MONICA, CALIFORNIA

*There is no need to go to Paris to enjoy the finest of French cuisine, as French-born chef René Robin is wont to point out to his customers. He proves his point with entrées such as this regional dish from southwestern France.*

chopped parsley. Drain off any juices that may have accumulated on the serving platter and pour the sauce over the fish.

GOURMET PASTA

—

ALBERTSON,
LONG ISLAND

*The Benjamin family used to live in Rome, where they owned an American restaurant called The Cowboy. Seven years ago, back in the United States, they opened Gourmet Pasta on Long Island and have now expanded to New York City.*

## FILLET OF SOLE WITH CREAMED SPINACH AND PEARS

*Serves 6 to 8*

2 Bartlett pears, peeled and sliced
1 cup pear nectar
1 pound fresh spinach, chopped
2 tablespoons butter
1 teaspoon flour
½ cup heavy cream
12 small fillets of sole
Salt and pepper to taste
Paprika

In a skillet, heat the pears and the nectar. Reduce the liquid by half and add the chopped spinach, 1 tablespoon of the butter, the flour, and the cream. Mix well until smooth and cook for 3 to 4 minutes. Remove from the heat and keep warm.

Place 6 of the fillets on the bottom of a buttered baking dish and spoon the spinach-pear mixture on top of each until the mixture is all gone. Arrange the other fillets beside the first, setting them on their edges so that they fall over the spinach filling, leaving a small amount of the spinach exposed. Melt the remaining butter and pour it over the top. Sprinkle with salt and pepper and paprika and bake in a 350° oven until the sole turns white, about 35 minutes.

## GREY SOLE IN CARROT AND
## SHERRY SAUCE

*Serves 6*

2½ pounds grey sole fillets
½ lemon, sliced
⅓ cup dry white wine
⅓ cup water
Chopped fresh parsley to taste
4 bay leaves
Pinch of thyme
A few peppercorns
½ small yellow onion, sliced
2 cloves garlic, crushed

CARROT AND SHERRY SAUCE

3 tablespoons butter
2 carrots (about ¼ pound), finely grated
⅓ cup dry sherry
1½ tablespoons all-purpose flour
⅓ cup light cream
Approximately half the cooking liquid from the fish
Salt and pepper to taste
Chopped fresh parsley to taste
2 tomatoes, peeled, seeded, and chopped, for
    garnish

Roll the sole fillets and place in a shallow buttered baking dish. Top the fish with the sliced lemon and pour a mixture of the remaining ingredients (except the sauce) over it. Bake, covered with foil, in a 350° oven for 20 to 25 minutes. Drain off and reserve the cooking liquid, discard the onions, bay leaves, and peppercorns, and keep the fish warm, covered, on a heated platter.

While the fish is cooking, prepare the sauce. Melt the butter, add the carrots, and sauté for a few minutes, until the carrots are tender. Add the sherry and simmer for 5 minutes. Add the flour,

THE
FISHMONGER
—
CAMBRIDGE

*At The Fishmonger, many of the carry-out items are available from the freezer chest, and this is one of the "regulars." Other kinds of sole, or flounder, may be substituted for the grey sole.*

cook for 3 minutes, and slowly add the cream. Once the sauce has thickened, thin it to the desired consistency by adding small amounts of the fish cooking liquid. Add salt, pepper, and chopped parsley to taste. Sauce the fish and garnish the platter with chopped tomatoes.

## LEONARDI'S INTERNATIONAL, INC.

—

### FORT LAUDERDALE

*Chef Rick Kitten named this succulent fish dish for his Philippine-born wife, Orphie. The macadamia nut sauce nicely complements the delicate snapper.*

## *SNAPPER ORPHIE*

*Serves 6*

6 6-ounce skinned snapper fillets
Flour for dredging
2 eggs, beaten
1 cup (2 sticks) butter
1 to 1½ cups macadamia nuts, in halves and pieces
Juice of 1 lemon
2 cups chopped fresh parsley
Salt and pepper to taste
Lemon slices for garnish

Dip the snapper fillets in flour, in the beaten egg, then in the flour again. Heat half the butter in an 8-inch sauté pan over low heat, making sure that it does not burn. Sauté the snapper in the butter until the fillets are golden brown on both sides. Remove the fish from the pan and keep it warm.

Heat the rest of the butter in a saucepan over medium heat. Add the nuts, lemon juice, parsley, and a pinch of salt and pepper. Again, do not let the butter burn. Place each snapper fillet on a heated plate and top with the sauce. Serve immediately, garnishing each plate with lemon slices.

## CALAMARI SESAME

*Serves 6*

½ cup dry breadcrumbs, seasoned with
     salt and pepper
½ cup sesame seeds
6 5-ounce tenderized squid steaks
1 egg, beaten
1 cup (2 sticks) clarified butter (see recipe)
About 1 cup Garlic Lime Butter (see recipe below)
1 sweet red pepper, julienne-cut, for garnish

On a large plate or cutting board, mix the bread-crumbs and sesame seeds. Dredge each squid steak in the egg and then in the breadcrumb mix-ture. In a large heavy skillet or sauté pan, heat the clarified butter and quickly pan-fry the squid steaks, a few at a time, until they are golden brown, 2 to 3 minutes to a side. (Do not overcook or they will be tough.) Arrange the steaks on in-dividual dinner plates and top each with a pat of Garlic Lime Butter. Garnish the plate with the julienne of red pepper.

### Garlic Lime Butter

*Makes 2 cups*

1 pound unsalted butter, at room temperature
Juice of 3 limes
1 heaping teaspoon minced garlic
¼ teaspoon salt
⅛ teaspoon cayenne pepper
¼ bunch parsley, minced

In an electric mixer, whip the butter for 2 min-utes at medium speed. Slowly incorporate the lime juice and then add the remaining ingredi-ents. Pack the butter into a rectangular container

PIRET'S
—
SAN DIEGO

*Squid steak is a favorite entrée at Piret's bistros and carry-outs. The steaks, which taste a lot like abalone and are cooked in a similar fashion, come from very large squid caught by commercial fishermen. The steaks are tenderized and frozen at sea. If you have trouble finding squid steaks in your area, check with a fish wholesaler, or try boned chicken breasts instead of the squid.*

CLARIFIED BUTTER

To clarify butter, place it in a saucepan and heat it over medium heat until the butter begins to froth and white milk solids sink to the bottom. Skim off the foam and carefully pour out the clear yellow liquid (the clarified butter), leaving the white residue in the pan. Clarified butter is less likely to burn during frying and sautéing.

and refrigerate until cold enough to slice. The leftover butter can be refrigerated for several days, tightly wrapped, or frozen for 2 to 3 months. It is delicious on chicken and other fish dishes.

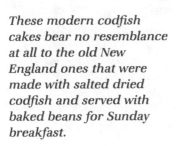

*These modern codfish cakes bear no resemblance at all to the old New England ones that were made with salted dried codfish and served with baked beans for Sunday breakfast.*

## CODFISH CAKES WITH GINGER

*Serves 4*

2 pounds cod fillets
2 eggs, slightly beaten
⅔ cup fresh white breadcrumbs (about 5 slices of
    bread)
2 tablespoons chopped cilantro (fresh coriander)
1 tablespoon grated fresh ginger root
¼ cup mayonnaise
1 teaspoon hot pepper oil
Salt to taste
½ cup (1 stick) butter for sautéing

Steam the cod over moderate steam for 7 minutes. Drain off any excess liquid and combine the fish with the other ingredients, mixing gently. Melt the butter in a skillet. Shape the codfish mixture into 7 or 8 patties and sauté them over moderate heat for about 3 minutes on each side, until brown.

## REDFISH MILFORD

*Serves 4*

2 white onions, peeled and thinly sliced
Olive oil
Salt and pepper to taste
2 sweet red peppers, julienne-cut
4 ripe tomatoes, peeled and cut into wedges
¾ cup dry vermouth
½ cup basil pesto (see recipe, page 233)
4 8-ounce redfish or snapper fillets
Fresh lime juice
8 lime wedges and apple chutney for garnish
   (optional)

Sauté the sliced onions in olive oil in a large sauté pan until they are well coated with oil but not translucent. Sprinkle with salt and pepper. Leaving the onions in the pan, lay the red pepper strips over the onions, but do not mix them. Place the tomato wedges over the pepper strips. Pack the vegetables down lightly, but, again, do not mix them. Over medium-high heat, allow the onions to sizzle. When you are sure the pan is hot, add the vermouth and cover the pan quickly to take advantage of the steam the vermouth will produce. Reduce the heat to low for 10 minutes. Do not stir.

Spread 2 tablespoons of the basil pesto on each fish fillet and sprinkle with lime juice. Place a little of the vegetable mixture in a buttered baking dish and lay the fish on top, with the fillets about an inch apart. Cover the fish with the rest of the vegetable mixture and bake it in a 400° oven until the fish is tender, about 12 to 15 minutes. Serve the fish with Onion Cumin Rice (page 174) and pour the pan juices from the fish over both. Garnish with lime wedges and chutney, if you wish.

OUISIE'S
TABLE
—
HOUSTON

*Eighteen years ago Elouise Cooper began packing three-course brown bag lunches for reporters on the* Houston Chronicle *who couldn't leave their typewriters to go out to eat. Now she serves more than 250 patrons a day in her restaurant in Houston's Village area, near Rice University and the Texas Medical Center, but she is still providing lunches and dinners to go for the doctors, professors, and businesspeople of the neighborhood.*

*Chris Jonsson studied at cooking schools all over the world before returning to Dallas to open one of the city's first gourmet shops in 1982. Her shop includes an outdoor restaurant, where this piquant dish is a popular offering.*

## HOT PEPPERED SHRIMP

*Serves 4*

2 scallions
2 teaspoons minced ginger root
1 tablespoon ketchup
1 tablespoon hot sauce
1 tablespoon sherry
1 tablespoon soy sauce
1 teaspoon sugar
2 tablespoons peanut oil
1 clove garlic, crushed
1 pound shrimp, shelled and deveined
½ teaspoon salt
½ teaspoon cayenne pepper

Mince both the white and the green parts of the scallions, reserving the minced green part for garnish. Mix the white part of the scallions with the ginger, ketchup, hot sauce, sherry, soy sauce, and sugar. Set aside. Heat the oil in a wok or heavy skillet until it is very hot. Brown the garlic in the oil and discard. Add the shrimp to the oil and stir-fry just until the color changes. Add the seasoning mixture to the wok and mix well. Stir in the salt and cayenne.

Serve the shrimp immediately with hot boiled rice. Garnish with the minced green onion. Cucumbers mixed with rice wine vinegar, soy sauce, and a small amount of sesame oil make a cool accompaniment.

NOTE: If you want the shrimp to appear "glazed," add a mixture of 2 tablespoons water and 2 tablespoons cornstarch just before removing the dish from the wok.

## SHRIMP AND ARTICHOKE HEARTS IN PHYLLO

*Serves 8*

### TARRAGON SAUCE

½ cup (1 stick) butter
2 tablespoons chopped shallots
½ cup flour
2 cups light cream
¼ cup white wine
1 bay leaf
¼ cup chopped fresh tarragon
Salt and white pepper to taste

Melt the butter in a medium-size saucepan over low heat. Add the shallots and sauté them until they are translucent. Add the flour and stir for 3 minutes. Gradually whisk in the cream. Continue whisking until the mixture thickens and comes to a boil. Remove the pan from the heat.

In a small saucepan, heat the white wine with the bay leaf and let it simmer for 2 or 3 minutes. Discard the bay leaf and gradually add the wine to the cream sauce. Add the tarragon and season the sauce to taste with salt and white pepper.

### ASSEMBLY

24 sheets phyllo dough, thawed
½ pound butter, melted
1½ pounds cooked small shrimp
1 10-ounce package frozen artichoke hearts, thawed

Place a sheet of phyllo dough on a work surface with one of the short sides of the pastry facing you. (Keep the remaining sheets covered with a damp towel.) Brush the pastry sheet with butter. Place a second sheet on top of the first and brush

REX'S
—
SEATTLE

*Chef Susan Grant views her approach to food as eclectic. Sometimes she takes full advantage of the fresh seasonal produce of the Pacific Northwest. At other times, she turns to the convenience of frozen artichoke hearts and frozen phyllo dough for her culinary creations.*

it with butter. Repeat so that you have a stack of three sheets. Make light indentations on the pastry to divide it in thirds lengthwise, but do not cut it. Put ¼ cup of the tarragon sauce, 3 or 4 shrimp, and 3 artichoke hearts in the center section, starting 2 inches in from the edge nearest to you. Spread the filling up toward the middle of the dough, keeping the side sections free of filling.

Fold the right and left sections over the center section. Brush the top with butter. Beginning at the edge nearest you, roll the filled dough to form an eggroll-shaped package. Place the package seam side down on a baking sheet that has been brushed with butter or lined with parchment paper. Brush the top of the package with butter. Repeat the process with the remaining pastry sheets until 8 packages have been created. Bake in a 350° oven for about 15 minutes or until golden brown. Cool for 5 minutes before serving.

## SHRIMP AND RICE ARABELLA

*Serves 8 to 10*

1 cup uncooked white rice
1 cup uncooked wild rice
1 cup (2 sticks) butter
1 cup chopped onions (about 2 small onions)
4 stalks celery, chopped
1 medium green pepper, chopped
½ pound mushrooms, sliced
½ cup flour
1½ cups milk, heated
½ cup white wine
3 tablespoons chopped canned pimientos
¼ cup chopped parsley
½ teaspoon Tabasco
¼ teaspoon cayenne pepper
Salt to taste
1½ to 2 pounds cooked medium shrimp
¼ cup sliced almonds
½ pound grated Cheddar cheese

Cook both kinds of rice according to the package directions. Over medium heat melt the butter and sauté the onions, celery, pepper, and mushrooms until onions are translucent. Add the flour, blending well until the mixture forms a paste. Then add the heated milk, white wine, and pimientos. Cook over low heat until the sauce is thick, 5 to 8 minutes. Then add the parsley, Tabasco, cayenne, salt, and shrimp. Remove from the heat and add both kinds of rice and the almonds, mixing well. Spread the mixture in a greased 9-by-13-inch casserole and cover with the cheese. Bake at 350° for 20 to 25 minutes, or until the cheese is completely melted and golden brown.

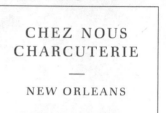

CHEZ NOUS
CHARCUTERIE
—
NEW ORLEANS

## THE WATERGATE CHEFS

—

WASHINGTON, D.C.

*Dijon mustard adds the special fillip to this seasonal dish that The Watergate Chefs make with fresh Maryland crabs. It is equally good hot or cold.*

## SOFT-SHELL CRABS DIJON

*Serves 6*

¼ cup salad oil
¼ cup Dijon mustard
6 soft-shell crabs, bought live and cleaned at the
　　market

BREADCRUMB MIX

2 cups finely crumbled stale bread
1 teaspoon tarragon
1 teaspoon basil
1 teaspoon oregano
½ teaspoon salt
½ teaspoon freshly cracked pepper

In a flat-bottomed bowl combine the oil and mustard. Dip the crabs one by one in the oil-mustard mixture. Drain off the excess oil. Dredge the crabs in the breadcrumb mix, being sure that each is well coated. Place them on a baking sheet and bake at 375° for about 10 minutes or until brown.

## MARYLAND BACKFIN CRAB IMPERIAL

*Serves 6*

2 tablespoons butter
1 medium green pepper, seeded and finely chopped
1 teaspoon finely chopped garlic
2 pounds backfin crabmeat
2 whole canned pimientos, finely chopped
1 tablespoon Dijon mustard
½ teaspoon salt
1 teaspoon white pepper
2 eggs
1 cup Hellmann's mayonnaise
Mayonnaise for topping
Paprika

Melt the butter in a small skillet and sauté the green pepper and garlic until they are tender. Set the pan aside to cool. Place the crabmeat in a large bowl. Combine the pimientos, mustard, salt, pepper, eggs, and mayonnaise and fold them into the crabmeat gently, so as not to break up the lumps.

Divide the mixture among six individual scallop shells or ramekins. Top each with a dollop of mayonnaise and sprinkle with paprika. Bake at 350° for 15 minutes.

## CAFÉ 21
—
NORFOLK,
VIRGINIA

*Crab imperial is a specialty of the Midatlantic region, and it even appears on the mostly Italian menu at Café 21.*

## PASTA & COMPANY

—

### VIRGINIA BEACH, VIRGINIA

*At Pasta & Company the five chefs are encouraged to add their own creations to the menu—hence Regina Richard's version of the Chesapeake Bay's most popular native dish.*

## REGINA'S CRAB CAKES

*Serves 6*

2 pounds fresh crabmeat, well picked over
1 cup finely chopped celery
1 cup finely chopped onion
4 cups freshly grated French bread crumbs
2 eggs, beaten
1 cup mayonnaise
2 tablespoons Dijon mustard
1 teaspoon cayenne pepper
2 tablespoons Texas Pete Hot Sauce
1 tablespoon fresh lemon juice
2 tablespoons Worcestershire sauce
2 tablespoons chopped fresh parsley
Salt and pepper to taste

PREPARATION FOR FRYING

1 cup flour
4 eggs, beaten
½ cup light cream
2 cups freshly grated French bread crumbs
½ cup vegetable oil (approximately) for frying

Mix together gently all the ingredients except the last five and form the mixture into 12 patties. Roll the patties in the flour, then dip in a mixture of the 4 eggs and ½ cup cream and finally in the 2 cups bread crumbs. Fry the crab cakes in a skillet containing ½ inch of hot vegetable oil until they are browned on one side, then turn and brown the other side. Drain the cakes on paper towels and serve hot with tartar sauce or cocktail sauce.

## OYSTERS IN FRESH TARRAGON CREAM

*Serves 2*

1½ cups heavy cream
Salt and white pepper to taste
1 teaspoon chopped fresh tarragon
1 teaspoon grated orange zest
2 dashes tarragon vinegar
16 oysters, shelled and patted dry
2 tablespoons minced ham
½ cup saltine cracker crumbs and grated Parmesan
   cheese combined (3 parts crumbs to
    1 part cheese)
Softened butter
6 ounces angel hair pasta

Reduce the cream to 1 cup by cooking it in a skillet over medium heat. Season the cream with the salt, pepper, tarragon, orange zest, and vinegar. Divide the oysters between two buttered ramekins and distribute half the minced ham over each portion. Spoon the tarragon cream on top, then top with a mixture of the cracker crumbs and cheese bound together with some softened butter.

Bake the oysters at 350° until the sauce is just bubbly and the edges of the oysters have begun to curl. Serve the oysters with angel hair pasta that has been cooked and placed in two rimmed soup plates. Slip the oysters out of their ramekins to top the pasta, being careful to keep the crumb topping in place.

## OUISIE'S TABLE

### — 

### HOUSTON

*These oysters go especially well with a good Chardonnay wine or champagne, followed by a light salad of mixed lettuces tossed with a dressing of toasted sesame oil and lime juice—a most elegant dinner for two.*

## BY WORD OF MOUTH

—

### FORT LAUDERDALE

*If you are lucky enough to get fresh Maine lobster, all you need is butter and lemon to make it delectable. But for rock lobster or frozen lobster tails, something more is necessary. This is a sinfully delicious treatment.*

ROUX

To make approximately ¼ cup of roux, melt 4 tablespoons of butter in a small skillet and add 4 tablespoons of flour, stirring constantly. Cook for 4 to 6 minutes, continuing to stir and making sure the mixture does not brown.

## KEY WEST LOBSTER

*Serves 6 to 8*

5 tablespoons finely minced shallots
4 tablespoons finely minced garlic
1½ cups (3 sticks) unsalted butter
6 pounds lobster tails, removed from the shell and
    cut into 1-inch pieces
2 cups dry sherry
½ cup Amaretto
½ teaspoon cayenne pepper
½ teaspoon black pepper
1 tablespoon kosher salt
2 tablespoons paprika
¼ cup roux (see recipe)
4 cups heavy cream
3 cups canned artichoke hearts, quartered
3 cups sliced mushrooms, lightly sautéed
Parsley for garnish

In a large pan sauté the shallots and garlic in the butter until the vegetables are translucent. Add the lobster pieces and cook over high heat for 5 minutes or until the lobster turns white, stirring constantly. Remove the lobster from the pan, cover, and set aside.

Add the sherry, Amaretto, cayenne, pepper, salt, and paprika to the pan juices. Bring the sauce to a boil and cook it for 5 minutes. Add the roux and continue to stir the sauce constantly until it thickens, about 5 minutes. Add the cream and continue to cook the sauce over low heat. Add the reserved lobster, the artichoke hearts, and the mushrooms. Serve the lobster over linguini or rice and garnish with chopped parsley.

## PASTA

Pasta Marco Polo
Cheese Tortellini with Marinara Sauce
Cavatelli with Eggplant Sauce
Not Your Mother's Macaroni and Cheese
Michelle's Pasta Primavera
Pasta Carbonara
Fettuccine con Pollo
Seafood Lasagna
Rigatoni with Hot and Spicy Seafood Sauce
Crabmeat Pasta Seashells with Tomato Cream
    Sauce
Lemon-Parsley Pasta with Bay Scallops
Pasta with Bay Scallops, Tomatoes, and
    Zucchini
Fettuccine with Smoked Salmon in Cream
Linguini with White Clam Sauce

## FETTUCCINE BROS.

—

### SAN FRANCISCO

*Fettuccine Bros. has a reputation for selling the best pasta in town at the most reasonable prices. Their shop specializes in fresh pasta, homemade sauces, and delicatessen items. Originally for take-out only, today their first shop (now one of three) serves lunch daily and dinner on Friday, Saturday, and Sunday nights. Partners Bob Battaglia and Don Woodall offer northern and southern Italian sauces and variations on the classics. This sauce is similar to pesto in that it is served at room temperature, tossed with hot pasta.*

## PASTA MARCO POLO

*Serves 6 (makes 4 cups of sauce)*

3 6-ounce cans chopped ripe olives
2 tablespoons minced garlic
3 tablespoons grated Parmesan cheese
1 tablespoon grated Romano cheese
4 tablespoons finely chopped fresh parsley
1 teaspoon basil
1 teaspoon oregano
Pinch of ground thyme
Pinch of ground rosemary
¼ teaspoon pepper
1½ cups olive oil
1 pound pasta, cooked according to
    package directions

Mix all the ingredients except the pasta in a large bowl and let the mixture sit for 1 hour before serving. At serving time, whisk the sauce well and toss with hot pasta. The sauce may also be added in small amounts to a green salad or spread on crackers for a canapé.

## CHEESE TORTELLINI WITH MARINARA SAUCE

*Serves 4*

¼ cup extra-virgin olive oil
1 large onion, diced
8 cloves garlic, minced
½ teaspoon kosher salt
1 cup red Zinfandel wine
1 28-ounce can plum tomatoes, including juice
¼ cup chopped fresh basil
1½ teaspoons oregano
1 teaspoon marjoram
1 teaspoon thyme
¼ teaspoon crushed red pepper flakes
½ teaspoon freshly ground black pepper
½ teaspoon sugar
½ pound cheese tortellini
Freshly grated Parmesan cheese for garnish

Heat the olive oil in a saucepan and add the onion and garlic. Sauté until the onion is translucent. Add the salt and wine and reduce the mixture by half. Add the tomatoes, break them up with a spoon, and add the juice from the tomatoes and the herbs, spices, and sugar. Simmer gently until the sauce thickens slightly, which will take from 20 to 50 minutes. Fresh or thawed small peas and sautéed diced prosciutto may be added to the sauce.

Cook the tortellini according to the instructions on the package if you are using dried, or for 5 to 8 minutes if you are using fresh. Toss the cooked pasta with a small amount of butter and spoon the marinara sauce over it. Serve with freshly grated Parmesan cheese.

### PETAK'S
—
NEW YORK CITY

*The marinara sauce in this recipe may be used with various kinds of pasta or as a base for eggplant Parmesan.*

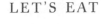

## LET'S EAT

—

TIBURON,
CALIFORNIA

*Cavatelli is a pasta made with ricotta cheese instead of flour, with a dumpling-like consistency. If you are unable to find it, spaghettini is a fine substitute.*

## CAVATELLI WITH EGGPLANT SAUCE

*Serves 4 to 6*

2 eggplants, approximately 1 pound each
Salt
1 cup vegetable oil
2 tablespoons olive oil
2 cloves garlic, minced
1 28-ounce can crushed tomatoes or diced tomatoes
    in purée
2 tablespoons minced fresh parsley
1 teaspoon basil
⅛ teaspoon cayenne pepper
1 pound cavatelli
½ cup chopped black olives, 1 tablespoon capers,
    and chopped fresh parsley for garnish

Cut the unpeeled eggplant into ½-inch dice. Sprinkle the cubes with salt and place them in a colander to drain for 30 minutes. Pat them dry with paper towels. Heat the vegetable oil in a skillet until very hot, just under smoking point. Fry the eggplant in batches until golden and drain on paper towels. Heat the olive oil in another skillet and sauté the garlic for about 3 minutes, being careful not to burn it. Add the tomatoes, parsley, basil, and cayenne and simmer the mixture for 25 minutes. Add the eggplant and cook for 5 minutes. Taste the sauce and correct the seasonings.

Cook the cavatelli in boiling salted water until *al dente* and drain. Reserve 1 cup of the eggplant sauce. Combine the balance of the sauce with the pasta and toss. Serve on a large platter or on individual serving plates, topped with the reserved sauce and garnished with the olives, capers, and chopped parsley.

## NOT YOUR MOTHER'S MACARONI AND CHEESE

*Serves 6*

1½ cups chicken stock
½ cup dry white wine
4 cups heavy cream
2 tablespoons olive oil
1 clove garlic, minced
2 teaspoons minced shallots
4 tablespoons Dijon mustard
4 ounces Appenzeller cheese, grated
4 ounces Gouda cheese, grated
4 ounces Gruyère cheese, grated
Salt and pepper to taste
1 pound fusilli pasta
1 tablespoon butter
3 ripe tomatoes, peeled, seeded, and chopped
Dash of cayenne pepper
Dash of Worcestershire sauce
4 ounces Parmesan cheese, grated

Butter a large rectangular baking dish and set it aside. Combine the stock and wine, bring the mixture to a boil, and reduce it to ¾ cup. Bring the cream to a boil and reduce it to 3 cups. Heat the oil in a heavy saucepan. Add the garlic and shallots and cook them until they are soft, 5 to 10 minutes. Add the reduced stock and cream. Whisk in the mustard. Reduce the heat to low and add the cheeses, stirring often until they have melted. Add salt and pepper to taste.

Meanwhile, cook the pasta in boiling salted water until it is *al dente*. Drain it and toss it with butter.

Add the tomato, cayenne, and Worcestershire sauce to the cheese mixture and heat the sauce thoroughly. Then pour it over the pasta, toss until well mixed, and transfer to the baking dish.

SUZANNE'S
—
WASHINGTON, D.C.

*"A person who truly enjoys macaroni and cheese is forced to eat alone in the dark."*
—GARRISON KEILLOR

*The inventive chef need have no fear serving this superlative version of macaroni and cheese in broad daylight or under the soft glow of candles at a dinner party.*

Sprinkle the top with the Parmesan cheese and run under the broiler until the cheese melts and is golden, about 5 minutes. Serve immediately.

PASTA NATALE
—
PHILADELPHIA

*The Market at New Market is a colorful collection of food stalls and fresh produce displays in the restored colonial section of Philadelphia. At Pasta Natale they conjure up all sorts of pasta dishes and sauces to carry out. This one uses tomato-basil linguini, but if it cannot be found, tomato linguini may be used instead and basil added to taste.*

## MICHELLE'S PASTA PRIMAVERA

*Serves 6*

½ cup (1 stick) butter
2 cloves garlic, peeled and crushed
1 medium zucchini, cut into bite-size pieces
1 medium yellow squash, cut into bite-size pieces
2 medium tomatoes, seeded and chopped
1 cup snow peas
1 pound fresh tomato-basil linguini (or tomato
   linguini)
1 cup broccoli flowerets
Salt and pepper to taste
Grated Parmesan cheese

Bring a 5-quart pot of salted water to a boil. Meanwhile, melt the butter in a large skillet and sauté the garlic, zucchini, yellow squash, tomatoes, and snow peas about 2 minutes. When the water reaches a boil, add the linguini and then the broccoli. Stir to keep separate and cook about 1½ minutes once the water has returned to the boil. Drain the linguini and broccoli, refresh in cold water, and add them to the vegetables in the sauté pan. Toss together until the pasta is coated with butter and the sauce juices. Season with salt and pepper if desired. Sprinkle liberally with grated Parmesan cheese and serve immediately.

## PASTA CARBONARA

*Serves 4 or 5*

1 pound lean bacon, cut in small squares
1 pound spiral egg pasta
2 eggs, well beaten
3 tablespoons olive oil
1 tablespoon bacon drippings
2 cups chopped fresh parsley
½ cup freshly grated Romano cheese
Freshly ground pepper to taste

Sauté the bacon until it is crisp, stirring it occasionally so the pieces cook evenly. Drain the bacon on paper towels, reserving 1 tablespoon of the drippings.

Cook the pasta in boiling salted water according to the instructions on the package. When the pasta is done, add cold water to the pot to stop the pasta from cooking and to allow the excess starch to rise to the surface. Then drain the pasta in a colander.

While the pasta is still warm, add the beaten eggs and toss lightly and quickly. Add the olive oil and bacon drippings and toss lightly again. Add the parsley, bacon, and cheese and toss once more. Serve the pasta at room temperature, topped with a grinding of black pepper.

### CRANBERRY HILL

—

MONTCLAIR,
NEW JERSEY

*Pasta Carbonara is perfect for Sunday night suppers or for those times when you think you have nothing in the house for dinner. If you don't have spiral pasta on hand, spaghetti or linguini will do just as well.*

CAMARGO
COOKING
COMPANY
AND CAFÉ

—

CINCINNATI

*At the Camargo Cooking Company and Café, Fettuccine con Pollo is often served for Sunday brunch. Accompanied by a green salad, crusty bread, and a white Burgundy or Chardonnay, it's a quick and simple evening entrée, too.*

## FETTUCCINE CON POLLO

*Serves 8*

4 whole chicken breasts
1 medium onion, julienne-cut
½ pound mushrooms, sliced
1 large clove garlic, minced
½ cup (1 stick) butter
½ pound spinach fettuccine
½ pound egg fettuccine
2 cups half-and-half
Salt and pepper to taste
Nutmeg to taste
¾ cup tomato purée
½ pound ham, julienne-cut

Poach and cool the chicken breasts. Sauté the onion, mushrooms, and garlic in as much of the butter as necessary until they are soft. Cook the pasta *al dente* according to the directions on the package and drain. Add the half-and-half, seasonings (be generous with the pepper), and what remains of the butter to the pasta, and mix. Add the tomato purée, vegetables, and ham. Tear the chicken into bite-size strips and add it to the fettuccine. Place the mixture in a shallow 9-by-13-inch casserole and bake at 350° for 30 minutes.

## SEAFOOD LASAGNA

*Serves 8*

2 pounds lasagna noodles
Olive oil and salt for cooking the noodles
1 pound fillet of flounder
1 pound Maryland backfin crabmeat
½ pound bay scallops
½ pound shrimp, peeled, deveined, and chopped
4 tablespoons butter
1 pound mushrooms, sliced
2 cups thin béchamel sauce (see recipe, page 168 )
1½ pounds ricotta cheese
1½ cups grated Parmesan cheese
4 eggs
12 ounces shredded mozzarella
2 tablespoons chopped fresh parsley

Bring 4 quarts of water with a little oil in it to a boil in a large pot and add 1 teaspoon salt. Drop the lasagna noodles one at a time into the boiling water. Cook for 4 or 5 minutes. (The noodles should be only half cooked.) Run the noodles under ice water and toss them gently in olive oil to prevent sticking, and set aside.

Chop the flounder into ½-inch squares and mix with the crabmeat, scallops, and shrimp in a large bowl. Melt the butter. Sauté the sliced mushrooms in the butter for about 2 minutes. Remove them from the heat and drain.

Combine the béchamel sauce, ricotta, and ½ cup of the Parmesan cheese with the eggs and mushrooms. Put a layer of noodles on the bottom of a buttered 9-by-12-inch casserole or baking pan. Put one third of the fish and one third of the cheese mixture on top of the noodles. Add one third of the mozzarella. Top with noodles. Repeat the process twice more, ending with a layer of cheese sauce. Sprinkle with the last of

## THE CHEF'S MARKET

—

PHILADELPHIA

*Most people think of tomato and meat sauce when they think of lasagna. This one is a seafood lover's delight.*

the mozzarella cheese and the parsley and bake at 325° for 1½ hours. Top with the remaining grated Parmesan at serving time.

GOURMET PASTA
—
ALBERTSON,
LONG ISLAND

## RIGATONI WITH HOT AND SPICY SEAFOOD SAUCE

*Serves 4*

½ clove garlic, finely chopped
2 anchovy fillets
2 tablespoons butter
1 16-ounce can crushed plum tomatoes
¼ cup chopped parsley
Pinch each of oregano and basil
Cayenne pepper to taste
8 jumbo shrimp, peeled
4 clams in their shells
½ cup bay scallops
1 pound fresh rigatoni

In a large pot, bring 4 quarts of salted water to a boil. Meanwhile, sauté the garlic and anchovies in the butter in a large saucepan. Add the tomatoes and herbs and cayenne. Bring the sauce to a light boil. Add the shrimp, clams, and scallops. When the clams open, the sauce is ready. Set it aside.

Add the fresh pasta to the boiling water. Cook for 3 minutes. Rinse the pasta under cold water, drain, place on a platter, and cover with the sauce.

## CRABMEAT PASTA SEASHELLS WITH TOMATO CREAM SAUCE

*Serves 6*

1½ pounds crabmeat
3 8-ounce packages cream cheese
¾ cup grated sharp cheese (Asiago, Romano,
    Parmesan, or a combination)
1 teaspoon minced garlic
¼ cup chopped shallots
Freshly ground pepper to taste
⅓ cup chopped fresh tarragon or fennel leaves
½ teaspoon crushed red pepper flakes
8 ounces large pasta seashells
2 ripe tomatoes, peeled, seeded, and chopped
Grated Parmesan cheese

CREAM SAUCE

4 cups heavy cream
2 teaspoons minced garlic
2 tablespoons chopped shallots
Salt and pepper to taste

Blend the first eight ingredients and adjust the seasonings. Cook the pasta shells according to the instructions on the package. Prepare the cream sauce by combining all ingredients in a saucepan and heating until the mixture is reduced by half.

Pour the reduced cream sauce into a shallow baking dish that will hold the shells in one layer. Stuff the shells with the crabmeat-cheese mixture, arrange them on top of the sauce, and bake, covered, at 400° for 15 to 20 minutes. Remove from the oven and top with the chopped tomato and grated Parmesan cheese.

NOTE: Pasta seashells are easily broken, so buy more than you think you will need.

RYAN'S
—
SAN FRANCISCO

*Lenore and Michael Ryan report that this dish is always a show stopper, whether served as an entrée or as a first course. The plump stuffed seashells topped with cream and chopped tomatoes make a beautiful presentation. A mixture of the first eight ingredients also may be used for canapés or as a spread for crackers.*

## PASTA NATALE

—

### PHILADELPHIA

*Many a weary Philadelphia office worker stops at Pasta Natale in the Market at New Market on the way home to pick up a fresh pasta dish or an imaginative sauce to put over the dried pasta in the pantry. Although this recipe calls for lemon-parsley linguini, if that is not available, plain linguini may be substituted and a little grated lemon peel and chopped parsley added at the end.*

## LEMON-PARSLEY PASTA WITH BAY SCALLOPS

*Serves 4*

1½ cups heavy cream
6 tablespoons butter
½ teaspoon salt
⅛ teaspoon nutmeg
Pinch of cayenne pepper
¼ cup grated Parmesan cheese
1 cup finely chopped mixed fresh herbs such as
    basil, mint, watercress, Italian parsley, and
    chives
1 pound bay scallops
1 pound fresh lemon-parsley linguini
Chopped fresh parsley for garnish

Combine the cream, 4 tablespoons of the butter, salt, nutmeg, and cayenne in a heavy saucepan and simmer for 15 minutes or until the sauce is slightly reduced and thickened. Whisk in the cheese and herbs and simmer for another 5 minutes. Correct the seasonings.

Sauté the scallops in the remaining 2 tablespoons of butter over high heat for 3 minutes. Add them to the sauce and simmer for 1 minute more. Remove the sauce from the heat.

Cook the fresh lemon-parsley linguini in boiling salted water for 1½ minutes. (If you are using dry pasta, cook it for 8 to 10 minutes.) Drain the pasta and toss it with half of the scallop-herb mixture. Turn it onto a platter; top it with the rest of the sauce and serve. Sprinkle with chopped parsley.

## PASTA WITH BAY SCALLOPS, TOMATOES, AND ZUCCHINI

*Serves 6*

1 tablespoon minced garlic
1½ cups chopped onions
1½ cups diced tomatoes, preferably fresh
1¼ teaspoons oregano
2 teaspoons basil
1½ teaspoons salt
½ teaspoon pepper
½ cup dry white wine
¼ cup capers, drained
1 pound bay scallops
¾ pound zucchini, julienne-cut
¾ pound mushrooms, thinly sliced
½ cup finely chopped fresh parsley
2½ cups chopped fresh tomatoes
⅔ pound fresh linguini, cooked *al dente*
Grated Parmesan cheese

Combine the garlic, onion, and diced tomatoes and cook them over high heat, stirring constantly. Turn the heat to low and cover. Simmer for 8 minutes, stirring occasionally. Uncover, raise the heat, and cook until most of the liquid has evaporated. Add the dried herbs, salt and pepper, white wine, and capers, and simmer for 5 minutes. Add the scallops, zucchini, and mushrooms, and cook for 2 to 3 minutes until the scallops are just done and the vegetables are hot and slightly wilted. Do not overcook. Add the parsley, the chopped tomatoes, and the pasta and heat through. Divide among six plates, topping each serving with Parmesan cheese.

This may also be served cold as a salad with lemon or vinegar added to taste.

## THE MARKET OF THE COMMISSARY

—

### PHILADELPHIA

*The Market of the Commissary specializes in developing "enlightened" recipes for people who want to eat well and stay thin. In this case, fresh vegetables replace some of the pasta that would ordinarily be used.*

## GOURMET PASTA

—

### ALBERTSON, LONG ISLAND

*The pasta business is booming, and Bryn Benjamin, the owner of Gourmet Pasta, admits that he's doing his part by eating two pounds of pasta a week himself. This recipe for fettuccine devised by his chef, Kenneth Morakkabi, suggests why.*

## FETTUCCINE WITH SMOKED SALMON IN CREAM

*Serves 4 to 6*

¼ cup cognac
½ cup fish stock, or ¼ cup clam juice plus
    ¼ cup water
1 tablespoon chopped fresh dill
½ teaspoon butter
1 cup heavy cream
4 thin slices smoked salmon, cut in strips or bite-
    size pieces
1 pound fresh fettuccine
Pepper to taste
2 tablespoons caviar for garnish (optional)

In a skillet, heat the cognac for about 1 minute until the alcohol has evaporated. Add the fish stock, dill, and butter. When it reaches a boil, add the heavy cream. Cook until thick and add the salmon. Remove the sauce from the stove.

Cook the fresh fettuccine in boiling salted water for 3 minutes. Rinse it in cold water. Drain it and put it on a platter. Pour the sauce over the pasta. Add pepper to taste and sprinkle the top with caviar if desired.

## LINGUINI WITH WHITE CLAM SAUCE

*Serves 6*

1 cup white wine
4 dozen littleneck or cherrystone clams, scrubbed
¾ cup olive oil
8 cloves garlic, minced
2 cups bottled clam juice
½ cup finely chopped fresh parsley
2 teaspoons oregano
¾ cup sun-dried tomatoes, julienne-cut
Salt and pepper to taste
1 pound linguini, cooked

Put the white wine and the clams in a large pot and cook till the shells open. Remove the clams from the shells; strain the cooking liquid and reserve. Chop the clams.

Heat the oil in a deep, heavy kettle. Add the garlic and cook over low heat until tender, about 5 minutes. Combine the reserved liquid and the clam juice and add this to the kettle along with the parsley, oregano, sun-dried tomatoes, and salt and pepper. Simmer for 10 minutes. Add the chopped clams and heat briefly. Serve tossed with linguini and garnished with a few clams left in the steamed open shells.

## SAVOIR FARE

—

EDGARTOWN,
MASSACHUSETTS

*Clams are always available on the island of Martha's Vineyard, and Scott and Charlotte Caskey make good use of them in this sauce for linguini.*

## VEGETABLES AND RELISHES

Pizzoccheri
Spinach Casserole
Turban of Eggplant with Four Cheeses
Black-Eyed Peas with Salsa
Cavolini Gratinati
Roast Onions
Pepperoni Arrostiti Gratinati
Carrot Mousse
Squash Fritters
Zucchini Pancakes
Sautéed Snow Peas and Shiitake Mushrooms
Onion Cumin Rice
Couscous Pilaf
Zucchini Relish
Cranberry Chutney
Green Tomato Chutney

## *PIZZOCCHERI*

*Serves 8*

2 pounds cabbage, spinach, or Swiss chard,
 chopped
½ pound potatoes, cut into small cubes
1 pound pizzoccheri pasta
Salt to taste
½ cup (1 stick) butter
2 leaves fresh sage, minced, or ½ teaspoon
 dried sage
3 cloves garlic, chopped
1 large red onion, chopped
⅓ pound Taleggio cheese, cubed
¼ pound Parmesan cheese, grated

Put the chopped cabbage, spinach, or Swiss
chard with the potatoes into a large pot of boiling
water. Boil it for 5 minutes and add the pasta.
Salt the water to taste and continue cooking for
12 to 15 minutes.

In a separate pan, melt the butter with the
sage, garlic, and onion. With a skimmer, transfer
one third of the pizzoccheri mixture to a large
bowl. Toss it with one third of the cheese and
the butter mixture. Repeat until all ingredients
have been mixed. Serve hot.

NOTE: Any kind of fettuccine may be substituted
for the buckwheat pizzoccheri.

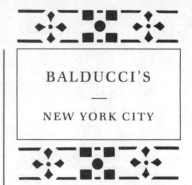

### BALDUCCI'S
### —
### NEW YORK CITY

*The Balducci family has
been serving New Yorkers
with fine foods from
around the world for more
than forty years. By now
their Greenwich Village
market is an epicurean
landmark in New York City,
selling fine produce, meats,
baked goods, and all
manner of carry-out dishes.*

*There is a threesome behind this Louisiana carry-out shop—owners Edwina Costley and Ann Stauss and chef Ronnie Thompson. Regular customers often stock up on their favorite specialties of the day, which they take home for dinner or freeze for future occasions.*

## SPINACH CASSEROLE

*Serves 6*

½ cup (1 stick) butter
1½ cups chopped onions
1 cup sliced mushrooms
2 cloves garlic, minced
3 10-ounce packages frozen chopped spinach, thawed and with excess liquid squeezed out
1 teaspoon Worcestershire sauce
1 8-ounce package cream cheese
¼ cup half-and-half
½ teaspoon salt
¼ teaspoon pepper
½ cup breadcrumbs
1 teaspoon Tabasco
½ pound Gruyère cheese, grated

In a heavy skillet, melt the butter over medium heat. Add the onions and sauté them until they are clear. Add the sliced mushrooms and garlic and cook until the mushrooms give up their liquid. Add the spinach and Worcestershire sauce. Cook until the spinach loses its bright green color. Add the cream cheese, half-and-half, and seasonings, and cook until the cream cheese has melted. Stir in the breadcrumbs and add the Tabasco. Grease a 6-by-8-inch casserole and pour in the spinach mixture. Sprinkle with the grated Gruyère and bake, uncovered, for 15 minutes in a 375° oven or until the top is golden brown. This casserole goes particularly well with poultry and beef dishes.

NOTE: If you wish to assemble the casserole ahead of time, note that it will take a half hour for the mixture to heat and brown.

## TURBAN OF EGGPLANT WITH FOUR CHEESES

*Serves 6*

3 large (or 6 small) eggplants
Salt as needed
¼ to ½ cup olive oil
1 pound feta cheese
2 cups ricotta cheese
½ cup grated Romano or Asiago cheese
½ cup grated Parmesan cheese
½ cup chopped fresh parsley
1 cup chopped scallions
2 large eggs
3 tablespoons lemon juice
½ teaspoon white pepper
½ teaspoon grated nutmeg

Trim off the ends of the eggplants. Slice each eggplant lengthwise into ⅛- to ¼-inch slices. Arrange them in a colander, salting each slice with a pinch of salt on each side. Set them aside for an hour. Then rinse off the salt and pat the slices dry. Dredge them in olive oil and place them on baking sheets. Bake them at 400° for 15 minutes, but do not allow them to brown. Cool.

In a food processor or blender, in two batches, blend the combined cheeses, parsley, scallions, eggs, lemon juice, and seasonings. Butter a straight-sided charlotte mold or a porcelain soufflé dish, and overlap the eggplant slices on the sides and bottom to form one layer. Alternate layers of the cheese mixture with the remaining slices to fill the mold, ending with the eggplant.

Cover the mold with buttered parchment paper topped with a pie plate or tin foil, and put it in a warm water bath going three quarters of the way up the mold. Bake at 375° for 1 hour. Let the mold cool in the water for an hour or two. Run a knife around the side of the turban and

## METROPOLIS
—
### CHICAGO

*The glass showcases in this café/carry-out/bakery on the Near North Side offer an eclectic display of hearty dishes—seafood sausages, mustard roast chicken, creole jambalaya, and this Turban of Eggplant with Four Cheeses.*

invert it onto a platter. Slice and serve with warm tomato sauce.

PASTA & CO.
—
SEATTLE

*This flavorful dish can be made as hot as you like. Most customers at Pasta & Co. like it with a good dose of jalapeño fire. Served at room temperature, it makes a fine accompaniment to grilled meats.*

## BLACK-EYED PEAS WITH SALSA

*Serves 6 to 8*

PEAS

1 pound dried black-eyed peas
½ cup lemon juice
1 cup olive oil
1 clove garlic
1 scant teaspoon oregano
2 teaspoons fresh lime juice
1 teaspoon salt

Soak the peas overnight, then cook them in salted water until they are very tender. Drain the peas and rinse them with cold water. Process the other ingredients in a food processor or blender, and toss the cooked peas with the dressing.

SALSA

1 medium onion, quartered
⅓ green pepper, seeded and cut in pieces
1 to 2 ounces fresh jalapeño peppers (both green
   and red if possible), tops removed but unseeded
⅓ bunch cilantro (fresh coriander), stems removed
Slices of lime for garnish

Gently sauté the onion in a small amount of olive oil until it is translucent. When the onion is cool, add it and both kinds of peppers and the cilantro to the food processor bowl and purée. Add the purée to the pea mixture. Salt to taste and garnish with the lime slices.

## CAVOLINI GRATINATI

*Serves 6*

2 pounds Brussels sprouts
3 tablespoons butter
4 ounces prosciutto, thinly sliced
5 ounces mozzarella, thinly sliced
1 cup canned peeled tomatoes, drained and
    chopped
2 cups béchamel sauce (see recipe)
½ cup finely grated Parmesan cheese
¼ cup breadcrumbs

Trim the base of each of the Brussels sprouts with a knife and make a cross in it. Remove any wilted leaves and wash the sprouts in cold water. Drop the sprouts into boiling salted water and boil slowly, uncovered, for about 8 minutes or until they are nearly tender. Drain the sprouts well and set them aside.

    With 1 tablespoon of the butter, grease the bottom and sides of a shallow casserole large enough to hold the sprouts in one layer. Put the sprouts in the casserole. Cover them with a layer of prosciutto, then a layer of mozzarella. Spread the tomatoes over the mozzarella and cover the tomatoes with the béchamel sauce. Sprinkle with the Parmesan cheese and dot the casserole with the remaining 2 tablespoons of butter. Sprinkle the breadcrumbs on top and bake the dish in a 350° oven for 30 minutes or until the sauce is bubbly. Serve immediately.

CONVITO
ITALIANO
—
CHICAGO

BÉCHAMEL SAUCE

Melt 4 tablespoons of butter in a heavy-bottomed saucepan. Add 4 tablespoons of flour and cook, stirring constantly, until the mixture becomes a thick, bubbly paste (do not let it brown). Add 2 cups of hot milk, stirring constantly as the sauce thickens. Bring to a low boil and season with salt and pepper to taste. Simmer for 2 or 3 minutes more, again stirring constantly.

*This simple but delicious recipe is a favorite with owner-chef Carlo Middione's clientele. The onions can be eaten hot with roasts or stews and are equally good served at room temperature, as an antipasto or a garnish for cold foods.*

## ROAST ONIONS

*Serves 6*

6 Spanish onions, about 3 inches in diameter,
    of uniform size
3 tablespoons olive oil
Salt and pepper
⅓ cup balsamic vinegar

Leave the brown skins on the onions and rub them gently with olive oil all around. Sprinkle them with salt and pepper. Place the onions in a baking pan and bake them in a 375° oven for 1 hour or more. They should be soft but not mushy. Remove the onions to a serving platter. Cut them in half vertically, being careful to leave the brown skin in place.

On the baking pan will be quite a bit of caramelized natural sugar from the juice of the onions, exuded during baking. To deglaze the pan, place it over medium heat on top of the stove. Pour in the balsamic vinegar and scrape the pan well to dislodge all of the "caramel." Let the vinegar alcohol burn off for about 4 minutes.

Push aside any large pieces of outer onion skin that may be left in the pan. Using a pastry brush, brush the sauce over the open cut faces of the onion halves on the serving platter. Serve hot or at room temperature.

NOTE: Any leftover sauce is delicious brushed on chicken or fish.

## PEPPERONI ARROSTITI GRATINATI

*Serves 6 to 8*

6 sweet red peppers, or 3 red and 3 yellow
⅓ cup extra-virgin olive oil
¼ cup chopped fresh parsley
3 cloves garlic, minced and mashed
Salt to taste
4 green stuffed olives, sliced
⅓ cup grated Parmesan cheese

Rub the peppers with some of the oil and roast them in a 550° oven until the skin blackens. Remove the peppers from the oven and peel them. Cut them in half or in slices. Combine the rest of the oil, the parsley, and the garlic. Dip the peppers in the parsley-garlic mixture. Salt them and arrange in a shallow gratin dish. Sprinkle the sliced olives and the Parmesan cheese on top. Bake until heated through, 3 to 4 minutes, and until the cheese is brown. Serve hot.

## CARROT MOUSSE

*Serves 8*

10 large carrots, peeled and sliced
½ cup (1 stick) butter
2 cups heavy cream
4 large eggs
Salt and pepper to taste
Nutmeg to taste

Cook the carrots slowly in a covered saucepan. Cool them slightly and purée them in a food processor with the rest of the ingredients. Pour the

### DDL FOODSHOW

—

LOS ANGELES

*In any production, the people behind the scenes are important. At a foodshow, it is they who actually put on the show. This recipe comes from the chefs who make movie producer Dino De Laurentiis' DDL Foodshow possible.*

### MONTICELLO GOURMET

—

WASHINGTON, D.C.

*Most people think that cooked carrots need a little doctoring. This*

*mousse turns them into a downright alluring vegetable.*

FIREHOUSE
NO. 4

—

CHARLESTON,
WEST VIRGINIA

*These fritters are wonderfully versatile. They can be served as an appetizer, as a main course for a brunch, or as a side dish for dinner.*

purée into a buttered baking dish or individual molds.

Bake in a water bath in a 350° oven until a knife comes out clean, about 1½ hours. Spoon the mousse out or unmold it, depending on the dish used.

## *SQUASH FRITTERS*

*Serves 4*

2 unpeeled medium summer squash, grated
1 medium onion, grated
1 cup grated sharp Cheddar cheese
1 egg, beaten
¼ teaspoon pepper
½ cup self-rising flour
¾ teaspoon salt
2 tablespoons vegetable oil, or more as needed

Combine all the ingredients except the oil and mix well. Heat the oil in a large skillet. Drop the batter by large tablespoonfuls into the hot oil and fry until golden. Turn and fry the other side. Drain on paper towels and serve warm.

## ZUCCHINI PANCAKES

*Makes 20 1½-inch pancakes*

1 egg
2 cups grated unpeeled zucchini
2 tablespoons chopped fresh parsley
1 teaspoon salt
¼ teaspoon pepper
½ cup flour
1 teaspoon baking powder
Oil for frying

Beat the egg and mix it thoroughly with the zucchini. Add the parsley, salt, and pepper and mix again. Combine the flour and the baking powder and add them to the zucchini mixture. Let the batter sit for 30 minutes.

Heat 1 inch of oil in a frying pan. Drop the batter into the oil by tablespoonfuls. When the edges are firm and brown, turn the pancakes and cook the other side. Drain and serve hot.

## VIVIAN'S KITCHEN

—

WESTFIELD,
NEW JERSEY

*Vivian Collyer Bucher's kitchen is smack in the middle of her carry-out shop—on purpose. After a dozen years of catering from her home, she tired of working alone and wanted to be near the action. This recipe has been a favorite of Vivian's clients since the days when she used to trade her homemade goodies for a neighbor's extra zucchini.*

THE CHEF'S
MARKET

—

PHILADELPHIA

## SAUTÉED SNOW PEAS AND SHIITAKE MUSHROOMS

*Serves 6 to 8*

3 tablespoons sesame oil
1 clove garlic, minced
½ pound fresh shiitake mushrooms, stems removed
    and discarded, caps sliced
1½ pounds snow peas, ends removed
1 sweet red pepper, seeded and diced
¼ cup light soy sauce
2 tablespoons Chinese plum sauce
1 tablespoon rice wine vinegar
1 tablespoon sesame seeds
White pepper to taste

In a large sauté pan, heat the sesame oil. Add the garlic and sauté for 2 minutes. Add the mushrooms, snow peas, and red pepper and cook for another minute. Add all the other ingredients, toss quickly, and serve.

## ONION CUMIN RICE

*Serves 4*

2 yellow onions, thinly sliced
Olive oil
6 whole cloves
½ teaspoon red pepper flakes
1 cup uncooked long-grain rice
3 tablespoons ground cumin
1 tablespoon coriander
1 tablespoon ground ginger
1 cinnamon stick
Salt to taste
¼ cup fresh lime juice
2½ cups hot chicken stock

Sauté the onions in a small amount of olive oil until they are lightly browned. Push the onions to one side of the pan and pour a little more olive oil into the middle of the pan. The oil must be hot enough for the cloves to sizzle when you add them. Test with one clove before adding the others. Allow the cloves to sizzle for about 30 seconds, but do not let them scorch. Add the pepper flakes and the rice. Sauté until the rice is lightly colored. Then add the cumin, coriander, ginger, cinnamon stick, and salt to taste. Combine well and heat. Add the lime juice and chicken stock, stirring to blend, and cover the pan.

Cook over the lowest possible heat for 15 minutes, without removing the lid. Remove the cinnamon stick and cloves and serve the rice immediately.

## OUISIE'S TABLE
## —
## HOUSTON

*This spicy dish is the perfect accompaniment for Ouisie's Redfish Milford (page 138) or any plain grilled fish.*

## FÊTE ACCOMPLIE
—
WASHINGTON, D.C.

*This couscous pilaf makes a
fine vegetarian entrée or
may be served as a side
dish with roasts or stews.*

## COUSCOUS PILAF

*Serves 6 to 8*

1 leek, white part only, cleaned and sliced
4 tablespoons butter
2 cups chicken stock
Salt and pepper to taste
1 carrot, sliced
1 turnip, diced
1 sweet red pepper, seeded and diced
1 19-ounce can chickpeas, drained
1 medium zucchini, quartered and sliced
1 14-ounce box precooked couscous

Sauté the leek in the butter until it is soft. Add
the chicken stock, salt, and pepper and bring the
stock to a boil. Add the carrot and turnip and
cook for 8 minutes. Add the red pepper, chickpeas, and zucchini and cook for 2 minutes
longer. Add the couscous, stir, cover, and steam
for 5 minutes. If the mixture seems dry, add more
hot chicken stock. Serve hot.

## ZUCCHINI RELISH

*Makes 4 to 5 pints*

8 cups diced zucchini
2 cups sliced onions
1 tablespoon salt
½ cup diced sweet red pepper
1 cup cider vinegar
1¾ cups sugar
½ teaspoon celery seed
½ teaspoon mustard seed

Mix the zucchini, onions, and salt in a bowl and set them aside for an hour. Mix the rest of the ingredients in a saucepan and bring them to a boil. Drain the squash and onion mixture and add it to the boiling liquid. Bring the mixture back to a boil. Remove it from the heat and chill. This relish can readily be canned or will last a week or two in the refrigerator.

### THE GOODIE SHOPPE

—

LANCASTER, PENNSYLVANIA

*If you have a summer garden overflowing with zucchini, putting them into this condiment to serve as a side dish is a fine way to make use of them. Jackie Parker of The Goodie Shoppe finds it a fine accompaniment for potato and macaroni salads or for hamburgers.*

## CRANBERRY HILL

—

### MONTCLAIR, NEW JERSEY

*As one might expect, cranberries are a favorite ingredient at this shop. This condiment is a specialty at holiday time.*

## CRANBERRY CHUTNEY

*Makes 6 pints*

1 cup apricot preserves
1 cup cider vinegar
1 cup dark brown sugar
1½ teaspoons curry powder
1 teaspoon ground ginger
2 3-inch cinnamon sticks
12 whole cloves
3 cups water
2 limes, blanched in boiling water for 2 minutes, seeded, and finely chopped
2 firm pears, peeled, cored, and diced
2 apples, peeled, cored, and diced
6 cups cranberries, carefully picked over
1 cup raisins
1 cup roughly chopped walnuts

In a 3½-quart enamel saucepan, combine the preserves, vinegar, sugar, curry powder, ginger, a cheesecloth bag containing the cinnamon sticks and cloves, and water. Bring the mixture to a boil, stirring until the sugar is dissolved. Add the chopped limes, pears, and apples and simmer for 10 minutes, stirring occasionally. Add the cranberries and raisins and simmer for 20 minutes, until the mixture is thick, stirring occasionally. Remove the pan from the heat and stir in the walnuts. Remove the cheesecloth bag.

The chutney will keep for up to 3 weeks in the refrigerator or may be packed in hot, sterilized jars and sealed with hot paraffin.

## GREEN TOMATO CHUTNEY

*Makes 2 pints*

2 pounds green tomatoes, finely diced
2 pounds cooking apples, cored and finely diced
½ pound onions, chopped
1 pound raisins
1½ pounds dark brown sugar
1 tablespoon chopped garlic
3 fresh green jalapeño peppers, seeded and
    finely diced
1 tablespoon ground ginger
1 tablespoon allspice
1 tablespoon black pepper
4 cups white vinegar
2 tablespoons salt (or less, to taste)

Combine the diced tomatoes, apples, and onions with the raisins, brown sugar, garlic, jalapeño peppers, and spices (but not the salt) in a heavy copper, steel, or enamel pan. Pour half the vinegar over it all. Bring the mixture to a boil, stirring well. Turn it to a high simmer and cook it down to a syrupy state. Add the rest of the vinegar in stages during the cooking. The process should take from 2 to 3 hours. When the mixture is syrupy and dark, taste it and adjust the seasonings.

    This chutney will keep indefinitely if the containers are well sealed and refrigerated.

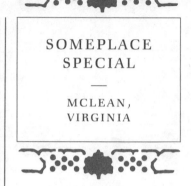

## SOMEPLACE SPECIAL
—
MCLEAN, VIRGINIA

*Combined with cream cheese, this chutney makes an excellent canapé. By itself, it is a nice complement to fresh roasted pork or ham.*

# PART 3

—

# SALADS

—

**MEAT AND POULTRY SALADS**

**SEAFOOD SALADS**

**PASTA AND RICE SALADS**

**VEGETABLE SALADS**

## MEAT AND POULTRY SALADS

Flank Steak Salad
Pommery Beef Salad
Beef, Walnut, and Roquefort Salad
Mandarin Beef Salad
Spicy Pork Meatballs with Buckwheat Noodles
Greek Lamb Salad
Marinated Lamb Salad
Sweetbread and Asparagus Salad
Kielbasa Vinaigrette
Mango Chicken with Broccoli
Grilled Chicken Breasts with Vietnamese-Style
    Dressing
Chicken, Avocado, and Bacon Salad
Raspberry Chicken Salad
Wolferman's Chicken Salad
Bombay-Style Chicken Breasts
Moroccan Chicken Salad
Apricot Ginger Chicken Salad
Cobb Salad
Brazilian Chicken Salad
Chicken Salad Valentino
Mexican Chicken Salad
Chicken Pesto Salad
Smoked Chicken Salad
Jerilyn's Turkey Salad with Tarragon and
    Hazelnuts
Oriental Duck Salad

## FLANK STEAK SALAD

*Serves 6*

1 pound flank steak
½ cup plus 2 tablespoons olive oil
2 tablespoons corn oil
¼ cup red wine vinegar
1½ teaspoons lime juice
½ teaspoon oregano
½ teaspoon thyme
2 tablespoons brown sugar
1 teaspoon Oriental chili sauce
2 tablespoons soy sauce
3 medium red potatoes
1 large yellow onion
3 green peppers
3 sweet red peppers
1½ teaspoons rosemary
1½ teaspoons salt
1 teaspoon pepper

DRESSING

4 tablespoons soy oil
2 tablespoons red wine vinegar
½ teaspoon salt
½ teaspoon rosemary
1 tablespoon crushed garlic

Trim the excess fat off the flank steak. Cut the meat into eighths and marinate it overnight in 2 tablespoons of the olive oil, the corn oil, vinegar, lime juice, oregano, thyme, brown sugar, chili sauce, and soy sauce.

Cut the potatoes in half lengthwise and then slice them. Cut the onion into thin slices and cut the green and red peppers into julienne strips. Toss all the vegetables with the rosemary, salt, pepper, and the remaining ½ cup of olive oil and roast them on cookie sheets at 425° until they are slightly browned but still crunchy.

MOVABLE FEAST
—
WASHINGTON, D.C.

*This hearty salad must be started a day ahead of serving, since the meat has to marinate overnight.*

Sauté the flank steak over high heat. Cool it and cut it into strips against the grain. Combine the meat with the vegetables.

Whisk together all the dressing ingredients. Toss the dressing with the salad meat and vegetables. Chill well before serving.

LA PRIMA

—

WASHINGTON, D.C.

*The makers of Pommery mustard claim that it has been served at the tables of the kings of France since 1632. The recipe was transmitted to the Pommery family in the eighteenth century by a superior of the ancient religious order of Meaux. Brillat-Savarin called it the mustard for gourmets, and said, "If it isn't Meaux, it isn't Mustard."*

## POMMERY BEEF SALAD

*Serves 6*

1¼ pounds cold roast beef
3 tablespoons sesame seeds
1 sweet red pepper, seeded and julienne-cut
1 green pepper, seeded and julienne-cut
½ yellow pepper, seeded and julienne-cut
⅓ cup olive oil
⅓ cup cooking oil
⅔ cup wine vinegar
2½ teaspoons salt
2½ teaspoons pepper
1 tablespoon Pommery mustard
5 cups cooked white rice, at room temperature
Lettuce

Trim any fat from the roast beef. Slice it thin and cut it into ¼-inch-wide strips. Toast the sesame seeds in an open pan in a 350° oven until they are golden brown, checking frequently. Combine all the ingredients except the rice and lettuce and let the salad sit at room temperature for at least 2 hours. Before serving, drain off the excess dressing. Place a lettuce leaf on each serving plate. Top the lettuce with a mound of white rice and a portion of the salad.

## BEEF, WALNUT, AND ROQUEFORT SALAD

*Serves 4*

1 pound medium-rare roast beef, julienne-cut
½ cup broken walnuts
4 to 6 ounces Roquefort cheese, broken into pieces
Watercress and tomatoes (preferably cherry) for
  garnish

VINAIGRETTE

¾ cup olive or any other good vegetable oil
¼ cup red wine vinegar
1 tablespoon Dijon mustard
¼ teaspoon freshly ground pepper
½ teaspoon salt
1 teaspoon dried herbs (thyme, crushed bay leaf,
  rosemary)

Combine the roast beef, walnuts, and Roquefort. Make the vinaigrette by mixing the oil and vinegar with the seasonings. Toss the roast beef mixture with the vinaigrette, adding the dressing gradually, and serve the salad with a garnish of watercress and tomatoes.

## MANDARIN BEEF SALAD

*Serves 12*

3 pounds flank steak
⅓ cup Kikkoman soy sauce
⅓ cup honey
⅓ cup pineapple juice
1 clove garlic, minced
1 teaspoon minced fresh ginger root

CAFÉ EXPRESS

—

HOUSTON

*Houston's Café Express is bright and trendy with an art deco feeling to it. And its food is inventive, like this roast beef salad made crunchy with walnuts and given pizzazz by the addition of Roquefort.*

THE GOODIE
SHOPPE

—

LANCASTER,
PENNSYLVANIA

SALADS

*In 1980, The Goodie Shoppe, then operating in present owner Jackie Parker's home, became known as the place where really special desserts were made. Now the shop has outgrown her home and has a location all its own. Along with the "goodies," delectable and ingenious fresh salads are being prepared.*

Lettuce leaves
12 oranges, sectioned, with the membranes
   removed
1 small red onion, thinly sliced
½ cup toasted slivered almonds

POPPY SEED DRESSING

¾ cup sugar
1 teaspoon dry mustard
1 teaspoon salt
⅓ cup cider vinegar
2 tablespoons finely minced onion
1 cup salad oil
1½ tablespoons poppy seeds

Marinate the flank steak overnight in a mixture of the soy sauce, honey, pineapple juice, garlic, and ginger. The next day, broil the steak until medium done (some center pinkness should remain). Chill and slice the steak thin.

In a food processor, combine the first five ingredients for the dressing and process until well combined. Gradually drizzle in the oil while the machine is running. The mixture should be thick and smooth. Stir in the poppy seeds.

Line a large platter or individual serving plates with leaf lettuce and arrange beef slices and orange sections on it. Top with red onion rings and the toasted slivered almonds. Drizzle the dressing over the salad and serve.

NOTE: This dressing keeps well, covered, in the refrigerator.

## SPICY PORK MEATBALLS WITH
## BUCKWHEAT NOODLES

*Serves 6*

2 cloves garlic
1 2-inch piece peeled fresh ginger root
2 teaspoons crushed red pepper flakes
½ teaspoon salt
1½ pounds ground pork
1 bunch broccoli
4 ounces snow peas
¼ cup rice wine vinegar
¾ cup sesame oil
1 sweet red pepper, julienne-cut
1 bunch scallions, chopped
4 tablespoons chopped cilantro (fresh coriander)
4 tablespoons toasted sesame seeds
½ pound Japanese buckwheat noodles, prepared
     according to the package directions

Pound the garlic, ginger, pepper flakes, and salt
to a paste with a mortar and pestle. Add half of
the paste to the ground pork and mix it in well.
Reserve the rest to use later. Shape the pork into
1-inch meatballs and arrange them on a baking
sheet. Bake at 350° for 15 minutes. Cool.

Cut the broccoli into flowerets. Peel and slice
the stems. Cook the flowerets and stems in boiling salted water for 3 minutes. During the last 30
seconds add the snow peas. Drain the vegetables
and refresh them under cold water. Drain well.
Put the reserved ginger paste in a small bowl, add
the rice vinegar, and whisk in the sesame oil.
Combine the meatballs, vegetables, cilantro, sesame seeds, and noodles in a large bowl and toss
with the ginger dressing. Serve the salad at room
temperature.

TAKE ME HOME
—
WASHINGTON, D.C.

*Red pepper, broccoli, snow
peas, and scallions add a
range of bright colors to
this attractive Oriental
salad.*

## MOVABLE FEAST
—
WASHINGTON, D.C.

*If you like lamb but not its high price, this salad helps a little go a long way.*

### GREEK LAMB SALAD

*Serves 10*

2½ pounds roasting lamb
1½ cups artichoke hearts, halved
1 cup fresh green beans, blanched
½ cup sliced red onion
½ cup black olives, halved
½ cup julienne-cut sweet red pepper
2 tablespoons chopped fresh parsley
2 tablespoons chopped fresh mint
1 teaspoon oregano
Pinch of rosemary

DRESSING

1¼ cups olive oil
⅓ cup red wine vinegar
1 tablespoon Pommery mustard
Salt and pepper to taste

Roast the lamb 30 to 40 minutes at 375°. Cool, cut in strips, and combine with the vegetables and herbs. Set the mixture aside. Combine all the dressing ingredients and toss gently with the meat and vegetables. Chill well before serving. Adjust seasonings if necessary.

## MARINATED LAMB SALAD

*Serves 8*

¾ pound green beans
1½ pounds cooked leg of lamb, cut into julienne
    strips 2 inches by ¼ inch
2 green peppers, julienne-cut
¼ cup cornichons, chopped
1 medium red onion, diced
2 tablespoons Dijon mustard
2 tablespoons red wine vinegar
½ cup olive oil
1 teaspoon salt
¼ teaspoon freshly ground pepper
3 cloves garlic, crushed
3 medium red-skinned potatoes (unpeeled), cubed
    and steamed

Cook the beans in boiling salted water for 3 minutes, until just tender, drain, refresh, and drain again. In a large bowl combine the lamb, green beans, green peppers, cornichons, and onion.

In a small bowl, whisk together the mustard, vinegar, oil, salt, pepper, and garlic. Add the potatoes to the salad, pour over enough dressing to coat well, and toss gently. Cover the salad and let sit for 1 hour before serving.

## SWEETBREAD AND ASPARAGUS SALAD

*Serves 4 to 6*

1 pound sweetbreads
½ cup white vinegar
1 bay leaf

### LE ST. GERMAIN TO GO
—
LOS ANGELES

*Located in a small cottage on a pie-shaped corner of Santa Monica Boulevard, Le St. Germain to Go is a community outreach program of one of the city's oldest and finest restaurants. There is no Hollywood dazzle in its décor—just basic steel and glass serving counters and a pair of wooden tables and benches. All the dazzle is in the food.*

### LE PETIT CHEF
—
MINNEAPOLIS

1 sprig parsley
Salt and pepper to taste
1 pound fresh asparagus
1 tablespoon chopped parsley
1 teaspoon chopped truffles (optional)
12 leaves Boston lettuce

VINAIGRETTE

2 teaspoons olive oil
2 teaspoons soy oil
1 teaspoon vinegar
1 teaspoon Dijon mustard
¼ teaspoon salt
Dash of white pepper

Soak the sweetbreads overnight in the refrigerator in cold water. The next day, blanch the sweetbreads in water to cover, to which the vinegar, bay leaf, parsley sprig, and salt and pepper have been added. Gently remove the sweetbreads from the water. Chill well in the refrigerator and cut them into bite-size pieces, removing any membrane.

Blanch the tender part of the asparagus spears in lightly salted water for 7 minutes. Drain off the water and cover the asparagus with ice. When it is thoroughly chilled, cut the asparagus into ¾-inch pieces and toss gently with the sweetbreads.

Whisk together the ingredients for the vinaigrette, adjusting the amount of salt and pepper. Add the vinaigrette, along with the chopped parsley and truffles (if desired), to the asparagus-sweetbread mixture. Place the lettuce leaves on individual chilled plates and top with the salad. Serve at once.

## KIELBASA VINAIGRETTE

*Serves 8 as a main course or 15 to 20 as an appetizer*

3½ pounds kielbasa sausage
1 4-ounce jar chopped pimientos, drained
1 6-ounce can pitted black olives, drained and sliced
1 bunch scallions, sliced
1 cup chopped fresh parsley
1½ cups Herb Vinaigrette (see recipe below)

Put the kielbasa in a large pot and add enough water to just cover the sausage. Bring it to a boil over high heat. Reduce the heat and simmer the sausage for 10 minutes. Drain it in a colander and let it sit just until the sausage is cool enough to handle.

Slice the sausage with a serrated knife at ½-inch intervals on a sharp diagonal. Put the sausage in a large mixing bowl with the pimientos, olives, scallions, and parsley. Toss with the dressing and serve.

### Herb Vinaigrette

*Makes about 3½ cups*

4 cloves garlic, finely minced
3 tablespoons Dijon mustard
¾ cup red wine vinegar
2 cups olive oil
½ cup vegetable oil
3 tablespoons mixed Italian herbs
Salt and freshly ground pepper to taste

In a mixing bowl, whisk together the garlic and Dijon mustard. Whisk in the red wine vinegar. Combine the olive oil and vegetable oil and slowly whisk them into the mustard mixture, pouring in a thin, steady stream. Season with the

## QUE SERA SARAH

—

### NANTUCKET, MASSACHUSETTS

*Sarah Leah Chase, who opened Que Sera Sarah on Nantucket Island in 1981, created this summer salad to reflect her Polish heritage. Whether the kielbasa is served as a main course salad or simply speared with toothpicks as an hors d'oeuvre, the flavors are best at room temperature.*

salt, pepper, and herbs. Let the flavors mellow at room temperature for a few hours. Store the vinaigrette in the refrigerator and use as needed, always bringing it back to room temperature before using.

## SHEER'S SIMPLY DELICIOUS

—

### ATLANTA

*This "gentle" chicken curry dish can be prepared a day in advance and still look crisp and inviting if the broccoli isn't blanched and added until just before serving time. Save a few flowerets to decorate the top. A rice salad and cherry tomatoes are good accompaniments, or for a special presentation, serve the salad in papaya halves.*

## MANGO CHICKEN WITH BROCCOLI

*Serves 10*

3 large mangoes, sliced
1 8½-ounce jar mango chutney
1½ cups mayonnaise
4½ heaped teaspoons curry powder
5 pounds skinless, boneless chicken breasts,
    poached, chilled, and cut into strips
6 cups fresh broccoli flowerets
1 large sweet red pepper, julienne-cut

Chop the mangoes and chutney in a food processor for 15 seconds. Combine the mayonnaise and curry in a small bowl and blend well. Stir in the chutney and mango mixture. Cover and chill. When chilled, add the chicken.

Blanch the broccoli flowerets for about 45 seconds and immediately plunge them into cold water. Toss them with the chicken, the pepper, and the dressing, adding more mayonnaise if the mixture seems too dry. Chill until ready to serve.

## GRILLED CHICKEN BREASTS WITH VIETNAMESE-STYLE DRESSING

*Serves 6*

¾ cup honey
6 tablespoons Pickapeppa Sauce
3 whole chicken breasts, skinned, boned, and halved
12 leaves red leaf lettuce
½ head green leaf lettuce, cut into strands
2 stalks celery, thinly sliced on the diagonal
1 medium red onion, thinly sliced
1 cucumber, thinly sliced
9 thin slices lemon
1 sweet red pepper, julienne-cut
About 1 cup Vietnamese-Style Dressing (see recipe, page 193)
3 tablespoons toasted sesame seeds

Combine the honey and Pickapeppa Sauce and warm the mixture in a small noncorrosive saucepan. Place the mixture in a glass or ceramic baking dish large enough to hold the six chicken breast halves in one layer and cool to room temperature. Add the chicken, and marinate in the refrigerator for 2 to 4 hours.

Remove the chicken from the marinade and grill on an outdoor barbecue or under the broiler indoors, for about 4 minutes per side. Cool the chicken to room temperature.

Arrange the red leaf lettuce, two leaves per serving, on individual luncheon plates. Attractively arrange green lettuce, celery, red onion, and cucumber slices on each plate. Cut the lemon slices in half and place them in a fanlike arrangement on one half of the plate and the julienne of red pepper on the other half. Slice the cooled chicken breasts on the diagonal and place one breast, slightly fanned out, in the center of each plate. Spoon several tablespoons of the

## PIRET'S
## —
## SAN DIEGO

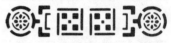

*Here is a "composed" salad that combines three popular aspects of today's cuisine—grilled meats, Oriental flavors, and artful presentation. The Picka-peppa Sauce called for is made in Jamaica and is available in most specialty food stores. It is a spicy sweet sauce containing tomatoes, onions, sugar, cane vinegar, mangoes, raisins, tamarinds, and spices.*

dressing over each salad, making sure that each serving gets some of the carrots. Garnish with the sesame seeds.

## Vietnamese-Style Dressing

*Makes about 1½ cups*

6 tablespoons sugar
½ cup champagne vinegar
½ cup Fish Sauce (available in Oriental markets)
½ cup water
⅛ cup carrots, very finely julienne-cut

Place the sugar and vinegar in a small bowl and stir to melt the sugar. Add the remaining ingredients and blend well with a whisk. Store in a covered container at cool room temperature, or in the refrigerator. (The dressing should be served at room temperature.)

## CHICKEN, AVOCADO, AND BACON SALAD

*Serves 8*

8 skinless, boneless chicken breast halves
8 strips bacon
2 avocados
1 tablespoon lemon juice
⅔ cup mayonnaise
⅓ cup sour cream
Salt and pepper to taste

Gently poach the chicken in water or stock to cover for about 15 minutes, or until cooked through. Cool and cut into 1-inch cubes. Cook the bacon until crisp, drain on paper towels, and crumble into bite-size pieces. Peel and dice the avocados and cover with the lemon juice.

In a food processor or blender, blend the mayonnaise, sour cream, and one quarter of the diced avocado until smooth. Fold the chicken, the remaining diced avocado, and the bacon into the dressing. Season with salt and pepper.

## RASPBERRY CHICKEN SALAD

*Serves 6 to 8*

6 small whole chicken breasts, poached, skinned, and boned
2 sweet red peppers, julienne-cut
2 green peppers, julienne-cut
1 cup chopped scallions
¼ cup raspberry vinegar
¾ cup peanut oil
1 tablespoon Herbes de Provence
Salt and pepper to taste

| FÊTE ACCOMPLIE |
| --- |
| WASHINGTON, D.C. |

| CROSBY'S |
| --- |
| LENOX, MASSACHUSETTS |

*Especially if you grow your own berries, you may want to take advantage of the*

*economy of making your own raspberry vinegar. Simply combine 1 cup of fresh raspberries with 3 cups of white wine vinegar in a quart jar. Cover the jar tightly and store in the refrigerator. The vinegar will be ready to use after a week and will keep indefinitely in the refrigerator.*

WOLFERMAN'S
GOOD THINGS
TO EAT
—
FAIRWAY,
KANSAS

*For almost a century Wolferman's has presented a tradition of specialty grocery shopping in Kansas City. Today its offerings include serving breakfasts and lunches on its balcony, packing picnic baskets and box lunches, and catering dinners and banquets.*

Tear the chicken into bite-size pieces and combine with the vegetables. Mix the vinegar, oil, herbs, and salt and pepper, and add the dressing to the chicken until the salad is adequately coated. Blend carefully and adjust the seasonings. Serve at room temperature.

## WOLFERMAN'S CHICKEN SALAD

*Serves 6 to 8*

3 cups cooked and cubed chicken
1 cup diced celery
½ cup diced white onion
¾ cup sliced water chestnuts, drained
¼ cup pimientos, drained and diced

DRESSING

1 cup mayonnaise
½ cup sour cream
1 tablespoon mustard
2 teaspoons sugar
1 teaspoon salt
1 teaspoon white pepper
1 tablespoon lemon juice

Combine the chicken, celery, onion, water chestnuts, and pimientos in a large bowl and set aside. Mix together all the ingredients for the dressing, and pour it over the chicken mixture. Toss well and chill before serving.

## BOMBAY-STYLE CHICKEN BREASTS

*Serves 6*

1 tablespoon safflower oil
2 tablespoons curry powder
1 13-ounce can chicken broth
3 whole chicken breasts, skinned, boned, and halved
8 ounces seedless grapes
2 bananas
2 apples, preferably Granny Smith, peeled
1 large papaya, peeled
2 ounces crystallized ginger
½ cup broken walnuts
1 cup heavy cream
2 cups mayonnaise
⅔ cup grated coconut, preferably frozen
1 bunch fresh mint for garnish

In a small casserole, heat the oil lightly and add the curry powder. Simmer briefly and add the chicken broth and chicken breasts. Simmer for 25 to 30 minutes. Remove the breasts and pat them dry with a paper towel.

Reduce the chicken stock to one fourth of its original amount over high heat. Wash the grapes and pick them off the stems. Slice the bananas and core and quarter the apples. Then slice the apples thin. Halve and seed the papaya and slice it lengthwise. Chop the ginger and walnuts separately. Prepare the dressing by whipping the heavy cream and in a separate bowl combining the mayonnaise, ginger, reduced chicken stock, grapes, bananas, apples, and coconut. Fold the whipped cream into the mayonnaise and fruit mixture.

Serve the chicken breasts on papaya slices with the dressing poured over and the walnuts sprinkled on top. Garnish with sprigs of fresh mint.

*Caffè Quadro opened in late 1985, an adjunct to Joyce Goldstein's acclaimed San Francisco restaurant, Square One. Mediterranean pizza, sandwiches, salads, and homemade pastries and ice cream are available for eating in or taking away. Joyce Goldstein was head chef and manager of the celebrated café at Chez Panisse in Berkeley for three years.*

## MOROCCAN CHICKEN SALAD

*Serves 8*

4 large whole chicken breasts, skinned and boned
2 green peppers, sliced in ¼-inch-wide strips
2 small red onions, thinly sliced
¼ cup chopped fresh parsley
¼ cup chopped cilantro (fresh coriander)
2 cloves garlic, finely minced
Watercress
Chopped black olives for garnish (optional)

VINAIGRETTE

1 to 1½ cups olive oil
¼ cup lemon juice
¼ cup red wine vinegar
1 teaspoon paprika
1 teaspoon ground cumin
¼ teaspoon cayenne pepper
Salt and pepper

Poach the chicken breasts in chicken stock or cook them over a grill. Cool the chicken, then slice in ¼-inch-wide strips. Combine the chicken, peppers, onions, chopped herbs, and garlic. Mix together the ingredients for the vinaigrette. To the chicken mixture, add enough vinaigrette to coat the chicken and vegetables, tossing lightly with your hands. Adjust the seasoning to taste. You may want more paprika and cumin and/or less vinegar and more lemon. Serve on a bed of watercress and top with chopped black olives if you wish. This salad also makes a great sandwich, stuffed in pita bread.

## APRICOT GINGER CHICKEN SALAD

*Serves 6 to 8*

5 cups diced cooked chicken breasts
4 small carrots, peeled, quartered, and blanched
3 oranges, peeled to remove both outer and inner
   skin, and cut into bite-size pieces
½ pound dried apricots, cut in half
⅔ cup slivered almonds, browned in 2 tablespoons
   butter
½ pound sweet red peppers, cut into ¼-inch
   julienne

DRESSING

1 cup sour cream
1 cup mayonnaise
8 ounces cream cheese
Juice and grated zest of 2 oranges
1½ teaspoons salt
1 teaspoon curry powder
4 ounces sweetened coconut
2 ounces crystallized ginger, chopped

Prepare the salad ingredients and mix them together in a large bowl. Process the dressing ingredients, except the coconut and ginger, in a blender or food processor. Stir in the ginger and coconut. Pour the dressing over the salad mixture in small amounts and toss until the salad is adequately coated.

### FORMAGGIO KITCHEN

---

CAMBRIDGE

*Formaggio's owner, Norma Wasserman, reports that her customers have become more and more sophisticated over the years. Those who felt experimental when they bought chicken salad with grapes and walnuts four years ago are now choosing Apricot Ginger Chicken Salad without blinking an eye.*

## BAREFOOT
## CONTESSA

—

### EAST HAMPTON,
### LONG ISLAND

*Ina Garten, who has operated a fancy food market in Westhampton Beach since 1978, recently opened a second shop in East Hampton. Scrubbed pine cupboards and dressers serve as checkout counters and display cases at the front of the store. As customers make their way from front to back, they encounter an enticing array of cheeses, coffees, homemade baked goods, exotic fruits and vegetables, fancy groceries, and delicious prepared foods.*

## COBB SALAD

*Serves 6*

4 whole chicken breasts, skinned and boned
¼ pound bacon
1 avocado, sliced
1 large beefsteak tomato, diced
2 ounces blue cheese, preferably Danish, diced
Salt and pepper to taste

VINAIGRETTE

¼ cup champagne vinegar
¾ cup corn oil
¾ cup olive oil
2 cloves garlic, minced
2 teaspoons oregano
1 teaspoon salt
1 teaspoon pepper

Poach the chicken breasts in water or chicken stock for 10 minutes, until the pink color is just gone. Drain, cool, and cut the chicken in julienne strips. Cook the bacon, drain it well, and crumble. Mix the chicken and bacon with the avocado, tomato, and blue cheese and season with salt and pepper.

Combine the ingredients for the vinaigrette and shake or whisk well. Gradually add it to the salad until the proper coating is achieved. The flavor of the salad improves if it is allowed to stand for a few hours before serving.

## BRAZILIAN CHICKEN SALAD

*Serves 4*

1 whole chicken breast, skinned and boned
2 green peppers
1 sweet red pepper
3 hearts of palm
1 seedless orange

DRESSING

6 tablespoons olive oil
⅓ cup orange juice
2 tablespoons lime juice
4 tablespoons red wine vinegar
1 teaspoon crushed dried chilies, or to taste
Pinch of cayenne
1 teaspoon Tabasco, or to taste
Pinch of sugar
Salt and pepper to taste

Bake the chicken breast at 375° for 12 minutes. Let the chicken cool and cut it into julienne strips. Cut the peppers into julienne strips, sprinkle them with salt, and set them aside for 10 minutes. Drain the peppers, rinse, and pat dry.

Slice the hearts of palm on the bias. Peel the orange, quarter it, and cut into ¼-inch slices. Reserve several slices of the hearts of palm and orange for garnish. Combine the chicken, peppers, hearts of palm, and orange and toss gently.

Blend together the ingredients for the dressing in a blender or food processor. Add enough dressing to the chicken mixture to coat it and again toss gently. Garnish with the reserved hearts of palm and orange slices and a small amount of crushed dried chilies.

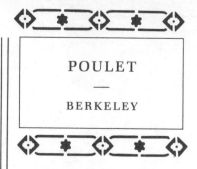

POULET

—

BERKELEY

*Shai Yerlick, the chef at Poulet, is Israeli and lived for a while in Brazil, the inspiration for this recipe. If you feel intimidated by the quantity of chilies and Tabasco he calls for, don't hesitate to cut down on the amounts.*

## SUZANNE'S
—
WASHINGTON, D.C.

*It wasn't for the great Hollywood lover of the twenties, Rudolph Valentino, that this salad was named. Valentino was just one of those names that pop into a chef's mind; but all who try the salad do love it, so Rudolph would be pleased.*

## CHICKEN SALAD VALENTINO

*Serves 4 to 6*

3 whole chicken breasts (approximately 3½ pounds), cooked and cut into bite-size pieces
2 sweet red peppers, julienne-cut
1 large head broccoli, cut into flowerets
12 slices bacon, cut into 1-inch lengths
Salt and pepper to taste

DRESSING

½ cup sour cream
½ cup mayonnaise
3 tablespoons Dijon mustard
3 tablespoons raspberry vinegar
4 tablespoons finely chopped fresh dill

In a large bowl combine the chicken and red peppers. Set aside. Blanch the broccoli in a pot of boiling salted water for 2 to 3 minutes, until tender but still crisp. Drain the broccoli and refresh it in cold water. Drain again. Add the broccoli to the chicken and peppers. Sauté the bacon until crisp. Drain it and add it to the chicken mixture.

Whisk together the ingredients for the dressing, pour it over the chicken and vegetables, and mix well. Adjust the seasonings and serve.

## MEXICAN CHICKEN SALAD

*Serves 12 to 14*

6 whole chicken breasts
Salt and pepper to taste
¼ cup balsamic vinegar
Several dashes of Tabasco
1 16-ounce can chickpeas, drained and rinsed
1 sweet red pepper, diced
1 green pepper, diced
3 stalks celery, diced
1 red onion, finely diced

DRESSING

4 cups sour cream
2 tablespoons chili powder
2 teaspoons ground cumin
2 jalapeño peppers, seeded and finely chopped
1 small bunch cilantro (fresh coriander), finely
    chopped
Salt and pepper to taste

Lay the chicken breasts flat on a baking sheet. Salt and pepper them and bake them in a 350° oven for 30 to 40 minutes, until done. When they are cool, discard the skin and remove the chicken from the bones in long strips. Put the chicken in a bowl and mix it with the vinegar, Tabasco, chickpeas, and vegetables.

Mix the dressing. Pour it over the chicken and vegetables and mix all together very well. Serve the salad immediately or let it chill. It will keep well for several days.

### WORD OF MOUTH

—

NEW YORK CITY

*It's cozy and friendly in Christi Finch's Word of Mouth on Lexington Avenue, and the fragrances that emanate from the shop are tantalizing indeed. Mexican Chicken Salad is among its tried-and-true favorites, with neighborhood hosts and hostesses stopping in regularly to order it for their luncheon parties or summer suppers.*

*Twenty years ago Val's was a very small, homey meat market, started by Bruce and Val Stahle. It is still homey but no longer small. Today Val's sells gourmet items as well as soups, salads, and quiches pre-pared on the premises for take-out. Their wine department is one of the finest on Florida's west coast, with weekly wine tastings and classes conducted by Val's son Mark.*

## CHICKEN PESTO SALAD

*Serves 6 to 8*

2 whole chicken breasts (about 2 pounds)
Celery leaves, parsley, and tarragon
½ pound rotelli (spinach, tomato, and egg combination), cooked according to the package directions
¾ cup cubed zucchini
¾ cup seeded, diced tomatoes
½ cup chopped celery
4½ teaspoons dried basil
1 teaspoon oregano
2 tablespoons chopped fresh parsley
¾ teaspoon salt
⅛ teaspoon pepper
½ cup sour cream
½ cup mayonnaise
1½ teaspoons lemon juice
Sprinkling of chopped walnuts or toasted pine nuts

A day before you wish to serve the salad, cook the chicken with celery leaves, parsley, and tarragon to flavor it. Refrigerate.

Remove the skin and bones from the chicken and cube the meat. (There should be about 2½ cups.) Combine the chicken with the pasta, zucchini, tomatoes, and celery and set aside.

Combine the herbs and salt and pepper with the sour cream, mayonnaise, and lemon juice, and fold it into the pasta and chicken mixture along with the walnuts or pine nuts. Chill the salad at least 4 hours before serving on lettuce leaves.

## SMOKED CHICKEN SALAD

*Serves 4*

¾ pound *jícama*, julienne-cut
¾ pound carrots, julienne-cut
¾ pound smoked chicken or turkey, julienne-cut
Juice of 3 oranges
½ cup champagne vinegar
1 tablespoon soy sauce
4 tablespoons honey
Grated zest of 1 orange
Dash of white pepper
Romaine lettuce

Blanch the julienne pieces of *jícama* in boiling water for 30 seconds. Drain in a colander under cool running water for a few seconds. Follow the same procedure for the carrots. Combine the remaining ingredients except the chicken and lettuce in a jar, cover, and shake well to make the honey-orange vinaigrette.

To serve the salad, combine the *jícama* and carrots and place the mixture in a square in the middle of a serving platter. Place the strips of chicken or turkey in the center of the vegetable mixture. Surround the edge of the platter with a chiffonade of romaine lettuce. Sprinkle the salad with salt and pepper to taste and a small amount of dressing and pass the remaining vinaigrette.

MIRABELLE

—

DALLAS

*Chicken salads and anything chocolate remain favorites at Mirabelle, though Chris Jonsson is pleased with the way Dallasites are taking to her more innovative offerings. The* jícama *and the honey-orange dressing in this recipe make an interesting difference. Though native to the Southwest,* jícama *is now available in produce sections in many parts of the country. Smoked turkey works as well as smoked chicken in this recipe and may be easier to find.*

## BRUSSEAU'S

—

### EDMONDS, WASHINGTON

*Jerilyn Brusseau's original idea was to open her own homespun bakery and café in the charming waterfront community of Edmonds, just north of Seattle. Today "brusseau's" has become the favorite daytime bakery-café in the Puget Sound area, offering a tempting variety of local farm ingredients combined to create interesting and delicious breakfasts, lunches, pastries, and desserts.*

## JERILYN'S TURKEY SALAD WITH TARRAGON AND HAZELNUTS

*Serves 6*

2 pounds roasted turkey breast, cut into bite-size
　　pieces
1 small red onion, coarsely chopped
4 stalks celery, coarsely chopped
6 tablespoons chopped fresh tarragon (or 2
　　tablespoons dried)
Sprinkling of salad oil
4 tablespoons finely chopped fresh parsley
½ cup hazelnuts, roasted and skinned (see note)
½ cup low-fat yogurt
¼ cup mayonnaise
Salt and pepper to taste

Toss all the ingredients except the yogurt, may-onnaise, and salt and pepper in a large bowl. Mix the yogurt and mayonnaise and add until the proper coating is achieved. Season to taste.

NOTE: To prepare the hazelnuts, shell the nuts and roast them in a 375° oven for 12 minutes. Place them in a brown paper bag and shake it to help loosen the skins. Leave the nuts in the bag for about 10 minutes to further steam the skins, then peel away the skins with the help of a terrycloth towel.

## ORIENTAL DUCK SALAD

*Serves 6 to 8*

2 4½- to 5-pound ducklings
1 head broccoli (flowerets only)
4 medium tomatoes, diced
6 scallions, diced
½ cup toasted sesame seeds
4 cloves garlic, minced
¾ cup salad oil
1 teaspoon sesame oil (optional)
½ cup soy sauce
Salt and pepper to taste

Preheat the oven to 425°. Roast the ducklings for 45 minutes, basting them every 10 minutes. Remove them from the oven and let them cool. Carve the meat from the carcasses and cut it into bite-size strips, but don't remove the skin. Put the meat in a large mixing bowl and add the raw broccoli flowerets and the diced tomatoes and scallions. Combine the remaining ingredients and toss with the duck and vegetables.

SOIGNE
—
EDGARTOWN,
MASSACHUSETTS

*Ronald Cavallo takes a tip from the Chinese and makes sure that the crisp roasted skin is always included in his duck salad.*

## SEAFOOD SALADS

Salade Coquilles St. Jacques
Wolf Fish and Fruit Salad
Maine Lobster and Morel Salad
Lobster Salad
Shrimp Salad with Grapefruit
Rice Seafood Salad
Mesquite-Grilled Tuna with Lemon-Tarragon
  Mayonnaise
"Tuna Tonight"
Mediterranean Tuna Salad
Shrimp with Sautéed Celery Root
Crawfish and Snow Pea Salad
American Café Crabmeat Salad
Whitefish Salad

## SALADE COQUILLES ST. JACQUES

*Serves 6*

1½ pounds fresh sea or bay scallops
2 cups dry white wine
⅜ cup lemon juice
¾ cup sun-dried tomatoes, with their own oil (about
⅓ cup)
½ red cabbage, cut in half, cored, and shredded
½ head lettuce, cut into slivers
1 cucumber, thinly sliced
1 bunch cilantro (fresh coriander)
2 limes, cut into 12 wedges, for garnish

Wash the scallops thoroughly under cold running water, remove the small muscle from each, and pat dry with paper towels.

In a medium saucepan, combine the wine and lemon juice. There should be enough liquid to just cover the scallops. Bring the liquid to a boil, then reduce the heat to simmer. Add the scallops and poach them lightly for 3 to 4 minutes, being careful not to overcook them; they should remain slightly translucent. Remove the scallops with a slotted spoon. Pour the poaching liquid into a clean bowl.

Cut the sun-dried tomatoes into julienne strips, reserving the oil for the dressing. When the poaching liquid has reached room temperature, add the tomato oil. Whisk to blend well. Keeping the scallops, tomatoes, cabbage, and lettuce in separate bowls, add enough dressing to each to lightly coat.

On each luncheon plate arrange a bed of shredded lettuce (chiffonade) on one half of the plate and shredded cabbage on the other. Ladle some of the leftover dressing over both. Arrange the scallops and tomatoes on the chiffonade and garnish each salad with cucumber slices and

*Piret and George Munger began their extensive specialty food business by opening a pan store—The Perfect Pan—in 1975. Today the business includes numerous shops in southern California, combining bistro-restaurants, carry-out foods, cookware, and a cooking school. The bistros, called Piret's, started as a way of familiarizing patrons with the foods available for carry-out. This salad is one of the many that appear on the eat-in and take-out menus at Piret's. Either sea scallops or bay scallops may be used, though if you use the former, cut them in half crosswise.*

sprigs of cilantro. Add two wedges of lime to each plate and serve the salad immediately.

NOTE: If the scallops must be purchased a day ahead of serving, clean them and refrigerate them in a bowl filled with enough milk to cover. This helps to retain the sweet, fresh taste.

---

*Fishmonger owner Dorothy Batchelder has a mission to educate her customers about the benefits of the so-called underutilized species. Monkfish, pollock, and wolf fish are less expensive than the more standard scrod, halibut, and haddock and are equally nutritious and more readily available. Often they can be used in combination with more expensive fish to create an affordable dish for entertaining. This salad makes the point very well.*

## WOLF FISH AND FRUIT SALAD

*Serves 6*

2 pounds wolf fish (or monkfish, cusk, or any firm-fleshed white fish)
¾ pound seedless green grapes, halved
2 navel oranges, peeled and divided into sections
1 grapefruit, peeled and divided into sections
1 banana, sliced
1 kiwi fruit, peeled and sliced
¾ cup toasted slivered almonds
1 head Boston lettuce

LIME-GINGER DRESSING

½ cup fresh-squeezed lime juice
½ cup sour cream
½ cup mayonnaise
3 tablespoons honey
3 tablespoons finely minced fresh ginger root
2 tablespoons chopped fresh mint for garnish

Cut the fish into bite-size chunks. Fill a sauté pan halfway with water, bring the water to a simmer, and add the fish. Poach for 5 minutes, until the chunks become firm and no pink color remains. (Time from the point when the water returns to a simmer.) Remove the fish with a slotted spoon and drain on paper towels to absorb excess moisture. Refrigerate until well chilled,

In a large bowl combine the fruits. In a separate bowl prepare the lime-ginger dressing by whisking together all the ingredients.

Toss the fish and almonds with the fruit and add the dressing until the mixture is well coated. Serve the salad on a bed of Boston lettuce on individual plates or a platter, garnished with chopped mint.

## MAINE LOBSTER AND MOREL SALAD

*Serves 4*

2 whole 1½-pound Maine lobsters
Court bouillon (see recipe, page 211)
1 cup fresh morel mushrooms
½ cup raw fresh spinach
4 leaves Boston lettuce
½ cup celery root (celeriac), julienne-cut
2 teaspoons chopped truffles
5 tablespoons of your favorite vinaigrette dressing

Bring the court bouillon to a boil, add the lobsters, and cook for 15 minutes. Remove the pan from the heat, but leave the lobsters in the water.

Wash the morels, spinach, and lettuce well and drain them thoroughly. Slice the morels and finely cut the spinach.

Remove the lobsters from the water and the lobster meat from the shells. Slice the meat into pieces about 1½ inches thick. Mix the lobster meat with the vegetables and add the vinaigrette.

Lay the lettuce leaves on individual chilled plates and put some of the salad on top. Sprinkle

LE PETIT CHEF
—
MINNEAPOLIS

*Minnesota is morel country, and Jean-Claude Tindillier, tired of always combining them with meat, devised this dish—even though the lobsters have to be imported from New England.*

the salad with truffles and serve at once. The lobster should not be completely cold.

## Court Bouillon

½ cup chopped onions
½ cup chopped celery
2 sprigs parsley
2 tablespoons butter
6 peppercorns
2 cloves
1 bay leaf
1 tablespoon salt
¼ cup vinegar
3 quarts water

Sauté the vegetables and parsley in the butter. Remove them to a large pot and add the rest of the ingredients. Cover and simmer for 5 minutes.

## LOBSTER SALAD

*Serves 4 to 6*

½ pound snow peas, stems and strings removed
1 8-ounce can water chestnuts, drained and thinly
    sliced
¾ pound cold cooked lobster, cut into 1-inch
    chunks
¼ cup Sesame Vinaigrette (see recipe below)
Romaine lettuce
½ cup chopped roasted unsalted cashews for
    garnish

Place snow peas in a strainer and submerge in
boiling salted water for 1 minute. Refresh in cold
water and drain. Place the remaining ingredients
except the lettuce and cashews in a bowl and
toss with Sesame Vinaigrette until the lobster and
vegetables are well coated. Arrange the salad on
a bed of sliced romaine and sprinkle the top with
the cashews.

### Sesame Vinaigrette

*Makes about 2 cups*

Juice of 1 lemon
⅓ cup white wine vinegar
½ teaspoon salt
½ teaspoon sugar
Freshly ground pepper
1 clove garlic, crushed
1½ cups light vegetable oil
1 teaspoon sesame oil

Combine all ingredients in a jar and shake well.
The leftover dressing will keep well in the refrigerator.

### THE GREEN GROCER

—

NORFOLK,
VIRGINIA

*The flavors of sesame and
Oriental vegetables give this
lobster salad an interesting
new twist.*

## LE ST. GERMAIN TO GO

—

### LOS ANGELES

## *SHRIMP SALAD WITH GRAPEFRUIT*

*Serves 4 to 6*

2 large grapefruits
2 whole Belgian endives
1 pound cooked medium shrimp
6 tablespoons mayonnaise
4 tablespoons plain low-fat yogurt
½ cup fresh chopped dill
1 teaspoon fresh lemon juice

Cut the grapefruits in half, spoon out the fruit meat, and cut it in small chunks. Trim the endives and cut them in small chunks. Combine the shrimp, grapefruit, and endive in a salad bowl.

Make the sauce by whisking together the mayonnaise and yogurt and then adding the dill and lemon juice. Pour the sauce over the salad and serve immediately.

## RICE SEAFOOD SALAD

*Serves 24*

1½ pounds uncooked pearl or arborio rice
¼ teaspoon crushed saffron threads
1½ pounds shrimp or bay scallops, lightly cooked
1½ pounds squid, cleaned, julienne-cut, and lightly cooked (including tentacles)
1 28-ounce can clams, drained, or equivalent amount of cooked fresh clams
10 ounces (about 2 large) fire-roasted and julienne-cut sweet red peppers (peppers in jars may also be used)
20 leaves fresh basil, chopped
½ cup chopped fresh parsley

DRESSING

1¾ cups extra-virgin olive oil
⅔ cup fresh hand-squeezed lemon juice
1¼ teaspoons salt (or less, to taste)
½ teaspoon freshly ground pepper

Cook the rice according to the instructions on the package, using fish or chicken stock instead of water if you wish, along with the saffron. Prepare the dressing and toss with the rice, seafood, peppers, and herbs just before serving, making sure that the dressing is at room temperature.

VIVANDE
PORTA VIA
—
SAN FRANCISCO

*Carlo Middione developed this dish out of respect for Italy's continuing love of the fruits of the sea. This is a Vivande favorite for a summer buffet, and the fact that it will serve a crowd makes it especially appealing. Feel free to vary the types and quantities of seafood called for, depending on what is available.*

*In the summer of 1985, Scott and Charlotte Caskey took over a fish market in the Martha's Vineyard resort town of Edgartown and transformed it into a gourmet take-out shop. Since they are just a stone's throw from the waterfront, it is understandable that many of their creations feature fish.*

## MESQUITE-GRILLED TUNA WITH LEMON-TARRAGON MAYONNAISE

*Serves 6*

2 pounds fresh yellow-fin tuna steaks, 1½ to 2
     inches thick
5 tablespoons fresh lemon juice
1 clove garlic, minced
2 egg yolks
4 tablespoons dried tarragon
½ cup capers, drained
Pepper to taste
2 cups olive oil
Lemon wedges, capers, or sprigs of tarragon for
     garnish

Sprinkle the tuna steaks with 1 tablespoon of the fresh lemon juice and grill them over charcoal and mesquite coals. Cook until the fish flakes to the touch and is no longer translucent. This will take about 8 minutes on each side. Let the fish cool and cut it into 1½-inch cubes.

In a food processor or blender, combine the rest of the lemon juice, the garlic, and the egg yolks. With the motor still running, add the tarragon, capers, and pepper to taste and then the oil in a slow, steady stream to make mayonnaise. Gently toss the tuna with the mayonnaise.

Put the salad on a bed of lettuce and garnish it with lemon wedges or slices, capers, or a few sprigs of fresh tarragon.

## "TUNA TONIGHT"

*Serves 4 to 6*

2 pounds tuna steaks
½ cup sesame seeds
2 tablespoons sesame oil
2 tablespoons tamari
½ pound mushrooms, sliced
3 stalks celery, finely chopped
2 sweet red peppers, cored, cut in half, and thinly
    sliced
4 scallions, thinly sliced on an angle (use both green
    and white parts)
2 tablespoons peeled and minced ginger root
Chopped fresh parsley for garnish

SESAME-TAMARI DRESSING

1 cup mayonnaise
3 tablespoons tamari or soy sauce
2 tablespoons sesame oil
2 tablespoons fresh lemon juice

Oil a baking dish large enough to hold the tuna steaks in one layer. Add the tuna and a small amount of water. Cover the baking dish with tin foil and bake at 350° for 30 minutes. While the tuna is cooking, put the sesame seeds in a shallow pan in one layer, and toast them in the lower part of the oven for 10 to 15 minutes, until they are golden brown. Remove the pan from the oven and set aside to cool. When the tuna is done, remove it from the oven and let it cool to room temperature.

Heat the sesame oil and tamari in a sauté pan over medium heat. Add the sliced mushrooms and sauté until the juices have dried up and the mushrooms are spongy, shaking the pan often to coat them with oil. Set aside to cool.

Prepare the dressing by combining all the ingredients.

## THE FISHMONGER

—

### CAMBRIDGE

*Peter Wolf, noted rock star–composer, lives near The Fishmonger and is a loyal customer. This salad—a far cry from the all-American rendition—is one of his favorites.*

In a mixing bowl combine the celery, red peppers, scallions, and ginger root. Add the mushrooms and sesame seeds. Break the tuna into pieces and add it. Toss the mixture well. Just before serving, add enough dressing to lightly coat the tuna and vegetables. Garnish the salad with chopped parsley.

FOODWORKS
—
CHICAGO

*Foodworks is a garden of earthly delights. Its fresh fruits and vegetables look like models for a Cézanne still life, and the take-out counter entices with several kinds of pâtés, spicy somosas, and imaginative salads, such as this tuna salad with Havarti.*

## MEDITERRANEAN TUNA SALAD

*Serves 4 to 6*

2 6½-ounce cans tuna in water, drained
¼ pound dill Havarti cheese, cut into ½-inch cubes
¼ cup pitted black olives, sliced
2 8-ounce packages tricolored vegetable fusilli, cooked according to package directions
1 bunch scallions, thinly sliced
1 small sweet red pepper, finely chopped
1 small green pepper, finely chopped

DRESSING

⅔ cup lemon juice
¾ cup olive oil
¼ teaspoon sea salt
¼ teaspoon oregano
¼ teaspoon parsley
¼ teaspoon basil
15 grinds fresh black pepper

Mix the ingredients for the dressing and set it aside. Combine the salad ingredients in a large bowl. Gradually add enough dressing to coat the mixture adequately. Toss gently and serve.

## SHRIMP WITH SAUTÉED CELERY ROOT

*Serves 4 to 6*

2 medium-large celery roots (celeriac)
½ cup vegetable oil
2 leeks, white part only, julienne-cut
24 cooked, peeled, and deveined medium shrimp
2 tablespoons balsamic vinegar
Salt and pepper to taste

Trim the celery roots and peel them. Dice the white part. Heat the oil in a sauté pan. Add the celery root and cook it until it is lightly browned. Put it in a bowl and add the leeks, shrimp, and vinegar. Add salt and pepper to taste and serve the salad at room temperature.

## CRAWFISH AND SNOW PEA SALAD

*Serves 6*

1 pound crawfish tails, peeled (or substitute shrimp)
1 medium onion, diced
4 cloves garlic, minced
able oil for sautéing
½ pound snow peas, stems removed
8 ounces long-grain rice
½ bunch scallions (only the green part, sliced thin)
¼ cup white wine vinegar
1 cup vegetable oil
1 teaspoon chopped fresh thyme, or ½ teaspoon
   dried thyme

MITCHELL
COBEY
CUISINE

—

CHICAGO

*"Resolve to diet another day,"* Travel & Leisure *magazine said of this pioneer among Chicago carry-out specialty food shops. Since 1977, it has been offering Chicagoans foods that range from homey to haute—from shortbread and chicken curry to chocolate mousse marjolaine.*

MAGAZINE
CUISINE

—

NEW ORLEANS

*In 1984, after several years of cooking in Aspen and Nantucket, Natchez-born Alixe Hugret got her heart's desire, her own shop on*

SALADS

## THE
## AMERICAN CAFÉ
## MARKET

—

WASHINGTON, D.C.

*Fresh crabmeat, carefully
picked over to make sure
all the bits of shell and
cartilage are removed, is of
course the best choice for
this salad. In Washington,
the crabs would come from
the Chesapeake Bay, the
source of the famous blue
crab.*

Salt and pepper to taste
Tabasco to taste

Sauté the crawfish tails, onion, and garlic in oil
for about 10 minutes. Drop the snow peas into
boiling salted water for about 1 minute. Drain
and refresh them in cold water. Cut each snow
pea in half.

Cook the rice according to the package directions. Cool it and combine it with the crawfish
mixture, the snow peas, and the scallions. Whisk
together the vinegar, oil, thyme, salt, pepper, and
Tabasco. Toss the dressing with the crawfish and
snow peas. Serve the salad cold.

## AMERICAN CAFÉ CRABMEAT SALAD

*Serves 4*

6 tablespoons chopped sweet red pepper
2 scallions, chopped
1¾ cups chopped celery
½ cup plus 2 tablespoons mayonnaise
1 teaspoon salt
½ teaspoon celery salt
½ teaspoon Old Bay seasoning
1 teaspoon Worcestershire sauce
2 tablespoons white wine
1 teaspoon lemon juice
½ teaspoon Creole mustard or Dijon mustard with
    seeds
¼ teaspoon cayenne pepper
1 pound lump or backfin crabmeat

In a large bowl, combine all the ingredients except the crabmeat and mix well. Then add the
crabmeat by handfuls, mixing gently. Serve on a
bed of lettuce or in a sandwich.

## WHITEFISH SALAD

*Serves 8 to 10*

4 pounds cooked whitefish (deboned by hand, with
    care)
1 small red onion, chopped
4 stalks celery, sliced
1 green pepper, chopped
1½ teaspoons salt
¾ teaspoon white pepper
½ to ¾ cup mayonnaise

Mix all the ingredients together and serve on a
lettuce leaf with fresh homemade rye bread or a
fresh bagel. Possible garnishes include cole slaw,
fresh fruit wedges, sliced tomato and onions,
olives, and lemon wedges.

## TOOJAY'S
## OF PALM BEACH
—
### HIGHLAND PARK,
### ILLINOIS

*Posters and neon-pink
plastic palm trees are the
decoration for this tongue-
in-cheek recreation of
TooJay's posh Florida
namesake. Though many of
the shop's creations border
on the decadent, chef Jim
Walsh's Whitefish Salad is
easy on the waistline.*

## PASTA AND RICE SALADS

Pasta Toss with Shrimp
Pasta alla Checca
Tortellini Salad with Blue Cheese Dressing
Tortellini Pesto Salad with Sun-Dried Tomatoes
Pumate Pasta Salad
Pasta Salad alla Caesar
Pasta Chicken Salad with Peanuts
Grilled Chicken with Fusilli in Green Sauce
Fusilli with Chicken and Vegetables
Sesame Pasta Salad
Riso al Pesto
Curried Rice Salad
Tortellini with Wild Rice
Wild Rice Salad
Wild Rice and Shrimp Salad
Wild Rice and Chèvre Salad
Wild Rice with Smoked Turkey and Oranges
Brown Rice Salad

## PASTA TOSS WITH SHRIMP

*Serves 5*

5 cups dry rotini
About ¾ cup of your favorite vinaigrette dressing
1 teaspoon salt
½ teaspoon freshly ground pepper
½ teaspoon Beau Monde seasoning
1 medium red onion, minced
6 scallions, chopped
1 sweet red pepper, chopped
4 tablespoons chopped fresh parsley
1 pound cooked cocktail shrimp
Paprika and black olives for garnish

Cook the rotini in boiling salted water for 11 minutes, uncovered. Drain them and coat them with the vinaigrette. Add the seasonings, the chopped vegetables and parsley, and then the shrimp. Toss the salad lightly and serve it on chilled plates, garnished with paprika and black olives.

## RIBBONS

—

TACOMA,
WASHINGTON

*Ribbons is in a turn-of-the-century red brick building that once housed a Tacoma cobbler shop. Not only is food on sale inside, but local art is too, and the menu is as eclectic as the two parts of the shop. Offerings in its display case are as homespun as Waldorf salad (though with flourishes such as grapes and sour cream) and as up-to-date as this pasta dish.*

*This is a lovely salad to prepare in advance. It has to mellow for a minimum of two hours, and an additional two or three hours won't hurt a bit.*

## PASTA ALLA CHECCA

*Serves 6 to 8*

8 firm ripe tomatoes, diced
8 stalks celery, minced
¼ cup grated Parmesan cheese
3 cloves garlic, chopped
⅛ teaspoon crushed red pepper flakes
8 large fresh basil leaves, chopped
Pinch of white pepper
Salt to taste
½ cup olive oil
1 pound pasta, cooked

Combine all the ingredients except the pasta and let them sit at room temperature for 2 or more hours. Add the cooled cooked pasta and garnish with additional basil leaves.

## TORTELLINI SALAD WITH BLUE CHEESE DRESSING

*Serves 8*

### DRESSING

½ cup wine vinegar
2 teaspoons sugar
¼ cup olive oil
¼ cup salad oil
1½ teaspoons garlic salt
1 teaspoon freshly ground black pepper
3 ounces blue cheese

Prepare the dressing by putting the vinegar and sugar in a container first so that the vinegar will melt the sugar. Shake. Add the oil, garlic salt, pepper, and crumbled cheese. Set aside.

### SALAD

1 pound cheese-filled tortellini, green and white
   mixed
3 carrots, julienne-cut
½ pound roast beef, julienne-cut
½ head broccoli, cut into flowerets
1 sliced onion and 1½ tomatoes, cut into wedges,
   for garnish

Cook the tortellini *al dente* in boiling salted water. Run it under cold water and drain. Blanch the carrot strips for 2 minutes. Mix the beef, carrots, tortellini, and broccoli flowerets. Add the dressing and chill for 30 minutes before serving. Line each plate with a lettuce leaf and top with a portion of salad garnished with onion rings and tomato wedges.

## LA PRIMA
—
WASHINGTON, D.C.

*This tortellini salad came into being when La Prima founder Gregory Leisch, a former business consultant who loves to eat and to cook, had some leftover tortellini one day, combined it with blue cheese vinaigrette, tossed in a few strips of roast beef to provide substance, and— presto—had a new salad. The roast beef notwithstanding, he calls it a light pasta salad because of the vegetables.*

## FORMAGGIO KITCHEN

—

### CAMBRIDGE

*Tortellini, the original "gourmet pasta," seems to be a perennial favorite. This recipe combines several familiar food specialties, and the result is a colorful and flavorful main dish salad that is particularly attractive on a buffet table.*

## TORTELLINI PESTO SALAD WITH SUN-DRIED TOMATOES

*Serves 6*

¼ pound sun-dried tomatoes
1⅓ cups olive oil
1½ cups dry cheese-filled tortellini
1 cup walnuts

DRESSING

⅓ cup champagne vinegar
⅔ cup lemon juice
3 cloves garlic, halved
3 tablespoons Dijon mustard
1 or 2 bunches fresh basil, depending on size of
    bunch
1 teaspoon salt
¼ teaspoon pepper
Oil from sun-dried tomatoes

Soak the sun-dried tomatoes in the olive oil overnight. The next day, drain the tomatoes and reserve the oil for the dressing. Cut the tomatoes into quarters. Cook the tortellini in boiling salted water until *al dente.* Drain and let cool. Mix the tortellini with the walnuts and tomatoes.

Combine the ingredients for the dressing and blend in a blender or food processor. Pour the dressing over the tortellini mixture in small amounts until the pasta is adequately coated, and toss well.

## PUMATE PASTA SALAD

*Serves 6 to 8*

6 cups penne pasta
2½ ounces *pumate* (about 6 pairs)
6 scallions
2 tablespoons grated Parmesan cheese
½ cup extra-virgin olive oil
⅓ cup balsamic vinegar
2 tablespoons Italian (flat) parsley

Cook the pasta in boiling salted water for 9 minutes. Run it under cold water and drain. Mince the *pumate* and scallions. Combine them with the pasta and cheese and adjust the seasonings.

This salad may be served either warm or cold, but if warm is your choice, an additional ¼ cup of extra-virgin olive oil will be needed.

## PASTA SALAD ALLA CAESAR

*Serves 10 to 12*

½ pound dried fusilli
Olive oil
½ head broccoli, flowerets only
2 medium zucchini, cut into chunks
¼ pound fresh green beans, cut diagonally into ½-inch pieces
½ bunch scallions, sliced
1 small sweet red pepper, diced
¼ pound pepperoni, diced
2 tablespoons minced fresh basil
2 tablespoons minced fresh parsley
2 tablespoons pine nuts, sautéed to brown
5 or 6 marinated artichoke hearts, halved

## PROVENDER

—

TIVERTON,
RHODE ISLAND

Pumate—*Italian plum tomatoes, dried and preserved in olive oil and herbs—are what make this pasta salad so exceptional. And it's pretty, too, served with a bright green vegetable like broccoli or marinated green beans. It's a fine accompaniment for broiled steak.*

## MARION CHEESE

—

LANCASTER,
PENNSYLVANIA

*As the name suggests, Marion Cheese began as a cheese shop, but by now owner Janice Stork spends much of her time with chef Anne Eshelman concocting original recipes for salads and appetizers and assorted other prepared foods.*

4 sun-dried tomatoes, julienne-cut
10 to 12 calamata olives
½ cup marinated mushrooms

DRESSING

4 anchovy fillets
2 cloves garlic, pressed
1½ teaspoons Dijon mustard
1½ teaspoons Worcestershire sauce
1½ cups olive oil
½ cup red wine vinegar
¼ cup fresh lemon juice
1 egg
Salt and pepper to taste
2 tablespoons grated Parmesan cheese

Drop the fusilli into boiling salted water and cook for 8 minutes. Run cold water over the pasta and drain it thoroughly. Toss it with a bit of olive oil to keep the pieces separated. Blanch the broccoli, zucchini, and green beans.

Prepare the dressing by placing the anchovies, garlic, mustard, and Worcestershire sauce in the bowl of a food processor and processing until the mixture is of paste consistency. In a separate bowl combine the oil, vinegar, lemon juice, egg, salt, pepper, and cheese. Whisk in the anchovy mixture and blend thoroughly.

Mix all the salad ingredients in a large bowl and pour enough dressing over the mixture to coat well but not drench. Use the remaining dressing to refresh the salad, as needed.

## PASTA CHICKEN SALAD WITH PEANUTS

*Serves 6*

3 whole small chicken breasts
1 pound linguini, broken into 6-inch lengths
1 small green pepper, julienne-cut
1 small sweet red pepper, julienne-cut
4 scallions, finely sliced
1 cup chopped salted, roasted peanuts

VINAIGRETTE

Juice of 1 lemon
2 tablespoons Dijon mustard
2 tablespoons brown sugar
2 cloves garlic, minced
2 tablespoons finely chopped fresh ginger root
¼ to ⅓ cup red wine vinegar
⅓ cup sesame oil
⅓ cup vegetable oil
⅓ cup olive oil
Salt and pepper to taste
Cucumber and watercress for garnish

Poach the chicken breasts in lightly salted water or chicken broth until done, about 10 minutes. (Or season the chicken with salt and pepper and bake it at 375° for 25 minutes.) When the chicken is cool, remove the meat from the bones and slice the meat thinly against the grain. Cook the linguini in salted water according to package instructions. Rinse with cold water to cool. Drain the linguini. Place the chicken, linguini, peppers, scallions, and peanuts in a large bowl.

Prepare the vinaigrette by whisking together all the ingredients. Gradually pour the dressing over the salad and mix well. Garnish the salad with cucumber slices (peel the cucumber, cut it in half, remove the seeds, and slice it) and sprigs of watercress.

EICHELBAUM
& CO.

—

SAN FRANCISCO

*Before opening his business in 1981, Stanley Eichelbaum studied at the California Culinary Academy. Although he had cooked all his life, he realized that he was in no way prepared to be a professional chef. The oldest student in his class, Eichelbaum felt he opened the door for people in his age bracket, many of whom have since become food professionals as a second career.*

J. BILDNER
& SONS
—
BOSTON

*The carry-out cuisine at Bildner's is only a part of Jim Bildner's answer to one-stop shopping. In 1984 he opened the first of several supermarkets—stores where one can buy truffles and smoked quail as well as tuna and paper towels. And where an order for delivery of a gourmet feast for two can include the videocassette of your choice.*

## GRILLED CHICKEN WITH FUSILLI IN GREEN SAUCE

*Serves 4*

A 3½-pound roasting chicken
1 clove garlic
½ teaspoon dried thyme, or 1 teaspoon minced fresh thyme
½ teaspoon dried rosemary, or 1 teaspoon minced fresh rosemary
3 tablespoons olive oil
¾ pound fusilli pasta
½ cup chopped plum tomatoes and fresh parsley, rosemary, and thyme for garnish

GREEN SAUCE

¼ teaspoon freshly ground pepper
3¼ cups chopped fresh parsley
1 tablespoon capers, drained
Yolks of 4 hard-boiled eggs
1 clove garlic
2 tablespoons red wine vinegar
1 tablespoon breadcrumbs

Rinse the chicken under cold running water and dry with paper towels. Crush the garlic and the dried herbs (or mince fresh herbs), and in a small bowl mix them with the olive oil to form a basting sauce for the chicken. Place the chicken in a roasting pan and place it in a 375° oven for approximately 45 minutes, basting several times. Cool the chicken and remove the skin. Slice the skin into thin strips and sauté the strips until crisp. Set aside. Thinly slice the chicken meat and set it aside.

To prepare the green sauce, combine all of the ingredients in a food processor.

Cook the fusilli in boiling water until it is *al dente*, rinse well, and place in a large bowl. Fold the sliced chicken into the pasta. Place the pasta-chicken mixture on a serving platter and pour some of the green sauce over it. Sprinkle the salad with the crispy chicken skins. Garnish with the chopped tomatoes and fresh herbs.

## FUSILLI WITH CHICKEN AND VEGETABLES

*Serves 6*

3 whole chicken breasts (2½ to 3 pounds), skinned and boned
1 13-ounce can chicken broth
8 ounces fusilli pasta
2 cups fresh green beans, cut in half
2 cups cauliflower flowerets
2 cups broccoli flowerets
2 cups julienne-cut fennel
½ pint cherry tomatoes, cut in half
Lettuce leaves
Black olives for garnish

DRESSING

1 cup mild olive oil
½ cup tarragon vinegar
2 cloves garlic, minced
¼ cup fresh basil leaves, chopped
¼ cup cilantro leaves (fresh coriander), chopped
3 tablespoons honey
1 teaspoon pepper
Salt to taste

Simmer the chicken breasts in the broth for 15 to 20 minutes. Remove the breasts from the broth, reserving the broth, and let drain on paper towels. Cook the fusilli in lightly salted boiling water

JIM JAMAIL
& SONS
FOOD MARKET
—
HOUSTON

*The pasta craze is not at all on the wane. Gourmands love its variety and versatility, nutritionists its wealth of complex carbohydrates. Although Italian manufacturers report that spaghetti is still their most popular product, there is an increasing demand for "short" pasta, such as ziti or the corkscrew fusilli.*

until it is *al dente*. Drain the pasta and let it dry on paper towels.

Blanch the vegetables (except the tomatoes) in lightly salted boiling water for 2 or 3 minutes or until just tender. Refresh them in cold water, drain, and pat dry.

Reduce the reserved chicken broth to one quarter of its original volume by boiling it down. Let cool and set aside.

Prepare the dressing by combining the reduced chicken broth with the dressing ingredients.

Cut each chicken breast into bite-size pieces and combine with the blanched vegetables, the cherry tomatoes, and the pasta. Pour the dressing over the mixture and let it marinate for 4 to 5 hours. Serve each portion on a lettuce leaf, garnished with black olives, making sure to drain off any excess dressing.

## SESAME PASTA SALAD

*Serves 8 to 10*

1 pound penne or fusilli pasta
1 cup broccoli flowerets
10 snow peas
1 sweet red pepper, julienne-cut
½ green pepper, julienne-cut
3 scallions, finely chopped (green part only)
¼ cup sliced water chestnuts

DRESSING

1½ teaspoons grated fresh ginger root
4 tablespoons tahini
2 tablespoons sesame oil
4 tablespoons corn oil
2 tablespoons rice wine vinegar
2 tablespoons sweet brown rice vinegar
2 tablespoons teriyaki sauce
1 tablespoon toasted sesame seeds

Cook the pasta in boiling salted water until *al dente.* Drain and cool. Blanch the broccoli and pea pods for 1 minute and refresh in cold water.

Combine all ingredients for the dressing except the sesame seeds in a blender or food processor. Blend until smooth. Toss the dressing with the pasta and vegetables, and add the sesame seeds. Chill well.

## MOVABLE FEAST
—
WASHINGTON, D.C.

*Prior to opening Movable Feast, Stacy DeLano pursued two decidedly different vocations— applying a college degree in Asian art and history at the Brookings Institution and running a plant interior decorating service. She got her start in catering and carry-out cuisine by helping friends who were giving parties, and before long she had embarked on a profitable third career. Now she's working her way toward a fourth—in addition to her Connecticut Avenue shop, she prepares food for the café at the Marjorie Merriweather Post mansion on the edge of the capital's Rock Creek Park.*

*Like many owners of gourmet food shops, Silvana La Rocca started her business after several years spent in other occupations. Beginning with a master's degree in international law, she subsequently worked in banking, taught school, and sold real estate. Made to Order opened in 1981, modeled after a combination of stores Silvana had seen and patronized over the years.*

## RISO AL PESTO

*Serves 6 to 8*

1 pound rice-shaped pasta
3 tablespoons good-quality olive oil
1½ cups pesto (see recipe below)
¾ cup dried currants
2 cups diced celery
1 tablespoon tarragon vinegar
½ cup pine nuts
Salt and white pepper

Cook the pasta in boiling salted water until *al dente*. Drain it in a colander and rinse it briefly in cold water. Place the pasta in a serving bowl. Add the remaining ingredients and toss well. Taste and add salt and white pepper as needed. Serve cold or at room temperature. This dish is equally good with strong barbecued or grilled meats and as a complement to simple poached fish.

### Pesto

*Makes about 1½ cups*

4½ cups basil leaves, loosely packed
4 cloves garlic, peeled
¾ cup good-quality olive oil
½ cup blanched almonds
½ cup good-quality grated Parmesan cheese

Place all ingredients except the cheese in a food processor. Process until finely chopped. Empty the mixture into a bowl, stir in the cheese, and mix until well blended.

## CURRIED RICE SALAD

*Serves 8*

2 cups uncooked white rice, preferably basmati
½ cup dried black currants, soaked in hot water
½ cup pistachio nuts, toasted
4 to 6 scallions, thinly sliced

DRESSING

1 cup peanut oil
¼ cup or more lemon juice
2 teaspoons salt
1 tablespoon curry powder
1 teaspoon ground cumin
½ teaspoon ground coriander
½ teaspoon pepper
Pinch of cayenne

Combine all the ingredients for the dressing. Cook the rice according to the instructions on the package (but do not overcook), and while the rice is still warm, pour over the dressing until the grains are well coated but not floating. Add the currants, pistachios, and scallions. Add more dressing if necessary and adjust the seasoning by adding salt, and perhaps more lemon juice, to taste.

This dish goes well with Caffè Quadro's Roast Loin of Pork in Ginger Marinade, page 129.

## CAFFÈ QUADRO
—
SAN FRANCISCO

*This salad is best when made with basmati rice, a product of Pakistan that is an integral part of the taste of authentic Oriental dishes. The grains of basmati rice are slender and will not burst during cooking. This ensures separate and fluffy grains that have a slightly nutty consistency as well. The natural minerals in the water from the Himalayas and the soil of the Punjab area of Pakistan are said to be responsible for giving basmati rice its distinctive aroma and taste. Who can resist such exotica, available in many specialty food shops?*

## PASTA & CO.

—

### SEATTLE

*For Marcella and Harvey Rosene, Pasta & Co. was "a midlife venture into entrepreneuring." She was a magazine editor and he a food chemist, and in their jobs they saw early signs of the growing market for carry-out cuisine. In 1981 they returned to their hometown to go into the food business and now own three shops.*

## TORTELLINI WITH WILD RICE

*Serves 6 to 8*

1 clove garlic, finely minced
5 tablespoons fruit vinegar
½ cup plus 2 tablespoons walnut oil
1 pound hazelnut-filled tortellini or other tortellini
Salt and pepper to taste
¾ cup uncooked wild rice, cooked until tender in
　　chicken stock
½ cup celery, sliced ⅛ inch thick
½ cup dried black currants, soaked in Amaretto or
　　Frangelico
½ cup chopped roasted hazelnuts
Hazelnuts, currants, and finely chopped fresh
　　parsley for garnish

Whisk together the garlic, vinegar, and oil. Cook the tortellini in boiling salted water until *al dente*. Toss with the dressing. Season with salt and freshly cracked pepper. Toss again with the wild rice, celery, currants, and hazelnuts. Garnish the salad with additional hazelnuts and currants and finely chopped parsley.

## WILD RICE SALAD

*Serves 6 to 8*

3 cups cooked wild rice (cooked according to
    package instructions)
1 cup chopped green pepper
1 cup chopped sweet red pepper
1 cup chopped scallions (both green and white
    parts)
½ cup pine nuts, toasted in a dry skillet
½ cup sliced water chestnuts
¾ cup olive oil
¼ cup lemon juice
Salt and pepper to taste

Combine the first six ingredients and set the mixture aside. Mix the olive oil and lemon juice and gradually add to the rice mixture. Season the salad with generous amounts of salt and pepper and serve it at room temperature.

NOTE: This recipe is fun to play with. One variation is to substitute 1½ cups of snow peas for the peppers. If you do, be sure to add the snow peas at the last minute, since they will lose their bright green color if left to sit in the dressing.

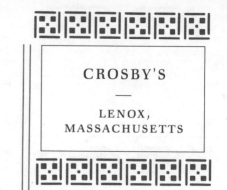

### CROSBY'S
—
### LENOX, MASSACHUSETTS

*People strolling down Church Street in Lenox can't help noticing Crosby's. It's the shop with the life-size Mr. and Mrs. Park Bench sitting in the window, commenting via comic-strip bubbles on everything from the weather to the rigors of making it through yet another Christmas. Once you have stopped to look, you can't help but go inside, and when you do you will inevitably find Wild Rice Salad in the carry-out case.*

## AN APPLE
## A DAY

—

### GLENCOE,
### ILLINOIS

*WILD RICE AND SHRIMP SALAD*

*Serves 10 to 12*

1 tablespoon turmeric
4 cups water
2 cups uncooked wild rice
¼ teaspoon salt
¼ cup pitted black olives, sliced
¼ cup diced sweet red pepper
½ cup diced artichoke hearts
½ cup sliced hearts of palm
¼ cup julienne-cut carrots, blanched
2 cups diced cooked shrimp (or smoked chicken)
½ cup green peas or snow peas, blanched

DRESSING

2 cups salad oil
¾ cup cider vinegar
½ cup lemon juice
1 teaspoon salt
1 tablespoon paprika
3 tablespoons fresh basil
1 tablespoon fresh dill
1 tablespoon black pepper, or to taste

Add the turmeric to the water and bring it to a boil. Add the rice and salt. Simmer the rice for 30 to 40 minutes, until it pops like popcorn. Chill. Add the remaining ingredients to the cold rice. Blend the dressing ingredients together well, using a wire whisk. Gradually add the dressing to the salad, and toss gently.

## WILD RICE AND CHÈVRE SALAD

*Serves 8*

2 cups uncooked wild rice, rinsed
6 cups cold water, salted
4 ounces goat cheese (such as Montrachet),
    crumbled
1 10-ounce package frozen peas, thawed

DRESSING

Grated rind of 1 orange
1 clove garlic, finely minced
1 teaspoon salt
1 teaspoon pepper
½ teaspoon dry mustard
2 tablespoons red wine vinegar
1 egg white
¾ cup extra-virgin olive oil

Place the wild rice in a saucepan with the cold water and bring it to a boil. Reduce the heat and continue to cook the rice at a low boil, uncovered, for about 40 minutes, or until the rice is tender but still firm. Be careful not to overcook it. Drain the rice and rinse it with cold water. Drain again. Let the rice cool. Then add the goat cheese and the peas.

In a small bowl, mix together the orange rind, garlic, salt and pepper, mustard, vinegar, and egg white. Beat with a wire whisk until well mixed and foaming. Gradually pour in the olive oil, continuing to whisk. Add the dressing to the rice mixture gradually until the proper coating is achieved. Toss well and correct the seasonings. Chill the salad for several hours before serving.

### REX'S
—
SEATTLE

*A few years ago, Rex McFadden, an executive with Seattle's Athletic Club, gave up his management position to open a gourmet delicatessen in the Pike's Place Public Market. He did so well that now he has a second shop, in Seattle's Broadway district. At both locations, Rex's Wild Rice and Chèvre Salad is a popular dish.*

## LA PRIMA
—
### WASHINGTON, D.C.

*Young professionals with discriminating taste make up much of the clientele at La Prima, credited by* Washingtonian *magazine in 1985 as having the best carry-out food in the capital.*

# WILD RICE WITH SMOKED TURKEY AND ORANGES

*Serves 10*

4 ounces (½ cup) uncooked wild rice
2 cups uncooked long-grain white rice
2 pounds smoked turkey, cut into ¼-inch julienne
    strips
5 oranges, peeled and sectioned
1 bunch parsley, finely chopped
1 orange, sliced, and parsley sprigs for garnish

VINAIGRETTE

1 teaspoon salt
1 teaspoon freshly ground pepper
1½ tablespoons Dijon mustard
¾ cup red wine vinegar
¾ cup olive oil
½ cup salad oil

Cook the wild and white rice according to the package directions and set them aside to cool. Place the turkey, cubed oranges, and chopped parsley in a bowl. Add both kinds of cooled rice and set aside.

Combine the ingredients for the dressing and whisk to blend well. Pour the vinaigrette over the turkey-rice mixture until the rice is well coated. Serve the salad on lettuce leaves, garnishing each portion with an orange slice and a sprig of parsley.

## BROWN RICE SALAD

*Serves 4 to 6*

2¼ cups water
Pinch of sea salt
1¼ cups uncooked brown rice
3 stalks celery, finely chopped
2 scallions, thinly sliced
3 level tablespoons dill pickle relish
¼ cup finely chopped parsley
2 teaspoons finely chopped fresh dill
3 to 4 radishes, sliced
¼ cup brown or Dijon mustard
1 tablespoon olive oil
1½ teaspoons seasoned salt

Bring the water to a boil and add the sea salt and rice. Cover and simmer for 1 hour. Chop the vegetables and herbs while the rice is cooking. Combine the rice with the rest of the ingredients. Chill for 1 to 2 hours.

## FOODWORKS
—
### CHICAGO

*This chewy brown rice salad with pickle relish and herbs is one of the talks of the take-out counter at Foodworks.*

## VEGETABLE SALADS

*Jícama* Salad
Summer Broccoli
Fresh Corn Salad with Vidalia Onion
Miniature Carrots and Zucchini Vinaigrette
Peperonata
Thomas Jefferson's Monticello Pepper Salad
Pepper, Olive, and Garlic Salad
Good and Hot Pepper Salad
Zucchini and Hearts of Palm
Beets with Walnuts and Oregon Blue
Green Bean Salad
Asparagus with Strawberry Vinaigrette
Lentil Salad
Lentil and Bean Salad Provençal
Marinated Vegetable Salad
Mediterranean Salad
Winter Salad
Watercress Slaw
Curried Cabbage Slaw
Garnet Potatoes
New Potato Salad
Potato Salad Madagascar
Sweet Potato Salad
Goat Cheese Salad with Kiwi Pear Vinaigrette
Three-Plum and Cucumber Salad with
     Goat Cheese Dressing

## JÍCAMA *SALAD*

*Serves 5 to 6*

1 medium *jícama,* peeled, split in half lengthwise,
    and cut into slices ⅛ inch thick
1⅓ cups zucchini, split in half lengthwise and cut
    into ⅛-inch slices
⅔ cup julienne-cut carrots
¼ cup half-moon slices of red onion
6 tablespoons olive oil
1½ tablespoons raspberry vinegar
1½ tablespoons rice wine vinegar
2 teaspoons honey
1 teaspoon Kosher salt
⅛ teaspoon cayenne pepper
1 teaspoon chopped cilantro (fresh coriander)

Combine the *jícama,* zucchini, carrots, and red onions. Mix the oil, vinegars, honey, salt, cayenne, and cilantro. Add the dressing to the vegetables until the proper coating is achieved, and mix well.

### THE AMERICAN CAFÉ MARKET

—

WASHINGTON, D.C.

Jícama *(pronounced* hih'- cama*) is a small root vegetable from the Southwest —slightly sweet and nutty in flavor, crunchy in texture. Like celery root (celeriac), it is a near-perfect salad ingredient because of the way it absorbs the flavors of a dressing.*

## FOODWORKS

—

### CHICAGO

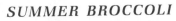

## SUMMER BROCCOLI

*Serves 4 to 6*

2 bunches broccoli
1 small sweet red pepper, chopped
1 small sweet yellow pepper, chopped
¾ cup pitted black olives, sliced
⅓ cup lemon juice
½ cup olive oil
1 teaspoon sea salt
7 grindings black pepper
½ teaspoon basil
½ teaspoon thyme
½ teaspoon tarragon
¼ teaspoon sage

Cut the broccoli into flowerets and diagonally cut 3 inches of the stems into thin slices. Blanch for 30 seconds in boiling salted water. Cool under cold, gently running water. Carefully mix all ingredients together and chill for 1 to 2 hours. This salad is best when used the same day, since the lemon juice will bleach the broccoli if it is left overnight.

## FRESH CORN SALAD WITH VIDALIA ONION

*Serves 6*

Kernels from 6 ears fresh corn
1 large Vidalia onion, chopped
2 medium zucchini, cubed
1 bunch scallions, chopped
1 sweet red pepper, chopped
1 green pepper, chopped
½ cup minced fresh parsley
2 teaspoons black mustard seed

DRESSING

1 clove garlic, minced
Salt and pepper to taste
2 teaspoons Dijon mustard
1 teaspoon ground cumin
2 teaspoons sugar
1 teaspoon Tabasco
⅓ cup cider vinegar
⅔ cup olive or vegetable oil

Cook the corn kernels in boiling salted water for 3 minutes. Drain thoroughly. When the kernels are cool, toss them with the other vegetables and the herbs. Set aside. Whisk together the ingredients for the dressing and gradually add the dressing to the salad vegetables until the mixture is adequately coated.

TAKE ME
HOME
—
WASHINGTON, D.C.

*This is a festive summer salad, ideal for a Fourth of July picnic if your native corn is in. The salad is best prepared a few hours in advance of serving, so the flavors can blend.*

*Instead of importing
miniature vegetables from
California, Denise Fugo and
Ralph Di Orio, owners of
Sammy's Tenth Street
Market, have convinced
local farmers to try growing
miniature varieties in Ohio.
Working with various
county agricultural agents,
their executive chef, Parker
Bosley, has found farmers
who are also willing to
supply specially raised
meats and poultry for the
gourmet trade.*

## MINIATURE CARROTS AND ZUCCHINI VINAIGRETTE

*Serves 4*

¾ pound miniature carrots, weighed with ¼ inch of
    stem left on
¾ pound miniature zucchini
Salt and pepper to taste
6 tablespoons olive oil
2 tablespoons white wine vinegar
1 tablespoon Dijon mustard
⅓ cup chopped fresh dill

Blanch the carrots, leaving on the ¼ inch of stem, in boiling salted water for 2 minutes. Plunge them immediately into ice water. When the carrots are chilled the skins will slip off easily. Remove all skins. Slit each zucchini twice from the flower end to within ¼ inch of the stem. Blanch for 1 minute in boiling salted water and then plunge into ice water. Pat the vegetables dry and season them with plenty of salt and freshly ground pepper.

To make the vinaigrette, combine the oil, vinegar, mustard, and salt and pepper. Just before serving, toss the vegetables with the vinaigrette and the chopped dill. Serve as a salad or as a first course.

## PEPERONATA

*Serves 4 to 6*

4 tablespoons olive oil
3 medium onions, halved vertically and cut into
　½-inch wedges
3 large cloves garlic, minced
2 medium fresh tomatoes, seeded and cut into
　2-inch wedges
2 medium green peppers, cut into ½-inch-wide
　strips
2 medium sweet red peppers, cut into ½-inch-wide
　strips
4 tablespoons chopped fresh basil leaves, or 2
　tablespoons dried basil
Salt and pepper to taste

Heat the olive oil in a large skillet or sauté pan
and add the onions, garlic, and tomatoes. Cover
the pan and cook the vegetables for 5 minutes.
Add the peppers, basil, and salt and pepper to
taste and cook the mixture for 5 minutes longer.
Serve at room temperature as a salad or leave hot
and toss with hot pasta.

NOTE: For a heartier entrée, add 1 can of tuna,
drained, or 1 cup of cooked and sliced Italian
sausage.

## THOMAS JEFFERSON'S MONTICELLO PEPPER SALAD

*Serves 6*

1½ green peppers
1½ sweet red peppers
1½ sweet yellow peppers

### FETTUCCINE BROS.

—

SAN FRANCISCO

*Before meeting Don
Woodall and opening
Fettuccine Bros. in 1981,
Bob Battaglia had a
checkered career on an
international scale—he was
a corporate marketing
manager in New York, a
men's fashion mogul in
Hong Kong, a pizza parlor
king in Manila, and, finally,
a purveyor of down
sleeping bags in San
Francisco. Although he has
never had formal cooking
training, Battaglia claims to
be happiest when he is in
the kitchen, and his
customers are happy to
keep him there.*

### OPPENHEIMER

—

SAN FRANCISCO

*The name for this colorful salad comes from the fact that Thomas Jefferson is credited with having been the first person to cultivate the sesame seed in this country, on his Monticello farm. Not surprisingly, he was also the first to produce sesame oil. Trivia, anyone? You won't think so after you try this recipe.*

THE PANTRY

—

WASHINGTON DEPOT, CONNECTICUT

*At The Pantry, specials for each day are written on a blackboard, and there are delectable choices for each course. This tasty salad can be prepared a day in advance and is marvelous with cold smoked turkey or roast veal (or* vitello tonnato, *if you are feeling ambitious).*

1½ sweet purple peppers
⅓ red onion

DRESSING

¾ cup roasted sesame seeds
⅓ cup olive oil
⅓ cup sesame oil
⅓ cup tarragon vinegar
1 tablespoon finely minced garlic
Pinch of salt and white pepper

Cut the peppers and onion in julienne strips and set aside. Mix the dressing ingredients in a jar or bowl and gradually add the dressing to the pepper and onion mixture. Serve the salad on a bed of lettuce.

## PEPPER, OLIVE, AND GARLIC SALAD

*Serves 4 to 6*

3 sweet red peppers
2 sweet yellow peppers
½ cup pitted calamata olives
2 cloves garlic, minced
⅓ cup virgin olive oil or any fine-quality fruity olive oil
Salt and pepper to taste

Slice the peppers very thinly using a food processor, mandoline, or electric slicer. Slice the olives in ⅛-inch slices and add them to the peppers. Add the garlic, olive oil, and salt and pepper to taste. Toss the mixture and let it marinate for at least 1 hour before serving.

## GOOD AND HOT PEPPER SALAD

*Serves 6*

3 tablespoons olive oil
3 tablespoons sesame oil
10 large peppers (green, yellow, and red), cut in
    ½-inch-wide strips
6 cloves garlic, finely minced
3 tablespoons soy sauce
1 tablespoon Hunan red chili paste (available at
    specialty food shops)
1 tablespoon red wine vinegar
¼ cup Marsala wine
1 tablespoon sugar
Grated rind of 1 lemon
Salt and pepper to taste

In a large skillet or wok, heat the oils until they
are very hot. Add the peppers and cook over high
heat, stirring constantly, until they begin to
soften, about 3 to 5 minutes. Add the remaining
ingredients and cook until the peppers are
tender and the liquids have nearly evaporated.

RYAN'S
—
SAN FRANCISCO

*This is a wonderfully
versatile recipe. The dish
may be served cold as a
salad or a topping for
almost any sandwich,
and it is equally delicious
reheated as a vegetable side
dish.*

## THE CHEF'S MARKET

—

PHILADELPHIA

## ZUCCHINI AND HEARTS OF PALM

*Serves 6 to 8*

4 medium zucchini, julienne-cut
1 14-ounce can hearts of palm, cut into strips (liquid reserved)
1 large pimiento, diced
Juice of 3 lemons
1 cup extra-virgin olive oil
Salt and white pepper to taste
1 tablespoon chopped fresh parsley

Combine the zucchini, hearts of palm, and pimiento in a large bowl. Set aside. To prepare the dressing, whip the lemon juice and the liquid from the hearts of palm into the olive oil, and then add the salt and pepper and parsley. Combine the dressing with the zucchini, hearts of palm, and pimiento, and let the salad marinate, unrefrigerated, for 30 minutes before serving.

## BEETS WITH WALNUTS AND OREGON BLUE

*Serves 4 to 6*

3 bunches medium beets
1 bay leaf
5 black peppercorns
1 teaspoon salt
1 tablespoon red wine vinegar
⅔ cup coarsely chopped toasted walnuts
Lettuce, preferably curly endive
2 to 3 ounces Oregon blue cheese, crumbled
Italian (flat) parsley, for garnish

DRESSING

2 tablespoons cider vinegar, or to taste
2 tablespoons walnut oil
⅓ cup peanut oil
Salt and white pepper

Cut off the tops and roots of the beets and wash the beets well. Place the beets in a saucepan and cover with cold water. Add the bay leaf, peppercorns, salt, and vinegar. Cook the beets until tender, at least 30 minutes. Cool, peel, and cut in julienne strips. Place the beets in a bowl. Whisk the ingredients for the dressing together and gradually pour it over the beets. Just before serving, add the walnuts and toss. Serve the salad on a bed of lettuce, preferably curly endive, and sprinkle the crumbled cheese on top. Garnish with the parsley.

NOTE: If you plan to make the Garnet Potatoes recipe on page 260, save the beet liquid from this recipe. It can be frozen for future use.

## NEIMAN-MARCUS

—

### PALO ALTO

*This salad travels well, so it makes a good picnic item. The walnuts and cheese can be packed separately and added at the last minute. If you can't find Oregon blue cheese, one from another state (or country) may be substituted.*

*This salad is a natural for the take-out business as well as for your own busy life, since it can be made ahead, although the beans will bleach somewhat once the dressing has been added.*

## GREEN BEAN SALAD

*Serves 4 to 6*

1½ pounds green beans, whole, with tips removed
1 small red onion, coarsely chopped
½ cup Lemon Vinaigrette (see recipe below)
¼ pound feta cheese
½ cup coarsely chopped walnuts

Plunge the beans into boiling salted water. Cook for 3 minutes. Drain and refresh with cold water. Drain the beans again. Toss the beans with the red onion and ½ cup of the vinaigrette. Using a slotted spoon, move the bean mixture to a shallow bowl. Crumble the feta cheese over the beans and sprinkle with chopped walnuts. Serve the salad chilled.

### Lemon Vinaigrette

*Makes about 1½ cups*

3 tablespoons lemon juice
3 tablespoons white wine vinegar
1 tablespoon Dijon mustard
Freshly ground pepper to taste
½ teaspoon sugar
¼ teaspoon salt
1 cup light vegetable oil

Whisk together all ingredients except the oil until well blended. Add the oil gradually, a few drops at a time, whisking until incorporated.

## ASPARAGUS WITH STRAWBERRY VINAIGRETTE

*Serves 6*

2½ pounds asparagus
2 cups hulled strawberries

DRESSING

¼ cup strawberry vinegar
1 tablespoon walnut oil
½ cup peanut oil
1½ teaspoons honey, or to taste

Trim the asparagus and steam it until it is tender but still crisp. Plunge it into ice water. Drain it and cut each stalk into thirds. Cut the strawberries in half. Combine the dressing ingredients and toss the asparagus and strawberries gently with the dressing. Chill well before serving.

MOVABLE
FEAST
—
WASHINGTON, D.C.

*What could be simpler—or more delicious—than spring's first asparagus combined with spring's first strawberries?*

## THE GOURMET GROCER

—

### PRAIRIE VILLAGE, KANSAS

*"Come in for lunch and take home your dinner" is the advice that Tom Anderson, owner of The Gourmet Grocer, gives his customers. This nutritious lentil salad is one of those dishes that frequently get taken home.*

## LENTIL SALAD

*Serves 8 to 10*

2 cups dried lentils
6 cups water
1 onion stuck with 2 cloves
2 bay leaves
1 tablespoon salt
1 red onion, diced
4 tablespoons chopped fresh parsley
2 carrots, julienne-cut and blanched
½ sweet red pepper, julienne-cut
½ green pepper, julienne-cut
Cherry tomatoes for garnish

### DRESSING

6 tablespoons olive oil
6 tablespoons grated onion
½ cup red wine vinegar
1 clove garlic, crushed
½ teaspoon salt
½ teaspoon pepper
¼ teaspoon oregano

Simmer the lentils in the water with the onion, bay leaves, and salt for 30 minutes, until the lentils are still crunchy but tender. Discard the onion and bay leaves and toss the drained lentils with the red onion, parsley, carrots, and peppers. Set aside.

Mix the dressing ingredients together. Gradually pour the dressing over the lentil mixture and toss lightly. Garnish with cherry tomatoes.

## LENTIL AND BEAN SALAD PROVENÇAL

*Serves 4 to 6*

½ pound small dried white beans
8 cups chicken stock
½ pound dried lentils
1 cup extra-virgin olive oil
⅓ cup red wine vinegar
4 tablespoons Herbes de Provence
1 clove garlic, chopped
4 or 5 sweet red peppers, roasted, peeled, and diced
Salt and pepper

Soak the white beans overnight in water before cooking them in 4 cups of the chicken stock for 1 hour. Salt the beans just before they are done. Drain off any liquid that has not been absorbed. Cook the lentils in the remaining 4 cups of stock for 10 to 15 minutes, being careful not to overcook. Drain off the stock.

Blend the oil, vinegar, herbs, and garlic in a blender or food processor for 5 seconds. In a large bowl combine the beans, lentils, and diced peppers and gradually pour the dressing over the mixture until the salad is adequately coated. Mix well and add salt and pepper to taste.

## NEIMAN-MARCUS
—
### PALO ALTO

*At Neiman-Marcus the salad menu changes every three months, though favorites are available by special order. The strong herb flavoring of this favorite salad makes it an especially good companion for cold roast pork or pâtés.*

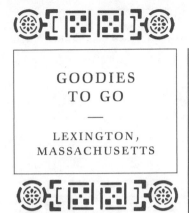

*In summertime, when the
vegetables are ripe in the
garden, what better salad
could there be than one
that combines them
colorfully? And this is a
salad that keeps well, too,
without the dressing.*

## MARINATED VEGETABLE SALAD

*Serves 6 to 8*

1 small head broccoli flowerets
2 carrots, thinly sliced
¼ pound green beans, tips removed
1 sweet red pepper, julienne-cut
1 green pepper, julienne-cut
2 cups cherry tomatoes, halved
1 small head cauliflower flowerets
1 red onion, thinly sliced
¼ pound snow peas, strings removed
1 zucchini, thinly sliced
1 summer squash, thinly sliced
½ red cabbage, shredded

DRESSING

4 cloves garlic, chopped
2 good-sized shallots, chopped
¼ cup red wine vinegar
1 tablespoon Dijon mustard
2 tablespoons fresh herbs (parsley, oregano, basil,
   thyme)
½ cup olive oil
Salt and pepper to taste

Blanch the broccoli, carrots, and green beans.
Add them to the remaining vegetables.

Combine all the dressing ingredients except
the olive oil in a bowl. Slowly add the oil, whisking thoroughly. Just before serving, lightly coat
the salad with the dressing.

## MEDITERRANEAN SALAD

*Serves 8*

4 cucumbers, peeled, cut in half, seeded, and cut in
⅓-inch-thick crescents
3 medium tomatoes, peeled and chopped in bite-
size pieces
1 green pepper, julienne-cut
1 sweet red pepper, julienne-cut
½ cup calamata olives, pitted
½ cup diced red onion
1 cup cubed feta cheese

DRESSING

1½ tablespoons oregano
⅓ cup red wine vinegar
1 cup olive oil
Salt and pepper to taste

Assemble the vegetables and cheese in a bowl.
Whisk together the dressing ingredients and
gradually add the dressing to the vegetables,
until the proper coating is achieved. Refrigerate
the salad until ready to serve. It will keep well for
8 to 12 hours.

PASTA &
COMPANY
—
VIRGINIA BEACH,
VIRGINIA

*Louise Nagourney and
Debbie Brannon are former
travel agents who had easy
access to specialty food
businesses all over the
world before starting their
own pasta shop in 1981.
Their operation now in-
cludes a complete line of
take-out foods and a
sophisticated café.*

## REBECCA'S
—
BOSTON

*Here is a versatile salad that makes a main dish for lunch or an accompaniment for any roasted meats or poultry for dinner. For a heartier salad, add julienne strips of roasted meat or chicken.*

## WINTER SALAD

*Serves 4*

1 head radicchio, torn into bite-size pieces
2 endives, sliced crosswise into bite-size pieces
½ pound fresh green beans, blanched
¼ pound mushrooms, sliced
2 ounces feta cheese, cut into small squares
1 medium tomato, cut into 8 wedges
¼ cup calamata olives
1 anchovy, mashed to a paste
1 clove garlic, minced
2 tablespoons vinegar
Pinch of oregano
3 tablespoons olive oil
¼ teaspoon mustard

Toss the radicchio, endives, green beans, mushrooms, feta cheese, tomato wedges, and olives gently in a large bowl. In a small bowl mix the anchovy paste, garlic, vinegar, oregano, olive oil, and mustard until they are well blended. Drizzle the dressing over the vegetables until the salad is lightly coated. Toss lightly and serve.

## WATERCRESS SLAW

*Serves 8*

1 2- to 2½-pound cabbage, tough outer leaves
   removed
1 large bunch watercress, rinsed, spun dry, and
   coarse stems discarded
1 large yellow onion
5 radishes, thinly sliced
⅓ cup rice wine vinegar or white wine vinegar
1 tablespoon sugar
Salt and pepper to taste

HORSERADISH DRESSING

1 cup mayonnaise
¾ cup sour cream
¼ cup heavy cream
1 tablespoon freshly grated horseradish or well-
   drained bottled horseradish

Cut the cabbage into thin wedges and remove
the core. In a food processor, chop the cabbage,
watercress, and onion, and transfer the mixture
to a large serving bowl. Add the radishes, vinegar,
sugar, and salt and pepper to taste and toss well.
Mix the dressing ingredients and add it gradually, stirring to coat the vegetables, and chill
the salad, covered, for at least one hour before
serving.

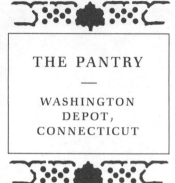

THE PANTRY
—
WASHINGTON
DEPOT,
CONNECTICUT

*Audrey and James Pat-
terson are examples of
the "urban dropouts" who
have become so prevalent
in New England. Their
first move away from urban
life was to buy the Chester
Inn in Chester, Vermont.
After several years of
round-the-clock innkeep-
ing and cooking three
meals a day, they decided
to cut back to part-time
"catering" and moved to
Washington Depot to
open The Pantry. The only
meal they serve is lunch,
but a thriving take-out and
catering business keeps the
Pattersons busy far more
than part-time.*

*At Rudi's Milk Street branch in the heart of downtown Boston, the upstairs café gives patrons an intimate view that is unbeatable in this era of super skyscrapers. The window tables overlook Old South Meeting House, Goodspeed's Book Shop, and the corner flower market.*

## CURRIED CABBAGE SLAW

*Serves 6*

1 medium green cabbage, thinly sliced
4 ounces frozen green peas, thawed
3 scallions, thinly sliced
4 tablespoons grated carrots
4 tablespoons minced fresh parsley
⅓ cup salted, roasted peanuts, chopped

### CURRIED ORANGE MAYONNAISE

2 egg yolks
4 tablespoons orange juice concentrate
2 tablespoons Dijon mustard
1 tablespoon curry powder
1 teaspoon minced garlic
Pinch of cayenne pepper and salt
½ cup plus 2 tablespoons soy oil

Prepare the Curried Orange Mayonnaise by placing all the ingredients except the oil in the bowl of a food processor. Turn on the processor and slowly add the oil until the mayonnaise has the proper consistency. Adjust the seasonings if necessary. Combine the vegetables, parsley, and peanuts in a large bowl and toss the salad with 10 tablespoons of the mayonnaise.

## GARNET POTATOES

*Serves 4 to 6*

3 pounds red potatoes
Beet cooking liquid to cover the potatoes
1 cup fresh peas
Pinch of sugar

DRESSING

1 teaspoon Dijon mustard
1 tablespoon caraway seeds
¾ cup olive oil
3 tablespoons lemon juice
Salt and white pepper to taste

Place the potatoes in a saucepan with cold water to cover and cook until tender. Peel the potatoes while they are still warm. Marinate the warm potatoes in the beet cooking liquid for 3 to 4 hours. Cook the peas in salted water with a pinch of sugar until they are barely tender, 2 to 3 minutes. Refresh under cold water and drain.

Prepare the dressing by combining all the ingredients in a jar or blender or food processor. Remove the potatoes from the beet juice. Slice the potatoes and toss gently with enough dressing to coat the slices. Add the peas and serve.

NEIMAN-MARCUS
—
PALO ALTO

*This is one of the first salads Neiman-Marcus offered to take-out customers, and it continues to be very popular. It is a great substitute for traditional potato salads, and the colors are spectacular. If you don't happen to have beet cooking liquid on hand, make a plan for canned beets and use the liquid they are packed in.*

## FISHER & LEVY

—

### NEW YORK CITY

*For Doug Fisher, who studied architecture at Pratt Institute before he went into the carry-out cuisine business, whether it's buildings or broccoli, design is important, and in the food business that includes color and texture particularly. That's why he likes new potatoes in potato salad. Their texture is firm, so they don't crumble, and in the bowl they give a pleasing aesthetic effect.*

## NEW POTATO SALAD

*Serves 12 to 16*

2 quart boxes new potatoes, peeled and sliced
    ¼ inch thick
½ cup chopped fresh parsley
4 tablespoons diced scallions
2 tablespoons finely chopped fresh dill
1½ teaspoons salt
½ teaspoon black pepper

DRESSING

1 egg
½ cup red wine vinegar
2½ teaspoons salt
½ teaspoon black pepper
½ teaspoon turmeric
⅓ cup mustard
1¼ cups soy oil

Place the potatoes in a steamer and steam for about 10 minutes, until they are tender but not soft. Remove and cool. Combine the potatoes, parsley, scallions, dill, salt, and pepper.

Put all the dressing ingredients except the oil in a bowl and mix with a whisk. Add the oil slowly and whisk rapidly. Add 1 cup of the dressing to the potato mixture. Mix and chill until ready to serve. Reserve the rest of the dressing for later use.

## POTATO SALAD MADAGASCAR

*Serves 6 to 8*

2 pounds red potatoes, boiled, peeled, and cut into
  small pieces
1½ cups pitted black olives, sliced lengthwise
1 small red onion, sliced lengthwise
¾ cup chopped Italian (flat) parsley

DRESSING

1 clove garlic, crushed
Salt and pepper to taste
½ cup sour cream
½ cup mayonnaise
3 tablespoons green peppercorns, drained and
  crushed

Combine the potatoes, olives, onion, and parsley.
Mix together the ingredients for the dressing,
and toss the dressing with the potato mixture.

BY WORD
OF MOUTH
—
FORT LAUDERDALE

*While she was a housewife
in New York, Ellen Cirillo's
enthusiasm for cooking
burgeoned into a full-blown
catering business. Now she
and partner James Caron
are established in Fort
Lauderdale, with eighteen
employees working full-
time in the Cirillo-Caron
kitchen. The island of
Madagascar is world-
famous for its spices, and
this tangy potato salad that
bears its name is enlivened
by green peppercorns and
black olives.*

## FORMAGGIO KITCHEN

—

### CAMBRIDGE

*This recipe is not to be believed, until you taste it! A perfect accompaniment to holiday hams and turkeys.*

## *SWEET POTATO SALAD*

*Serves 6 to 8*

3 pounds sweet potatoes, peeled and cut in
  ½-inch cubes
4 stalks celery, sliced
1 cup walnut halves
1 cup raisins
1 20-ounce can crushed pineapple, well drained

DRESSING

⅔ cup mayonnaise
1½ cups sour cream
Grated zest of 1 orange
1 teaspoon salt
2 tablespoons chopped crystallized ginger

Cook the sweet potatoes in boiling salted water for 10 to 15 minutes, until they are just tender. Drain and cool. Stir together the dressing ingredients. When the sweet potatoes are cool, mix them lightly with the celery, walnuts, raisins, and pineapple. Add the dressing gradually and toss carefully, so as not to mash the potatoes.

## GOAT CHEESE SALAD WITH KIWI PEAR VINAIGRETTE

*Serves 6*

### KIWI PEAR VINAIGRETTE

1½ Bartlett or D'Anjou pears
2 cups water
2½ teaspoons granulated sugar
Pinch each of cinnamon, cloves, and nutmeg, tied in
   cheesecloth
2 ripe kiwi fruits, peeled
2 tablespoons honey
½ cup raspberry vinegar
1¼ cups safflower oil
White pepper to taste

Peel the pears, cut them in half lengthwise, and remove the cores. In a small saucepan, bring the water, sugar, and spices to a boil. Add the pears, cover the pan, and lower the heat to simmer. Poach the pears for about 5 minutes, until fork-tender. Remove the pan from the heat and let the pears cool in the covered pan. Then drain the pears, reserving part of the liquid for use in the dressing. (Leftover poaching liquid can be used in chilled summer fruit soups or by itself as a terrific cold drink.)

Purée the pears and kiwi fruit in a blender or food processor. Add the honey, vinegar, and about 2 tablespoons of the pear poaching liquid and blend well. When the mixture is completely blended, slowly add the oil, with the machine running. Add white pepper to taste. The consistency of the dressing may be varied by adding more or less poaching liquid.

## PIRET'S
—
SAN DIEGO

*Chèvre has become a staple for take-out food operations, and American-produced goat cheeses are now sharing the limelight with French imports. The puréed fruit dressing on this salad provides a light and sweet counterpoint to the tang of the cheese.*

## GOAT CHEESE SALAD

9 ounces goat cheese (such as Montrachet) in logs
6 tablespoons dry breadcrumbs, seasoned with salt
    and pepper
1 bunch spinach
1 head red leaf lettuce (about 2 leaves per person)
6 thin slices red onion
1 bunch watercress, stems removed
1 sweet red pepper, julienne-cut

Slice the goat cheese logs into ¼-inch medallions (12 medallions in all). Roll the medallions in the seasoned breadcrumbs to coat well. Place the medallions on a baking sheet and warm them for a minute or two in a 300° oven or under the broiler. (Take care not to melt the cheese.)

Arrange the spinach leaves on individual salad plates and add shredded or torn red lettuce leaves. Top the greens with separated rings of the red onion slices and sprigs of watercress. Place two medallions of the warmed cheese on each plate and garnish with the julienne strips of red pepper. Ladle several tablespoons of the vinaigrette on each serving and serve immediately.

## THREE-PLUM AND CUCUMBER SALAD WITH GOAT CHEESE DRESSING

*Serves 4*

6 plums, of three different colors
2 medium cucumbers
½ pound goat cheese
1 small clove garlic, crushed
¼ cup red wine vinegar
2 dashes of pepper
2 tablespoons honey
½ cup vegetable oil
Chopped walnuts, for garnish
Lettuce or radicchio

Halve and stone the plums and slice them into very thin wedges. Peel the cucumbers, cut them in half, scoop out the seeds, and thinly slice. Crumble the goat cheese. Mix the plum slices, cucumber slices, and half of the goat cheese, tossing lightly, and set aside in the refrigerator.

In a food processor or blender, combine the garlic, vinegar, pepper, honey, oil, and the remaining goat cheese. Pour the dressing over the plum-cucumber mixture until the salad is adequately coated and garnish it with chopped walnuts. Serve the salad on a bed of greens or radicchio.

## J. BILDNER & SONS

—

### BOSTON

*The first of Bildner's seven Boston-area stores is located on the lower level of a Victorian mansion in the historic Back Bay. An authentic nineteenth-century look has been achieved by combining original details with quantities of imported green and white tiles and an abundance of polished brass. For many customers the pièce de résistance is the gilded cash register, a legacy from Jim Bildner's grandfather's Brooklyn grocery store, opened in 1917.*

# PART 4

—

# BREADS AND
# DESSERTS

—

BREADS, SCONES, AND MUFFINS

COOKIES AND BARS

CAKES, PIES, AND TARTS

MOUSSES AND PUDDINGS

## BREADS, SCONES, AND MUFFINS

Apricot Ginger Muffins
Cranberry Walnut Muffins
Cinnamon Apple Muffins
Butternut Squash Muffins
Bob Paroubek's Bran Muffins
Date Nut Muffins
Tri-Berry Muffins
Currant Scones
Cheddar Dill Scones
Cranberry Orange Anadama Rolls
Ham and Cheese Biscuits
Sausage Bread
Dill Bread
Focaccia
Spoonbread
Semolina Bread
Applesauce Bread
Cranberry Orange Bread
Elegant Picnic Date Bread
Coconut Bread

## APRICOT GINGER MUFFINS

*Makes 12*

1½ cups (3 sticks) unsalted butter
1 cup sugar
3 eggs
1½ teaspoons powdered ginger
3 cups all-purpose flour
1 teaspoon salt
1 tablespoon baking powder
½ cup milk
1 14-ounce can apricot halves, drained and chopped
3 ounces crystallized ginger, finely chopped

Cream the butter and sugar together well. Add the eggs and beat until the ingredients are thoroughly combined. Sift together the powdered ginger, flour, salt, and baking powder. Add the sifted dry ingredients to the butter mixture alternately with the milk, beginning and ending with the dry ingredients. Work quickly; do not overmix. Add the apricots and crystallized ginger and fold them in until just combined. Fill greased muffin tins to the top and bake at 350° for 20 minutes.

## CRANBERRY WALNUT MUFFINS

*Makes about 12*

2 cups all-purpose flour
¾ teaspoon salt
½ cup sugar
2 teaspoons baking powder
2 eggs
¾ cup milk
¼ cup melted butter
1 cup cranberries, chopped

BOND &
BURKHART

—

NEWTON,
MASSACHUSETTS

*Although it is indeed possible to make your own crystallized ginger,* The Joy of Cooking *describes it as "either a single long-day or an intermittent four-day procedure." At that rate the commercial version is a bargain no matter what the price.*

THE COOKERY

—

HUDSON, OHIO

*Owner Zona Spray has made The Cookery the headquarters for matters gourmet in northeastern Ohio. The shop carries a complete selection of cookware, sponsors classes and demonstrations by well-known chefs and cookbook authors, and offers an impressive carry-out menu. As for this recipe, Zona suggests that for bigger muffins you fill only eleven of the twelve muffin cups.*

PETAK'S
—
NEW YORK CITY

*There are no airs about this Madison Avenue storefront deli, but it surely has exquisite products in its showcases—smoked fish and delectable cheeses, towering chocolate cakes and plump muffins.*

½ cup walnuts, chopped
2 tablespoons grated orange rind

Sift together the dry ingredients. Beat the eggs with the milk and melted butter. Add the cranberries, walnuts, and grated orange rind to the dry ingredients. Quickly stir the milk and egg mixture into the dry ingredients, being careful not to overmix. Spoon the batter into well-greased muffin tins. If you wish, sprinkle a little sugar on top before baking. Bake for 20 to 25 minutes at 400°.

## CINNAMON APPLE MUFFINS

*Makes 12 3½-inch muffins or 18 2½-inch muffins*

3 cups all-purpose flour
1 cup sugar
1 teaspoon salt
4½ teaspoons baking powder
1 tablespoon cinnamon
1 Granny Smith apple, peeled, cored, and chopped
1 egg
1 cup buttermilk
½ teaspoon vanilla
½ pound butter, melted

In a large bowl, sift the flour, sugar, salt, baking powder, and cinnamon together. Mix in the chopped apple. In a small bowl, beat together the egg, buttermilk, and vanilla. Stir in the melted butter. Add these wet ingredients to the sifted mixture. Mix only until combined; if you overmix, the muffins will be tough. Fill greased muffin tins two-thirds full and bake the muffins 25 to 30 minutes in a 375° oven.

## BUTTERNUT SQUASH MUFFINS

*Makes about 2 dozen*

3½ cups all-purpose flour
2 cups sugar
1½ teaspoons salt
4½ teaspoons baking soda
1 teaspoon cinnamon
1 teaspoon nutmeg
1 teaspoon cloves
1 cup salad oil
½ cup water
4 eggs, beaten
2½ cups fresh butternut squash, cooked and
    mashed (or frozen squash, thawed)
1 teaspoon vanilla
1 cup chopped nuts (optional)

Into a large mixing bowl, sift together all the dry ingredients and set them aside. In another bowl, mix the oil, water, eggs, squash, vanilla, and nuts (if desired) until well blended. Make a well in the center of the dry ingredients and add the blended ones. Fold together just until all the flour has been incorporated.

Pour the batter into greased and floured muffin tins (or into tins lined with paper muffin cups) and bake for 30 to 35 minutes at 350° or until a toothpick comes out clean. Remove the muffins from the pans and let them cool on a wire rack.

SOIGNE

—

EDGARTOWN,
MASSACHUSETTS

## TOOJAY'S OF
## PALM BEACH

—

HIGHLAND PARK,
ILLINOIS

*These bran muffins make a nourishing breakfast or provide an energy boost with midmorning coffee.*

## BOB PAROUBEK'S BRAN MUFFINS

*Makes 26 to 28*

1 cup minus 1 tablespoon butter, softened
1¼ cups sugar
1½ cups all-purpose flour
1½ cups bread flour
2 teaspoons baking soda
Pinch of salt
1 teaspoon nutmeg
1½ teaspoons cinnamon
3 eggs
3 tablespoons honey
1 tablespoon molasses
1½ cups raisins
2½ cups bran cereal
1½ cups milk

In a large mixing bowl, cream the butter and sugar until fluffy. Add the two kinds of flour, baking soda, salt, nutmeg, and cinnamon. Mix well. Add the eggs, honey, and molasses. Blend well. Mix in the raisins.

In a medium mixing bowl, soak the cereal in the milk for about 5 minutes. Add it to the batter and mix it in well. Spoon the batter into greased muffin tins and bake in a 375° oven for 18 to 20 minutes.

## DATE NUT MUFFINS

*Makes about 2 dozen*

2¼ cups boiling water
1 cup chopped dates
3 cups all-purpose flour
1½ cups sugar
1½ teaspoons cinnamon
1½ teaspoons mace
1½ teaspoons baking powder
1 tablespoon baking soda
½ cup (1 stick) butter, melted
3 eggs, beaten
1 teaspoon vanilla
¼ cup brandy (optional)
Juice and grated rind of 1 orange
1 cup chopped walnuts

Pour the boiling water over the dates and set them aside. Sift together the dry ingredients into a large bowl. Add the melted butter to the dates and water and let the mixture cool to room temperature. Add the eggs and other wet ingredients, then fold them into the dry ingredients until the dry ingredients are just moist. Add the nuts. Pour the batter into greased and floured muffin tins (or tins lined with paper muffin cups) and bake them for 20 to 25 minutes at 350°, until a toothpick comes out clean. Remove the muffins from the tins and let them cool on a wire rack.

## SOIGNE

—

### EDGARTOWN, MASSACHUSETTS

*Back in the 1930s, George Benanchietti started the dining room in the prestigious Edgartown Yacht Club, and soon it was renowned for its fine fare. Now his grandson, Ronald Cavallo, and a partner, Diana Rabaioli, have opened Soigne, a carry-out shop for those who like to eat fine fare at home. This recipe is Diana's.*

## QUE SERA SARAH

—

NANTUCKET,
MASSACHUSETTS

*The secret of these muffins,
according to chef Sarah
Leah Chase, was invented
quite by accident one
morning. The batter for
the muffins was all mixed
and ready to bake when
suddenly it was discovered
that the sugar had been left
out. The serendipitous
result was that the sugar
was added at the last
minute, giving the muffins
the crunchy, crackled top
that is now their principal
characteristic. All three
kinds of berries may be
used or, if you prefer, any
one of the three.*

## TRI-BERRY MUFFINS

*Makes 20*

3 cups all-purpose flour
1 tablespoon baking powder
½ teaspoon baking soda
½ teaspoon salt
1½ teaspoons cinnamon
1¼ cups milk
2 eggs
1 cup (2 sticks) unsalted butter or margarine, melted
1 cup blueberries
½ cup diced strawberries
½ cup raspberries
1½ cups sugar

In a large bowl, stir together the flour, baking powder, soda, salt, and cinnamon. Make a well in the center of the flour mixture and add the milk, eggs, and melted butter or margarine. Stir the ingredients together quickly, just to combine them. Add the berries and the sugar and again stir quickly just to combine. Pour into muffin tins lined with paper liners, filling each cup almost to the top. Bake at 375° about 20 minutes, until crusty and brown.

## CURRANT SCONES

Makes 12

3 cups all-purpose flour
2½ teaspoons baking powder
1 teaspoon sugar
Pinch of salt
Pinch of nutmeg
½ cup (1 stick) unsalted butter, cut into pieces
½ cup currants
2 eggs
½ cup heavy cream
½ cup milk
Egg wash (1 egg yolk mixed with 1 tablespoon cream
   or milk)

Sift together the flour, baking powder, sugar, salt, and nutmeg, and place in the bowl of a mixer with the butter. Using the paddle, mix until the flour takes on a mealy texture. (If you do not have a mixer, cut the butter in with a pastry blender or two knives.) Add the currants. Set aside.

In a separate bowl, beat the eggs, cream, and milk with a whisk. Add the egg and milk mixture to the flour mixture. With the paddle, mix lightly. Turn the dough out onto a floured board and roll it to a ½-inch thickness. Using a 2-inch floured biscuit cutter, cut the dough into rounds. Place them on a greased cookie sheet and brush the tops with the egg wash. Bake the scones at 375° until they are light golden brown, about 15 minutes. Serve them hot.

## SARABETH'S KITCHEN
## —
## NEW YORK CITY

*When Sarabeth Levine was a child, she loved to visit her aunt's mother-in-law's house, where she headed straight for the cupboard with the Bell jars of orange apricot marmalade. Spread thickly with cream cheese on fresh bread, it was the best thing she ever ate. She liked the marmalade so much that the hitherto secret recipe was given to her with the comment, "One day you could make a business with this and become rich." After a tiresome foray in the insurance business, Sarabeth remembered the comment and began making marmalades, which she now sells in her two New York kitchen/restaurants.*

*Although one usually thinks
of eating scones for breakfast or at teatime, this
version—split, buttered,
and toasted—makes a
perfect accompaniment to
a tomatoey soup at lunch.
At Barefoot Contessa they
use a 3-inch square cutter
and then cut each square
in half diagonally to form
triangles.*

## CHEDDAR DILL SCONES

*Makes 14*

1¼ cups grated sharp yellow Cheddar cheese
¾ cup chopped fresh dill
2 cups all-purpose flour
1 tablespoon baking powder
½ teaspoon salt
¾ cup cold unsalted butter, diced
2 eggs, beaten
½ cup heavy cream
Egg wash (1 egg yolk mixed with 1 tablespoon
    heavy cream)

Combine the Cheddar and dill and set aside.
Place the flour, baking powder, and salt in the
bowl of a food processor. Add the butter and
pulse until the mixture is coarsely crumbled,
about 30 seconds. (The mixture should have
pieces of butter throughout.) Remove the mixture
to a medium bowl, add the eggs and cream, and
mix. Add the Cheddar-dill mixture and blend
until the dough is just soft and sticky. Do not
overmix.

Pat or roll out the dough on a well-floured
board to a thickness of ¾ inch. Cut with a floured
cutter. Place the scones 1 inch apart on a baking
sheet. Brush the tops with the egg wash and bake
at 425° for 15 to 20 minutes, until lightly browned.

## CRANBERRY ORANGE
## ANADAMA ROLLS

*Makes 18*

1½ cups cranberry juice
½ cup yellow cornmeal
4 tablespoons unsalted butter, at room temperature
⅓ cup plus 2 tablespoons dark molasses
1 teaspoon salt
1 package active dry yeast
½ cup lukewarm water
1 cup whole wheat flour
2½ cups cranberries
Zest of 1 orange, finely chopped
4 to 5 cups all-purpose flour
Egg wash (1 egg lightly beaten with 1 tablespoon
    water)
Additional cornmeal for dusting the tops of the rolls

In a small saucepan, heat the cranberry juice to just below the boiling point and gradually stir in the cornmeal. Reduce the heat to low and stir the mixture continuously with a wooden spoon until the mixture is thick and smooth like porridge (5 to 7 minutes). Remove the cornmeal mixture from the heat and immediately stir in the butter until it has melted. Add ⅓ cup of the molasses and the salt and set the bowl aside to cool to room temperature.

Meanwhile, proof the yeast with the lukewarm water in a large bowl for 10 minutes until it is bubbly. Stir in the whole wheat flour and the cooled cornmeal mixture.

Place the cranberries, orange zest, and the remaining 2 tablespoons of molasses in a food processor, and pulse the machine several times until the cranberries are coarsely chopped. (Or chop the cranberries by hand in a wooden chopping bowl.) Add the cranberry mixture to the bread mixture and stir until thoroughly incorporated.

# QUE SERA
# SARAH

—

NANTUCKET,
MASSACHUSETTS

*Ruby-colored cranberries abound in the bogs of Nantucket in the fall, and their tartness contributes to many a local recipe.*

If you have a mixer with a dough attachment, use it to incorporate the all-purpose flour. (If you have no mixer, use your hands and a wooden spoon.) Add the flour cup by cup to make a soft dough. Knead the dough for 10 minutes on a lightly floured board until it is smooth and elastic. Shape the dough into a ball and place it in a greased bowl, cover loosely with a plastic wrap, and let it rise in a warm place until it has doubled in bulk, about 1½ hours.

Punch the dough down and turn it out onto a lightly floured surface again. Tear off pieces of the dough and shape them into round balls, about 2 inches in diameter. Place them 2 inches apart on lightly greased baking trays. Put the rolls in a warm spot, cover loosely with damp towels, and let them rise until they have doubled in bulk, 30 to 45 minutes.

Heat the oven to 375°. Brush the rolls all over with the egg wash and sprinkle the tops lightly with cornmeal. Bake 20 minutes or until golden brown. Serve warm with plenty of sweet butter.

## HAM AND CHEESE BISCUITS

*Makes about 12 3-inch biscuits*

2 cups bread flour
2 cups cake flour
2 tablespoons baking powder
½ teaspoon salt
2 tablespoons sugar
½ cup (1 stick) butter
½ sweet red pepper, diced
1 small onion, finely chopped
1 teaspoon butter for sautéing
1½ cups buttermilk
½ pound ham, diced
¾ cup grated Cheddar cheese

Mix the dry ingredients in a large bowl. Cut in the ½ cup of butter with a pastry blender until the mixture is crumbly. Sauté the red pepper and onion in the teaspoon of butter and set aside. Add the buttermilk to the dry ingredients and mix until just blended. Add the sautéed pepper and onion, ham, and grated cheese and mix just enough to blend.

Roll the dough out on a lightly floured surface to a thickness of 1 inch. Cut into 3-inch biscuits (or whatever size you prefer) and bake them on a lightly greased baking sheet at 350° for approximately 30 minutes, or until the tops are lightly browned.

### REBECCA'S

—

### BOSTON

*Rebecca Caras originated the carry-out food business in Boston and she currently has shops and restaurants in three of Boston's most interesting and attractive neighborhoods—on Charles Street at the foot of Beacon Hill, on fashionable Newbury Street, and in the South End, with its streets and squares of reclaimed Victorian rowhouses.*

*Because of its perishability, this bread isn't kept on the shelves at Zabar's, but it's a favorite of the customers— and delectable, whether made with pepperoni or with hot Italian sausage, a variation on the original theme.*

## SAUSAGE BREAD

*Makes 2 loaves*

1 package active dry yeast
¼ cup lukewarm water
1 cup milk
½ cup (1 stick) unsalted butter, melted
1 teaspoon salt
2 tablespoons sugar
4 to 5 cups sifted cake flour
1 egg
½ pound pepperoni, sliced thin (or ½ pound hot Italian sausage, cooked, sautéed with ½ cup chopped onion, ½ cup chopped green pepper, and 2 to 4 cloves minced garlic)
Melted butter or salad oil

Dissolve the yeast in the warm water. Add the milk, ½ cup melted butter, salt, sugar, 2 cups of the flour, and the egg and beat well. Stir in enough flour to make a stiff dough. Knead on a floured board 8 to 10 minutes, until the dough is smooth and elastic. Place it in a greased bowl and turn the dough over to grease the top. Cover and let rise until doubled in bulk, about 1 hour.

Punch the dough down and remove it from the bowl. Cut it in half and roll each half into an 8-by-10-inch rectangle. Spread half the pepperoni slices (or sausage mixture) on each, and, from the short side, roll the dough up in jelly-roll fashion. Seal the edges. Brush the loaves with melted butter or oil, place them on a greased baking sheet, and cover them with a damp cloth. Let them rise until doubled in bulk again, 45 minutes to 1 hour. Bake the loaves in a 350° oven for 45 minutes to 1 hour, until they are golden brown and sound hollow when tapped on the bottom.

## DILL BREAD

*Makes 1 loaf*

1 package active dry yeast
¼ cup lukewarm water
1 cup creamed cottage cheese
2 tablespoons sugar
1 tablespoon dried minced onion
1 tablespoon butter
2 teaspoons dill seed
½ teaspoon salt
¼ teaspoon soda
1 egg
2½ cups sifted all-purpose flour
Coarse salt

Dissolve the yeast in the lukewarm water. Heat the cottage cheese to lukewarm and add it to the yeast mixture. Combine the sugar, onion, butter, dill seed, salt, soda, and egg in a bowl with the cheese and yeast mixture. Sift in the flour and mix. Cover and let the dough rise until doubled in bulk. Stir it down. Turn the dough into a greased 1½-quart casserole. Cover and let rise for 30 minutes. Bake at 350° for 40 to 50 minutes. Brush with butter and sprinkle with coarse salt.

## GRAHAM CATERING COMPANY

—

HOUSTON

*This simple dill bread is a favorite with soups at Cameron Graham's Catering Company.*

Focaccia *is a flat bread that developed in northern Italy. Like its pizza cousin, a southern dish, it can be topped with a variety of sauces, meats, and cheeses, or it can merely be sprinkled with fresh herbs, cut in squares, and served with roast meats or other entrées. It is also good split in half horizontally for sandwiches.*

## FOCACCIA

*Serves 6*

1 package active dry yeast
¼ teaspoon sugar
1 to 1¼ cups water, at room temperature
3½ cups bread flour
1¼ teaspoons salt
About 5 tablespoons extra-virgin olive oil
Fresh rosemary or sage

Dissolve the yeast and sugar in 1 cup of the water. Place the flour in a large bowl. Make a well in the center of the flour, pour the yeast mixture into the well, and begin to mix. Add 1 teaspoon of the salt and 1 tablespoon of the olive oil. Continue to mix until the dough forms a mass (more water may be necessary). Remove the dough from the bowl and knead it on a lightly floured surface until it is smooth. Form the dough into a ball and place it in a lightly oiled bowl, cover with plastic wrap, and allow to rise in a warm place until it has doubled in size (at least 1 hour). Then punch it down and remove it from the bowl.

Generously coat a jelly-roll pan with olive oil. Place the dough in the oiled pan, spreading it evenly with your fingertips into the corners of the pan. Brush the surface of the dough lightly with olive oil and sprinkle with fresh rosemary or sage and the remaining ¼ teaspoon salt. Allow the dough to rise until double in size. Bake at 400° for 15 minutes or until the top is a light golden brown. Remove the bread from the oven and brush the top lightly with olive oil.

## SPOONBREAD

*Serves 8*

1½ cups boiling water
1 cup yellow or white cornmeal
1 tablespoon butter, melted
3 egg yolks
1 cup buttermilk
1 teaspoon salt
1 teaspoon sugar
1 teaspoon baking powder
¼ teaspoon baking soda
3 egg whites

Pour the boiling water over the cornmeal and stir until it is cool to keep the meal from lumping. Add the butter and egg yolks. Stir until the yolks are well blended. Stir in the buttermilk. Blend in the salt, sugar, baking powder, and baking soda. Beat the egg whites and fold them in.

   Pour the batter into a greased 2-quart baking dish and bake 45 to 50 minutes at 375°. Serve hot with plenty of butter.

### SI BON
—
SANIBEL, FLORIDA

*Greg and Karen Seibert, the owners of Si Bon, are devotees of American regional cooking. This Southern spoonbread is an important part of their repertoire. It is delicious with roasted meats.*

*Semolina is a cream-colored, granular, protein-rich durum wheat flour that is customarily used for making pasta. It also makes a bread with a fine crumb, a loaf that is both tasty and easy to slice.*

## SEMOLINA BREAD

*Makes 2 loaves*

1½ cups water, at 80° to 90°
1 package active dry yeast
1 teaspoon sugar
2 cups semolina flour
2 teaspoons salt
About 2 cups all-purpose flour

In a medium-size bowl, mix the water, yeast, and sugar. Let the mixture rest for 10 minutes, then whisk in the semolina flour to form a batter. Add the salt. With a wooden spoon beat in 1 cup of the all-purpose flour. Sprinkle ¼ cup of flour on the work surface and ¼ cup of flour over the batter. Turn the dough out onto the work surface and knead for 8 to 10 minutes, adding flour as necessary. The dough should become soft and moist but not sticky.

    Place the dough in a clean, lightly oiled bowl. Cover and let rise in a warm, draft-free area for 1½ to 2 hours, or until the dough has doubled in size. Punch down the dough and form it into two French loaves. Place the bread on a baking sheet sprinkled with semolina flour. Let the loaves rise until doubled in bulk. Bake in a 400° oven for 20 to 25 minutes.

## APPLESAUCE BREAD

*Makes 1 loaf*

2 cups all-purpose flour
½ teaspoon baking powder
½ teaspoon baking soda
½ teaspoon salt
½ teaspoon cinnamon
½ cup unsalted butter
1½ cups sugar
2 eggs, beaten
1 cup applesauce
½ cup buttermilk or sour milk
1 teaspoon vanilla
1 cup chopped walnuts

Sift together the dry ingredients and set aside. Cream the butter and the sugar and add the eggs and applesauce. Alternately add the dry ingredients and the milk to the applesauce mixture. Stir in the vanilla and walnuts. Bake in a greased 9-by-5-inch loaf pan in a 375° oven for 50 minutes to 1 hour.

## CRANBERRY ORANGE BREAD

*Makes 1 loaf*

½ cup (1 stick) unsalted butter
1 cup sugar
2 eggs
Grated rind of ⅔ of an orange
½ teaspoon dried orange peel
½ teaspoon orange juice concentrate
2 cups all-purpose flour
1 teaspoon baking powder

## VIVIAN'S KITCHEN

—

WESTFIELD,
NEW JERSEY

*The applesauce and buttermilk in this recipe result in an especially moist bread. Spread with cream cheese, it makes a terrific brunch offering as well as an alternative to richer and sweeter desserts.*

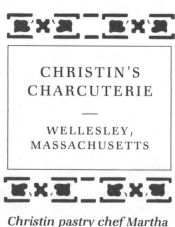

## CHRISTIN'S CHARCUTERIE

—

WELLESLEY,
MASSACHUSETTS

*Christin pastry chef Martha Burgess developed this*

*cranberry orange bread from a sour cream–cinnamon coffeecake recipe of her mother's. The cranberry relish used to marbleize the cake gives it a special fillip.*

1 teaspoon baking soda
¼ teaspoon salt
1 cup sour cream
1½ tablespoons cranberry liqueur
½ cup Cranberry Relish (see recipe below)

Cream the butter and sugar until smooth. Add the eggs and mix. Mix in the grated orange rind, peel, and juice concentrate. Sift together the dry ingredients and add them to the creamed mixture. Alternately with the sour cream, add the cranberry liqueur and mix. Pour the batter into a greased loaf pan. Pour the cranberry relish down the center of the batter, and with a knife, streak it through to marbleize the bread. Bake the loaf in a 350° oven for 45 to 60 minutes, until a toothpick comes out clean.

### Cranberry Relish

*Makes 2 cups*

1 12-ounce bag fresh cranberries
1 small orange, quartered
⅔ cup sugar
⅔ cup water
1 teaspoon Grand Marnier, or to taste

Reserve a quarter of the bag of cranberries and chop them coarsely. Combine the remaining cranberries with the quartered orange, sugar, and water in a saucepan. Cook the mixture until the berries pop, then set it aside to cool. Remove the quartered orange and purée two thirds of the cooked berries. Combine all the ingredients.

## ELEGANT PICNIC DATE BREAD

*Makes 1 large loaf or 2 medium loaves*

1½ cups sugar
2 tablespoons butter, softened
2 eggs
1 8-ounce box pitted dates
1½ teaspoons baking soda
1½ cups boiling water
1 cup walnuts
2½ cups all-purpose flour

Combine the sugar, butter, and eggs and beat until light and fluffy. Place the dates in the bowl of a food processor and pulse until they are finely chopped. Add the baking soda. With the machine running, add the boiling water and process until the mixture is well blended and has a pudding-like consistency. Stop the machine and add the walnuts. Pulse to chop the nuts but do not let them become pulverized.

Add the flour and the date mixture alternately to the creamed sugar and egg mixture, starting and ending with the flour. The batter will be thin. Pour the batter into 1 large buttered loaf pan or 2 medium-size pans. Bake the bread in a 350° oven for 1½ hours (or less for 2 loaves), or until a cake tester comes out clean. Let the bread cool in the pan. It will keep for a week wrapped in plastic and can also be frozen.

NOTE: This dark and moist date bread is a favorite not only for the picnic box but for gifts. At holiday time, try substituting chopped chestnuts for the walnuts. Whole wheat flour gives the bread a sweeter, nuttier taste.

## THE ELEGANT PICNIC
—
LENOX, MASSACHUSETTS

*Ted Weiant is a New York stage director who started coming to the Berkshires when his wife, Joan Stein, became managing director of the Berkshire Theater Festival in Stockbridge. Not wanting to accept directing assignments in other parts of the country during the summer months, Weiant turned to his second love, cooking, and launched The Elegant Picnic, which produces the ultimate in carry-out picnics. With a theatrical flair, Weiant ties a helium-filled balloon to the box containing a sumptuous five-course feast.*

## ADELAIDE'S CARRY-OUT CUISINE

—

### ATLANTA

*Along with the French baguettes and brioches and croissants that are made every day at Adelaide's, there is always a specialty bread of the week. This coconut bread blends nicely with curry or Thai dinners, or—slightly sweet as it is—it makes a new and different breakfast or tea bread.*

## COCONUT BREAD

*Makes 1 loaf*

1 cup grated sweetened coconut
2 cups all-purpose flour
¾ cup sugar
1 tablespoon baking powder
1 cup milk
¼ cup vegetable oil
1 egg, beaten
1 teaspoon vanilla

Spread the coconut on a cookie sheet and toast it in a 350° oven until it is lightly browned. Combine the coconut with the sifted flour, sugar, and baking powder in a large bowl. Mix the milk, oil, and egg with the vanilla in a small bowl. Add to the flour mixture and blend well. Pour into a buttered and floured 9-by-5-by-3-inch loaf pan and bake for 50 to 60 minutes, or until a cake tester comes out clean and the top is golden brown.

## COOKIES AND BARS

Mocha Chip Cookies
Chocolate Chubbies
Chocolate Chip Cookies
Almond Accidents
Jumbo Oatmeal Pecan Cookies
Molasses Cookies
Sesame Seed Cookies
Pepper Snaps
Lemon Puckers
Apricot Foldovers
Maple Shortbread Bars
Lemon Bars
Macadamia Nut Bars
Cookie Bars
Cognac Brownies
Chocolate Fudge Brownies
Wendy's Grand Marnier Brownies
Coconut Cream Cheese Balls
Jenny's Cream Cheese Brownies
Double Fudge Chocolate Chip Brownies
Brownies Ecstasy

REBECCA'S
—
BOSTON

*These delectable confections are a cross between chocolate chip cookies and meringues. They should be soft in the center, so be careful not to overbake them.*

## MOCHA CHIP COOKIES

*Makes 3 dozen*

½ cup (1 stick) butter
4 ounces unsweetened chocolate
3 cups semisweet chocolate chips
½ cup plus 2 tablespoons all-purpose flour
½ teaspoon baking powder
½ teaspoon salt
4 eggs
1½ cups sugar
4½ teaspoons instant coffee, powdered or crystals
2 teaspoons vanilla

Melt the butter, the unsweetened chocolate, and half the chocolate chips in the top of a double boiler over simmering water. Combine the flour, baking powder, and salt in a medium-size bowl. In another bowl beat the eggs, sugar, coffee, and vanilla at high speed for 2 minutes. Add the melted chocolate mixture to the egg-sugar mixture. Add the flour mixture and the remaining chocolate chips. Drop by tablespoonfuls onto an ungreased baking sheet. Bake at 300° for about 8 minutes. Leave the cookies on the baking sheets for 2 to 3 minutes before removing to a wire rack to cool.

## CHOCOLATE CHUBBIES

*Makes 3 dozen large cookies*

6 ounces semisweet chocolate
2 ounces unsweetened chocolate
5 tablespoons unsalted butter
¼ cup all-purpose flour
Scant ½ teaspoon baking powder
Pinch of salt
8 ounces (or more) semisweet chocolate chips
8 ounces (or more) broken pecans
8 ounces (or more) broken walnuts
3 eggs
Scant cup sugar

Break up the semisweet and unsweetened chocolate (not the chips) and cut the butter into small pieces. Melt them together over hot water. Mix and be careful not to burn the chocolate. Remove from the heat and cool the mixture to "baby bottle" temperature. Meanwhile, sift together the flour, baking powder, and salt. Set aside. In a separate bowl, combine the chocolate chips and nuts and set them aside.

When the chocolate has cooled, combine the eggs and sugar in a mixing bowl and beat until thick. Slowly add the chocolate-butter mixture, beating constantly. (If the mixture is too hot, the eggs will cook.) Add the flour mixture. Stir only until combined. Add the chocolate chips and nuts.

Grease two baking sheets well, and, using a tablespoon, drop the batter onto the sheets, leaving plenty of room between cookies. Bake in a 325° oven for 15 to 20 minutes.

SARABETH'S
KITCHEN
—
NEW YORK CITY

*When you're making these addictive cookies, it's important to use fine-quality semisweet chocolate. Add more nuts and chocolate chips, as you like. The more you add, of course, the chubbier the Chubbies (and those who eat them) will get, but the more delicious the results will be, too.*

## CROSBY'S

—

LENOX,
MASSACHUSETTS

*Everybody loves the origi-
nal Toll House cookies, and
this recipe is an admitted
adaptation. The Crosby's
version is super-buttery and
crisp and, not surprisingly
in this business, four
inches in diameter.*

## CHOCOLATE CHIP COOKIES

*Makes 30 to 36*

2 cups (4 sticks) unsalted butter, softened
3 cups light brown sugar
1 cup sugar
4 eggs
2 teaspoons vanilla
3½ cups all-purpose flour
1½ teaspoons salt
2 teaspoons baking soda
1½ cups semisweet chocolate chips

Cream the butter until smooth. Add both kinds
of sugar, beating well after each addition. Beat in
the eggs one at a time and add the vanilla. Sift
the flour with the salt and baking soda and fold
into the butter mixture. Add the chocolate chips.
For each cookie, drop 2 tablespoonfuls of batter
onto a greased baking sheet; place the cookies 2
inches apart. Bake for 8 minutes at 375°. Remove
the cookies from the pan immediately and cool
on racks.

## ALMOND ACCIDENTS

*Makes 35 to 40*

1 cup (2 sticks) butter
1¼ cups sifted confectioners' sugar
2½ cups cake flour
1 teaspoon almond extract
⅓ cup sliced almonds

Cream the butter and sugar. Sift the flour and add it to the butter-sugar mixture, mixing until just blended. Add the almond extract and the almonds and again mix until just blended, scraping the bowl often. Drop a tablespoonful of dough for each cookie on a lightly greased cookie sheet and bake at 350° for 12 to 15 minutes or until the cookies are lightly browned. Leave on baking sheet for 2 to 3 minutes before removing to racks to cool.

## JUMBO OATMEAL PECAN COOKIES

*Makes 2 dozen 4-inch cookies*

1½ cups (3 sticks) butter, softened
1½ cups packed dark brown sugar
½ cup white sugar
2 eggs
2 teaspoons vanilla
2 cups all-purpose flour
Pinch of salt
1 teaspoon baking soda
3⅓ cups rolled oats
1½ cups chopped pecans

Cream the butter with both kinds of sugar until well blended. Add the eggs and vanilla. Sift the

LET'S EAT
—
TIBURON,
CALIFORNIA

*These cookies are so named because they were meant to be the crust for a bar recipe, didn't work out, and were too good to let go.*

THE GREEN
GROCER
—
NORFOLK,
VIRGINIA

*King-size cookies are found near the checkout counter of many take-out shops, and these are a special favorite of Green Grocer customers. If you wish to*

*make smaller cookies, note that they will take less time to bake.*

flour with the salt and baking soda and add to the butter mixture. Mix until the flour is well incorporated. Stir in the rolled oats and nuts.

Using a very small ice cream scoop, place mounds of dough on a greased cookie sheet, making sure to leave room for 4-inch cookies. Flatten the mounds of dough with the wet heel of your hand.

Bake at 350° approximately 12 minutes, or until cookies are lightly and uniformly browned. Lift off the cookie sheets while still warm. Cool the cookies and store them in an airtight container.

## MATTERS OF TASTE

—

### ATLANTA

*Customers like Pamela Peterson's recipes because they are imaginative but unpretentious. These spicy molasses cookies are the perfect accompaniment to afternoon tea.*

## MOLASSES COOKIES

*Makes 4 dozen*

¾ cup (1½ sticks) butter, softened
1 cup dark brown sugar
1 egg
¼ cup molasses
2¼ cups all-purpose flour
2 teaspoons baking soda
¼ teaspoon salt
½ teaspoon cloves
1 teaspoon cinnamon
1 teaspoon ginger
Sugar for dipping

Cream the butter and sugar. Add the egg and molasses and stir. Add the sifted dry ingredients. Roll the dough into balls 1 inch in diameter. Dip them in granulated sugar and sprinkle them with water. Bake in a 375° oven for 10 to 12 minutes. When the cookies are cool, store them in an airtight container.

## SESAME SEED COOKIES

*Makes 2 dozen*

¾ cup (1½ sticks) unsalted butter, softened
1 cup light brown sugar
1 egg
1 teaspoon vanilla
1 cup all-purpose flour
¼ teaspoon baking powder
⅛ teaspoon salt
1½ cups toasted sesame seeds

Combine the butter, sugar, egg, and vanilla and beat until smooth. Sift together the flour, baking powder, and salt and add to the butter mixture. Stir until blended. Add the sesame seeds and blend well. Drop the dough by teaspoonfuls onto a greased baking sheet (or an ungreased sheet lined with parchment paper). Bake at 375° for 10 to 12 minutes. Watch carefully. Remove the cookies from the oven and transfer them to a wire rack for flat cookies, or roll them around the handle of a wooden spoon to form cylinders. (If the cookies become too crisp to roll, return the baking sheet to the oven to soften the cookies.)

## GOOD TASTE
—
BROOKLYN HEIGHTS,
NEW YORK

*In the South (and in the Middle East) these would be called benne seed cookies. Whatever the name, they are delicious, and even healthful, since sesame seeds are rich in calcium and protein. To toast the seeds, heat them in a dry skillet until they are golden and fragrant. Use the toasted seeds right away, since they tend to lose their flavor rapidly once toasted.*

## MADE
## TO ORDER

—

BERKELEY

*Here is an "adult" cookie
with an appealing bite.*

## *PEPPER SNAPS*

*Makes 18 to 24*

2¾ cups sifted all-purpose flour
2 teaspoons baking powder
1 teaspoon finely ground pepper
¼ teaspoon cayenne pepper
¼ teaspoon allspice
¼ teaspoon cloves
¼ teaspoon ginger
½ teaspoon salt
1 cup (2 sticks) unsalted butter
1 egg
1½ cups sugar

Sift together all the dry ingredients except the
sugar. Cream the butter in the large bowl of an
electric mixer. When the butter is creamy, beat in
the egg and sugar and mix well. With the mixer
at low speed, slowly add the dry ingredients to
the butter mixture. Continue beating until well
mixed. Refrigerate the dough for about 30 minutes.

Divide the dough into two or three portions.
Lightly flour the work surface and a rolling pin.
Working with one portion of dough at a time, roll
the dough to a thickness of ¼ inch and cut it into
circles with a cookie cutter. Transfer the circles
to an unbuttered cookie sheet. Continue with the
remaining portions of dough and the scraps.
Bake the cookies at 375° for 10 minutes, or until
they are a light golden brown. Cool on racks.

## LEMON PUCKERS

*Makes 3 dozen*

1 cup (2 sticks) butter, softened
3 ounces cream cheese
1 cup sugar
1 egg yolk
½ teaspoon grated lemon rind
2½ cups all-purpose flour
½ teaspoon salt
1 cup finely chopped walnuts
¾ cup sifted confectioners' sugar
3 tablespoons lemon juice (about 3 lemons)

Cream the butter and cream cheese. Add the sugar and then the egg yolk. Add the lemon rind and mix well. Mix the salt with the flour and add in small amounts to the butter-sugar mixture, blending well after each addition. Add the walnuts and refrigerate the dough for 2 hours.

When the dough is ready to bake, form it into three logs, each approximately 6 inches long, and flatten the logs slightly. Cut 12 1-by-3-inch ovals from each log. Bake the cookies on a lightly greased cookie sheet at 325° for 18 to 22 minutes, until they are lightly browned. Cool the cookies on racks and glaze with a mixture of the confectioners' sugar and lemon juice.

NOTE: This recipe can be doubled—a boon at holiday time.

LET'S EAT
—
TIBURON,
CALIFORNIA

*Next door to Let's Eat is Marsha Workman and Sharon Leach's original joint venture, a bakery called Sweet Things. The bakery provides pastries for retail sale and also supplies desserts for some of the Bay Area's finest restaurants.*

*Abigail Menard began cooking seriously while she was working at Massachusetts General Hospital as a technician. Feeling herself well paid, she spent some of her extra earnings on cooking classes and studied with Madeleine Kamman. Her co-workers benefited as she regularly brought in cakes and cookies to share.*

## APRICOT FOLDOVERS

*Makes 50*

1¼ cups unsifted all-purpose flour
6 tablespoons sugar
Pinch of salt
4 ounces cream cheese
4 tablespoons butter
3 tablespoons sour cream

FILLING

¼ cup orange juice
6 tablespoons sugar
8 ounces dried apricots, chopped in a
    food processor

In the bowl of a food processor, combine the flour, sugar, and salt. Process for 2 seconds, until blended. Add the cream cheese and the butter, cut into chunks, and process until crumbly. Add the sour cream 1 tablespoon at a time and process until the dough forms a ball (you may not need all of the sour cream). Wrap the dough in plastic wrap and refrigerate for at least an hour.

To prepare the filling, combine all of the ingredients in a small saucepan and cook over low heat until most of the orange juice has been absorbed, stirring frequently. Set aside to cool.

When you are ready to assemble the cookies, divide the dough into thirds. On a floured surface roll each batch of dough into a square ⅛ inch thick. Cut the dough into small squares, about 1½ inches on each side. Place a small amount of the apricot filling diagonally down the middle of each square. Pinch the opposite corners to the center and pinch closed. Place the foldovers on an unbuttered baking sheet. Repeat the process with the remaining dough. Bake the foldovers at 325° for 12 to 15 minutes or until they are lightly browned on the bottom. Let cool on a wire rack.

## MAPLE SHORTBREAD BARS

*Makes 16 bars*

### CRUST

2 cups all-purpose flour
½ cup sugar
¼ teaspoon salt
1 cup unsalted butter

Combine the flour, sugar, and salt in a bowl and cut in the butter with a pastry blender or two knives until the mixture is crumbly. Press the mixture onto the bottom of a greased 9-inch-square baking pan, bringing the crust up ½ inch around the edges. Bake at 350° for 15 minutes or until the edges begin to turn brown. Cool the crust.

### FILLING

1½ cups brown sugar
⅔ cup maple syrup
2 eggs
¼ cup melted unsalted butter
2 teaspoons vanilla
½ teaspoon salt
2 cups chopped walnuts

While the crust is baking, combine all the filling ingredients except the nuts. Mix until all lumps of brown sugar have been dissolved. Pour the filling mixture into the cooled crust. Sprinkle the top with the walnuts. Bake in a 350° oven for 50 minutes to 1 hour, until the filling is set. (Watch closely; if the top begins to turn too brown, cover the top of the pan loosely with tin foil.) When cool, cut into 16 pieces.

### FORMAGGIO KITCHEN

—

### CAMBRIDGE

*Maple syrup is New England's proudest export and is readily available, for a price, in any part of the country. One Yankee entrepreneur recently provided an opportunity to beat the high price by "leasing" rights to a sugar maple tree, or just one of its buckets, for a season.*

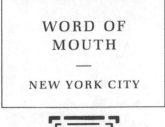
## LEMON BARS

*Makes 20 large bars*

PASTRY BASE

3 cups all-purpose flour
⅓ cup sugar
½ teaspoon salt
1 cup (2 sticks) margarine

Sift together the flour, sugar, and salt and cut in the margarine with two knives or a pastry blender until the mixture resembles coarse meal. Press into a buttered 11-by-17-inch baking sheet (a jelly-roll pan is ideal) and bake at 350° for 15 minutes. Cool it slightly. While the crust is baking and cooling, prepare the topping.

TOPPING

6 eggs
3 cups packed dark brown sugar
1½ cups chopped pecans
1½ cups coconut
1 tablespoon vanilla

Beat the eggs and blend in the sugar, pecans, coconut, and vanilla. Pour the mixture over the pastry. Bake 20 to 30 minutes at 350° until the topping is firm.

FROSTING

5 cups confectioners' sugar
Juice and grated peel of 3 lemons

Add the lemon juice and rind slowly to the confectioners' sugar until a proper frosting consistency has been reached. When the topping is done and has cooled, spread on the frosting. Let the pan cool completely and then cut into bars. Cover them if they are to be stored. They freeze very well.

## MACADAMIA NUT BARS

*Makes 12 to 16 bars*

CRUST

1 cup all-purpose flour
⅓ cup dark brown sugar
½ cup (1 stick) cold butter

Mix together the ingredients for the crust, using a pastry blender or two knives, until the mixture resembles meal. Press the crust into an 8-by-8-inch pan and bake for 20 minutes in a 350° oven.

TOPPING

2 eggs
1 cup dark brown sugar
1 teaspoon vanilla
⅓ cup all-purpose flour
½ teaspoon baking powder
1½ cups unsweetened coconut
1½ teaspoons lemon juice
1 cup macadamia nuts, toasted in a dry frying pan

Beat together the eggs, sugar, and vanilla. Mix the flour, baking powder, and coconut and add to the egg mixture, beating until smooth. Add the lemon juice and stir in the nuts. Pour the mixture over the crust and return the pan to the oven for 35 minutes. When cool, cut into bars.

GOOD TASTE
—
BROOKLYN HEIGHTS,
NEW YORK

*Although we have come to think of macadamia nuts as native to Hawaii, actually they first grew in the coastal tropical forests of northeastern Australia and were discovered there by a Dr. MacAdam (so much for exotic names!). They are costly, to be sure, so this recipe should be saved for a splurge.*

*This recipe allows you to dress up old-fashioned shortbread in four different ways.*

## COOKIE BARS

*Makes 12 to 15 bars*

### SHORTBREAD

¾ cup (1½ sticks) cold butter, cut in pieces
1½ cups sifted all-purpose flour
½ cup sugar

Combine the ingredients for the shortbread, using a pastry blender or two knives, and pat the mixture into a greased 11-by-17-inch jelly-roll pan.

### TOPPING

1 egg
½ cup brown sugar
6 ounces semisweet chocolate chips
1 cup chopped walnuts or pecans

Mix together the egg and the brown sugar. Add the chocolate chips and nuts and coat them well. Spread the topping over the shortbread and bake on the bottom rack of the oven at 350° for approximately 25 minutes.

### VARIATIONS

1. Substitute 6 ounces butterscotch chips, 1 cup coconut, and 1 cup chopped pecans for the chocolate chips and chopped walnuts.
2. Substitute 1 cup raisins for the chocolate chips, and use chopped walnuts.
3. Eliminate the topping and spread strawberry or raspberry jam over the shortbread.

## COGNAC BROWNIES

*Makes 32*

9 ounces unsweetened chocolate
9 ounces (2 sticks plus 2 tablespoons) butter
9 large eggs
4½ cups sugar
1 teaspoon vanilla
2 tablespoons cognac
2¼ cups all-purpose flour
1¼ teaspoons salt
2½ cups roughly chopped walnuts or pecans (or a
   combination)

Melt the chocolate and butter in the top of a double boiler. Set aside to cool somewhat. Beat the eggs and sugar in the bowl of an electric mixer at moderate to high speed or with a wire whisk, until the mixture is light and creamy. Add the vanilla and cognac to the egg mixture and blend well. Stir in the melted chocolate and butter and blend well with a rubber spatula.

Combine the flour and salt and fold into the chocolate mixture. Do not overmix. Stir in the chopped nuts.

Line an 11-by-17-inch jelly-roll pan with tin foil. Coat the foil well with butter. Spread the brownie mixture in the pan, using a rubber spatula and making sure all corners are filled. Place the pan in the lower part of a 325° oven and bake for 35 minutes. Remove the pan from the oven and let it cool.

When it is cool, turn the pan upside down onto a work surface and peel off the foil from the bottom. Using a warm knife and starting with two large halves, cut the brownie in half again and again until there are 32 pieces.

EICHELBAUM
& CO.
—
SAN FRANCISCO

*Though his first love is being a restaurateur, Stanley Eichelbaum has used the carry-out business to compensate for the limited revenue his small restaurant space can generate. No carry-out case is without brownies, and this recipe can be called the ultimate. It is definitely not for cholesterol or calorie counters.*

FISHER
& LEVY

—

NEW YORK CITY

*It's not only the food at Fisher & Levy that keeps customers like Burgess Meredith coming back and back. Atmosphere is important, too. It includes an earth resonance generator to help customers relax and spectrum lighting that is easy on the eyes.*

## CHOCOLATE FUDGE BROWNIES

*Makes 16*

2 cups light brown sugar
4 tablespoons melted butter
2 eggs
2 ounces unsweetened chocolate, melted and cooled to lukewarm
2 teaspoons vanilla
4 tablespoons unsweetened cocoa
1 cup all-purpose flour, sifted
⅛ teaspoon salt
¼ cup chopped walnuts

In the large bowl of a mixer, combine the brown sugar and butter on low speed until smooth. Add the eggs, chocolate, and vanilla and mix them in until smooth at low speed. Add the cocoa, flour, and salt sifted together and mix in at low speed until smooth. Add the walnuts and mix for 1 to 2 minutes, until they are evenly spread through the batter.

Pour the mixture into a greased and floured 8-by-8-inch pan and smooth the top with a wet spatula until flat. Bake at 350° for 20 to 25 minutes. Allow the brownies to cool in the pan. Then trim off any too-crisp outer edges, cut into squares, and serve.

## WENDY'S GRAND MARNIER BROWNIES

*Makes 1 dozen*

### BROWNIES

1 ounce unsweetened chocolate
6 ounces semisweet chocolate chips
7½ tablespoons unsalted butter
⅔ cup sifted all-purpose flour
¼ teaspoon baking soda
¼ teaspoon salt
2 eggs
⅔ cup sugar
2 tablespoons Grand Marnier
1 teaspoon vanilla
1 tablespoon grated orange rind
¾ cup ground almonds

Melt the chocolate, the chips, and the butter in the top of a double boiler over simmering water. Combine the flour, baking soda, and salt in a small bowl; mix well and reserve. In a separate bowl beat the eggs until they are light in color; gradually add the sugar. Beat in the Grand Marnier, vanilla, and orange rind. Stir in the chocolate-butter mixture and fold in the flour mixture and the ground almonds. Spread the batter in a greased 9-inch square pan and bake at 325° for exactly 22 minutes. Let the brownies cool in the pan before frosting.

### FROSTING

6 tablespoons unsalted butter, softened
2 teaspoons orange juice concentrate
1 teaspoon grated orange rind
1 cup confectioners' sugar

## TRUFFLES
—
### MARBLEHEAD, MASSACHUSETTS

*At Truffles, every dish is named for the person who created it. Wendy Ciarletta works on the retail side of the operation, but her Grand Marnier brownies have become the most requested of all Truffles desserts. They make a great finale for a buffet supper party—the recipe may be doubled, tripled, or quadrupled successfully.*

Whip the butter, orange juice concentrate, and orange rind together, until the mixture is smooth. Add the confectioners' sugar and beat until light and fluffy. Spread the frosting over the brownies.

GLAZE

4 tablespoons unsalted butter
⅓ cup semisweet chocolate chips

Combine the ingredients in a double boiler over low heat. Mix well. While the glaze is warm, gently pour it over the frosted brownies, spreading it evenly over the frosting. Chill the brownies until the glaze is firm.

*These creamy confections are closer to candy than cookies. If smoked almonds can't be found (or if you find them too special to cook with), slivered blanched almonds may be substituted.*

## COCONUT CREAM CHEESE BALLS

*Makes 28 1-inch balls*

8 ounces cream cheese
½ cup chopped smoked almonds
½ cup diced dried apricots
½ cup diced pitted dates
½ cup diced dried pears
¾ to 1 cup dried coconut

Combine all ingredients except the coconut in a mixing bowl and mix until the fruits and nuts are well distributed throughout the cheese. Form balls 1 inch in diameter and roll the balls in the coconut until the outer layer is covered and no longer sticky. If you do not wish to serve the cream cheese balls immediately, refrigerate them and remove them 15 minutes before serving time.

## JENNY'S CREAM CHEESE BROWNIES

*Makes 20 to 25*

BROWNIE BASE

4 ounces semisweet chocolate
3 tablespoons butter
2 eggs
¾ cup sugar
½ teaspoon baking powder
¼ teaspoon salt
½ cup all-purpose flour (do not sift)
½ cup coarsely chopped walnuts
¼ teaspoon almond extract
1 teaspoon vanilla

Melt the chocolate and butter together in a double boiler. Beat the eggs together, adding the sugar in small amounts until mixed well. Let the chocolate mixture cool slightly and add it to the egg mixture. Stir well. Combine the baking powder, salt, flour, and nuts and add to the chocolate mixture. Stir in the almond extract and vanilla.

TOPPING

3 ounces cream cheese
2 tablespoons butter
¼ cup sugar
1 egg
1 tablespoon flour
½ teaspoon vanilla

To make the topping, cream the cream cheese and butter together until smooth. Add the sugar and then the egg, flour, and vanilla.

To assemble the brownies, pour two thirds of the chocolate batter into a 9-inch square pan buttered and lined on the bottom with parch-

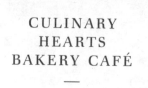

## CULINARY HEARTS BAKERY CAFÉ

—

WARREN,
NEW JERSEY

*People have asked whether this shop is related to the American Heart Association. Nothing could be further from the truth; in fact, it has been suggested that a sign be posted saying "Danger, High-Calorie Zone." Here's why.*

ment paper. Spread the topping mixture on top of the chocolate base. Then spoon the remaining chocolate batter over the cream cheese. Run a knife or spatula through the batter, marbleizing the two mixtures. Bake in a 350° oven for 35 minutes or until a cake tester comes out clean. Cool in the pan before cutting into squares.

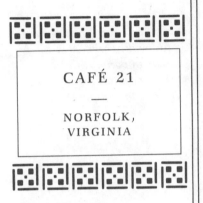

CAFÉ 21
—
NORFOLK,
VIRGINIA

*Before opening Café 21, Larry Epplein owned and operated the Lovitt Avenue Bakery, supplier of heavenly baked goods to many Norfolk restaurants and households. The bakery is now located in the rear of the restaurant and patrons are offered a wide selection of mousses, tortes, cakes, pies, and, of course, brownies.*

## DOUBLE FUDGE CHOCOLATE CHIP BROWNIES

*Makes 16*

5 ounces semisweet chocolate, broken into
    small pieces
1 cup (2 sticks) unsalted butter (or 1 stick butter plus
    1 stick margarine)
3 large eggs, at room temperature
1 cup sugar
1½ cups all-purpose flour
1 cup semisweet chocolate chips
1 cup chopped walnuts (optional)

In the top of a double boiler or in a microwave oven, melt together the chocolate pieces and butter. Blend well and set aside to cool. Beat the eggs until they are frothy and blend in the sugar. Add the chocolate mixture and blend well. Add the flour and stir until evenly mixed. Fold in the chocolate chips and the nuts.

Spread the mixture (it will be thick) into a buttered 9-by-13-inch baking pan. Bake in the center of a 350° oven for 25 to 35 minutes, until the top appears glazed and the edges pull away from the pan. Let the brownies cool in the pan, though they may be cut and served while still slightly warm.

## BROWNIES ECSTASY

*Makes 24*

8 ounces unsweetened chocolate
1 cup (2 sticks) unsalted butter
5 large eggs
1 tablespoon vanilla
1 teaspoon almond extract
¼ teaspoon salt
2½ tablespoons espresso coffee powder
3¾ cups granulated sugar
1⅔ cups sifted all-purpose flour
2 generous cups walnut halves

Line a 9-by-13-inch baking pan with foil, and butter the foil. Melt the chocolate and butter together in a heavy pan over low heat. Remove it from the heat and let cool.

In a large bowl, beat the eggs, vanilla, almond extract, salt, coffee, and sugar for 10 minutes at high speed. With the beater at low speed, add the chocolate mixture a little at a time, but beat only until mixed. Stir in the flour and the nuts and turn into the prepared pan. Bake in a 425° oven for 35 minutes. After 15 minutes rotate the pan to assure even baking. Do not cut the brownies until the next day.

## VAL'S
—
CLEARWATER,
FLORIDA

*Val's Brownies Ecstasy have a fudgelike interior but a crusty outside. Hungry travelers come from miles around to sample them.*

## CAKES, PIES, AND TARTS

Merry Cake
Apple Brandy Nut Cake
TooJay's Banana Cake
Rum Teacake
Torta Sabbiosa
Lemon Blueberry Loaf
Drogheda Oatmeal Cake
Torta Terramoto (Earthquake Cake)
Cheesecake Maison
Apricot Cheesecake
Yogurt Cheesecake
Raspberry Mousse Cake
Reine de Saba
Chocolate Roll
Coffee Hazelnut Cake
Date and Walnut Chess Pie
Fudge Walnut Pie
Pumpkin Pie la Toque
John's Grape Pie
Brandied Peach and Macaroon Strudel
English Lemon Tarts
Georgia Pecan Peach Tart
French Apple Custard Tart
Prune Plum Tart
Danish Puff
Pecan Dacquoise with Blueberry Fool

## MERRY CAKE

*Makes 1 loaf cake*

1 cup (2 sticks) butter, at room temperature
1 cup sugar
2 eggs
1 cup all-purpose flour
½ teaspoon baking powder
½ teaspoon salt
1 to 2 cups mixed fruit (ideally all fresh, but frozen
    raspberries, blueberries, and peaches will do,
    along with fresh bananas and apples)

Cream the butter and the sugar and add the eggs one at a time, beating well after each addition. Sift the flour with the baking powder and salt and add. Pour half the batter into a buttered and floured 9-by-5-inch loaf pan. Place the fruit on top. Pour the remaining batter on top of the fruit and bake at 350° for about 1 hour, until a toothpick or wooden skewer inserted in the center of the cake comes out clean. Let the cake cool on a rack before removing it from the pan.

## APPLE BRANDY NUT CAKE

*Makes 1 9-by-13-inch cake*

CAKE

4 cups peeled, cored, and medium-finely chopped
    Granny Smith apples
6 tablespoons brandy
2 cups all-purpose flour
2 teaspoons cinnamon
2 teaspoons baking soda

GOODIES
TO GO
—
LEXINGTON,
MASSACHUSETTS

*Improbable though this cake may seem on first glance, it's delicious—and the fruit doesn't sink to the bottom. It's an ideal accompaniment to strawberry— or another fruit-flavored—ice cream.*

METROPOLIS
—
CHICAGO

*Erwin and Cathy Drechsler, who own Metropolis in Chicago's Old Town, like*

*the idea of scaling up home-style cooking for their customers. Grandma might have made an apple nut cake with confectioners' sugar icing, but she wouldn't have put brandy in the cake nor cream cheese in the icing.*

1 teaspoon salt
1 teaspoon nutmeg
½ teaspoon cloves
2 cups sugar
½ cup vegetable oil
2 eggs
1 cup walnuts or pecans

Soak the apples in the brandy. Sift together the flour, cinnamon, baking soda, salt, nutmeg, and cloves. In the bowl of an electric mixer, combine the sugar, oil, and eggs. Mix together on low speed for 1 to 2 minutes. Mix only lightly. Do not incorporate a great deal of air into the batter. Add the sifted flour and spices and mix lightly. Stir in the apple-brandy mixture and the nuts. Pour into a buttered and floured 9-by-13-by-2-inch baking pan and bake about 1 hour. The cake should be firm to the touch when it is done. Cool completely before frosting.

ICING

8 ounces cream cheese, softened
½ cup (1 stick) unsalted butter, softened
1 cup confectioners' sugar
1 teaspoon vanilla
Pinch of salt

Cream the cheese until it is smooth. Add the softened butter and beat it in until the mixture is smooth. Add the confectioners' sugar gradually, beating until smooth. Add the vanilla and salt. Spread the frosting on the cooled cake. If you wish, sprinkle the frosting with additional nuts or cinnamon.

# TOOJAY'S BANANA CAKE

*Makes 1 8-inch layer cake*

CAKE

¾ cup (1½ sticks) butter
1½ cups sugar
2 eggs, beaten
1½ cups sifted cake flour
1 teaspoon baking soda
¼ cup sour cream
1 cup (2 medium) ripe bananas, mashed
1 teaspoon vanilla
1 cup chopped walnuts

In a medium-size bowl, cream the butter until fluffy. Gradually add the sugar and mix well. Add the eggs and mix well. In a small bowl, mix together the cake flour and baking soda. Add the flour mixture to the creamed mixture alternately with the sour cream. Blend well. Add the bananas, vanilla, and walnuts. Mix well.

Pour the batter into two 8-inch square buttered and floured cake pans and bake the cake in a 350° oven for 30 to 35 minutes. Let the cake cool in the pans about 15 minutes, then turn onto a cake rack until completely cool.

FROSTING

½ cup (1 stick) unsalted butter
1 cup firmly packed light brown sugar
¼ cup milk
1 cup confectioners' sugar, sifted

Melt the butter in a saucepan over medium heat. Add the brown sugar and melt it, stirring constantly for 1 to 2 minutes. Remove from heat. Add the milk and stir to blend. Return to the heat until the mixture begins to bubble at the edges. Cook over medium-low heat, stirring occasion-

## TOOJAY'S OF PALM BEACH

—

HIGHLAND PARK, ILLINOIS

*Before he got into the restaurant business, lawyer Bill Bronner was a marathon runner. Perhaps that's why so many of the baked goods he sells in his retail shop/deli/restaurant are such topnotch fuel— items like killer chocolate cake, homemade rye bread, bran muffins, and this buttery banana cake with caramel frosting.*

ally, for 3 minutes. Do not boil; the mixture should barely bubble. Remove it from the heat. Cool it to lukewarm. Then stir in the confectioners' sugar. Frost the banana cake.

## THE COOKERY
—
HUDSON, OHIO

APRICOT GLAZE

Rub 1 cup of apricot preserves through a sieve into a saucepan, add 2 tablespoons of sugar, and boil for several minutes, until the mixture falls in thick drops from a spoon. Keep the glaze warm over hot water until ready to use. If it seems too thick, add drops of hot water.

## RUM TEACAKE

*Makes 2 loaf cakes*

1 cup chopped candied fruits
⅓ cup raisins
Dark rum to cover the fruits and raisins
2 cups all-purpose flour
1 teaspoon baking powder
1 cup plus 2 tablespoons butter
1 cup plus 2 tablespoons sugar
4 eggs, at room temperature
Apricot glaze (optional) (see recipe)

Soak the fruits and raisins in rum to cover for 1 to 2 days, or heat the rum, flame it, and soak the fruits and raisins for 2 hours. Drain the fruits and raisins, reserving the rum.

Sift together the flour and baking powder and set aside. Cream the butter, add the sugar, and beat until light and fluffy. With a whisk, beat in the eggs all at once. Fold in the flour with a spatula and then the drained fruits and raisins, mixing carefully.

Spoon the batter into two 7¼-by-3¼-inch bread pans, buttered and lined with parchment paper. Bake for 50 to 60 minutes at 325°, until a toothpick inserted into the center comes out clean. Remove the cakes from the oven and immediately pour over them ⅓ cup of the reserved rum, heated. Turn the cakes out of the pans to cool. When cool, brush with an apricot glaze if you wish.

## TORTA SABBIOSA

*Serves 6*

3 eggs
1 cup sugar
¾ cup potato starch
2 tablespoons all-purpose flour
2 teaspoons baking powder
1½ tablespoons light rum
⅞ cup (1¾ sticks) butter, melted
Confectioners' sugar

Beat the eggs with the sugar in an electric mixer at high speed, until they are light and fluffy—as long as 10 to 15 minutes. Sift together the potato starch, flour, and baking powder. Gently fold the dry ingredients into the egg mixture. Pour the rum into the melted butter. Gently but thoroughly fold the butter mixture into the batter. Pour the batter into a greased and floured charlotte mold. Bake at 400° for 45 minutes or until a toothpick inserted in the center comes out clean. Cool the cake, remove from the pan, and dust with confectioners' sugar.

---

## MASSIMO DA MILANO

—

### DALLAS

*Massimo Albini's father, Roberto, is known as the Gucci of bread in his native Milan, and many of his products even bear a typical designer's signature stamp. The Albini formula for returning breadmaking to the art form of centuries past has been used in hundreds of bakeries throughout Europe and was brought to Dallas in early 1985. Massimo da Milano combines the warmth and authenticity of a nineteenth-century European bakery with the sophistication of an Italian café.*

## MORNINGSIDE CAFÉ

—

### HOUSTON

*When blueberries are in season, this lemon blueberry loaf is always among the offerings at the Morningside Café.*

## LEMON BLUEBERRY LOAF

*Makes 1 1-pound loaf*

⅓ cup butter
1 cup sugar
2 eggs
1½ cups all-purpose flour
1 tablespoon baking powder
1 teaspoon salt
½ cup milk
1 cup fresh blueberries
1½ teaspoons grated lemon rind

Cream the butter and the sugar. Add the eggs and mix. Sift together the flour, baking powder, and salt. To the butter-egg mixture, add the milk and the sifted ingredients. Stir in the blueberries and the lemon rind. Bake in a 7½-by-3¼-inch greased and floured loaf pan in a 350° oven for 30 minutes.

## DROGHEDA OATMEAL CAKE

*Makes 1 10-inch tube cake*

### CAKE

2 cups oats
2½ cups boiling water
1 cup (2 sticks) butter
2 cups sugar
2 cups light brown sugar
4 eggs
2 teaspoons vanilla
3 cups all-purpose flour
2 teaspoons baking soda
2 teaspoons salt
2 teaspoons cinnamon
1 cup nuts

Soak the oats in the boiling water for 30 minutes. In another bowl, cream the butter with both kinds of sugar. Add the eggs one by one, beating after each addition, and the vanilla. Add the oats.

Sift together the flour, baking soda, salt, and cinnamon. Stir the sifted ingredients into the batter until just mixed. Fold in the nuts. Pour the batter into a greased and floured 10-inch tube pan and bake at 350° for 55 to 60 minutes or until a cake tester inserted in the middle of the cake comes out clean. Let the cake cool before adding the topping.

### TOPPING

½ cup (1 stick) butter
½ cup brown sugar
½ teaspoon vanilla
¾ cup chopped nuts
½ cup heavy cream

## PROVENDER

—

### TIVERTON, RHODE ISLAND

*In a picturesque Victorian building that used to be a general store, Cynthia Baker Burns and her staff of chefs lure passers-by with the taste-tempting smells that seep out from under the front door and across the old-fashioned porch. This moist breakfast cake is the creation of chef Jody Adams.*

Mix all of the topping ingredients except the cream in a saucepan over low heat. When they are thoroughly combined, add the cream and remove from the heat. Pour the topping over the cake and put it under the broiler until just brown. Serve immediately.

*This recipe was taught to Carlo Middione by his friend Mirella Nasi, in Bologna, Italy. The potato starch gives a moist but light texture and makes the top of the cake glossy. The surface is supposed to crack—like earth in an earthquake!*

## TORTA TERRAMOTO (EARTHQUAKE CAKE)

*Makes 1 8-inch cake*

12 ounces semisweet chocolate
½ cup (1 stick) unsalted butter
4 eggs
1¼ cups confectioners' sugar
¼ cup potato starch

Melt the chocolate and butter together in the top of a double boiler. Remove from the heat and set aside to cool.

Beat the eggs with the sugar until a heavy ribbon forms when you lift the beaters. Lighten the chocolate mixture with a small amount of the egg mixture, and then fold the chocolate into the egg mixture, blending well. Add the potato starch and blend well. Pour into a buttered and floured 8-inch cake pan and bake in a 350° oven for about 30 minutes. Cool in the pan before turning out onto a serving plate.

## CHEESECAKE MAISON

*Serves 10 to 12*

CHEESECAKE

1 cup coarsely crumbled Italian-style macaroons
    (amaretti)
Flavorless vegetable oil
3 8-ounce packages cream cheese, softened
2 tablespoons vanilla
5 extra large egg whites
1 teaspoon cream of tartar
Pinch of salt
1 cup sugar

Grind the macaroons in a food processor. Coat
the bottom and sides of a 10-inch springform pan
with vegetable oil. Add the macaroon crumbs to
the pan, shaking it to distribute them evenly over
the bottom.

In a large bowl, beat the cream cheese with
the vanilla until it is smooth and creamy. In another large bowl, beat the egg whites, cream of
tartar, and salt with an electric mixer until soft
peaks are formed. Then gradually beat in the
sugar and beat the meringue until it holds stiff
peaks. Fold the egg whites into the cream cheese
until the mixture is just blended. Pour the mixture into the prepared pan and bake in a 350°
oven for 35 minutes. Transfer to a rack to cool for
1 hour.

TOPPING

2 cups sour cream
2 tablespoons sugar
1 tablespoon vanilla
1 cup finely chopped hazelnuts

Beat the sour cream with the sugar and the vanilla until smooth. Pour this mixture over the

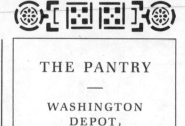

## THE PANTRY
—
WASHINGTON
DEPOT,
CONNECTICUT

*True to its name, The Pan-
try stocks domestic and
imported packaged foods,
including the Italian cookies that form the crust of
this very popular Pantry
dessert.*

cooled cheesecake, spreading evenly. Sprinkle the hazelnuts evenly over the top. Bake at 450° for 15 minutes. Let the cake cool completely in the pan on a rack, and chill it, covered, overnight before serving. This cheesecake keeps very well —up to five days.

MORNINGSIDE CAFÉ

—

HOUSTON

*Apricots are a most appealing taste with cream cheese, and this recipe proves it.*

## *APRICOT CHEESECAKE*

*Serves 10 to 12*

CRUST

**1½ cups crushed graham crackers**
**6 tablespoons melted butter**
**¼ cup sugar**

Blend the graham crackers, melted butter, and sugar together well, then press the crust mixture into a greased 9-inch springform pan, pressing evenly on the bottom and a little way up the sides of the pan. Set aside.

FILLING

**½ cup dried apricots**
**½ cup water**
**1⅓ cups sugar**
**3 8-ounce packages cream cheese**
**6 eggs, separated**
**1 tablespoon lemon juice**
**1½ teaspoons lemon zest**
**2 tablespoons vanilla**
**1 cup heavy cream**

Bring the apricots and water to a boil and boil until the apricots are soft. Process the drained apricots in a blender and add half the sugar.

Cool. In a separate bowl, beat the cream cheese and add the rest of the sugar. Add the egg yolks, lemon juice and zest, vanilla, and cream. Whip the egg whites until they are stiff and fold them in. Fold the apricot purée into the filling and pour into the prepared crust. Bake at 300° for 1 hour. Cool at room temperature for 1 hour. Refrigerate thoroughly before unmolding. Decorate with small pieces of apricot if desired.

## YOGURT CHEESECAKE

*Serves 6 to 8*

### CRUST

1½ cups graham cracker crumbs
¼ cup confectioners' sugar
6 tablespoons melted butter

Combine the ingredients well and press the mixture onto the bottom and up the sides (as far as possible) of an 8-inch springform pan. Chill for 1 hour before filling.

### FILLING

4 egg yolks
1 cup sugar
2 cups *labni* (yogurt cheese)
1 cup heavy cream
¼ cup all-purpose flour
2 tablespoons lemon juice
½ teaspoon vanilla
¼ teaspoon salt
Grated rind of 1 lemon
¼ cup golden raisins
4 egg whites, stiffly beaten

## GOOD TASTE

—

### BROOKLYN HEIGHTS, NEW YORK

Labni *(yogurt cheese) is available in Middle Eastern markets and is easy to make at home. Just put plain yogurt in a cheese-cloth bag and let it hang over a bowl in the refrigerator overnight. Remove the yogurt cheese from the bag and discard the liquid in the bowl. For this recipe you will need to start with 2 pounds of yogurt.*

In a large bowl, beat the egg yolks until they are well blended. Beat the sugar, ¼ cup at a time, into the yolks. Blend in the *labni*, cream, flour, lemon juice, vanilla, salt, and grated lemon rind. Beat until smooth and stir in the raisins. Gently fold in the egg whites. Pour the mixture into the crust and bake in a 350° oven for 1 hour. Do not be discouraged if the cheesecake sinks a bit during the baking and the cooling-off time. It is best made several hours before serving, or the night before.

## RASPBERRY MOUSSE CAKE

*Makes 1 9-inch cake*

RASPBERRY MOUSSE

2 eggs, separated
6 tablespoons sugar
⅔ cup drained frozen raspberries (or 1½ cups
    fresh), puréed and lightly sweetened
1½ teaspoons Framboise
4½ teaspoons unflavored gelatin
4½ teaspoons cold water
¾ cup heavy cream

Beat the egg yolks until thick, and gradually beat in the sugar. Stir in one third of the raspberry purée and place the mixture in the top of a double boiler over simmering water. Cook, stirring constantly, until the custard is thick enough to coat a spoon. Do not allow the mixture to come to a boil or the eggs will curdle.

Remove the pan from the heat and stir in the remaining raspberry purée, the Framboise, and the gelatin mixed with the water. Transfer the mixture to a large bowl, cover, and refrigerate for 2 hours. Whip the cream. In a separate bowl whip the egg whites until stiff but not dry. Fold the whipped cream and then the egg whites into the raspberry custard. Cover and refrigerate overnight.

GÉNOISE

1 cup all-purpose flour
¼ cup cornstarch
5 eggs
5 egg yolks
1 cup sugar

## CULINARY HEARTS BAKERY CAFÉ

—

WARREN,
NEW JERSEY

*This is the perfect dessert for a special occasion, but please note that the raspberry mousse part must be prepared the day before and refrigerated overnight.*

Sift together the flour and cornstarch four times. In a double boiler over simmering water, beat the eggs, the yolks, and the sugar until the mixture is warm to the touch (about 10 minutes). The mixture will be three times the original bulk. Remove the pan from the heat. Beat the mixture until it has cooled to room temperature (it will increase even more). Very gradually add the flour and cornstarch. Mix well. Pour the batter into a greased and floured 9-inch cake pan and bake in a 300° oven for 25 minutes, or until the center of the cake springs back when touched. Invert the cake onto a baking sheet lined with parchment paper and let it cool for 20 minutes before removing the pan.

ASSEMBLY

1 cup heavy cream
3 tablespoons confectioners' sugar, sifted

Slice the génoise in half. Spread with one third of the raspberry mousse. Top with the second layer of génoise. Cover the sides and top of the cake with the remaining mousse. Whip the cream and the confectioners' sugar. Spread the whipped cream on the sides of the cake and decorate the top with rosettes of cream.

## REINE DE SABA

*Serves 8 to 10*

### CAKE

5 tablespoons unsalted butter
2½ ounces bittersweet chocolate, chopped
½ cup plus 2 tablespoons unsweetened cocoa
    powder
½ cup cake flour
½ cup coarsely ground blanched almonds
1 tablespoon vanilla
⅛ teaspoon almond extract
2 tablespoons Myers's Dark Rum
4 eggs, separated
14 tablespoons sugar
⅛ teaspoon cream of tartar
Pinch of salt

Melt the butter and chocolate in the top of a double boiler over warm water, stirring until melted. Remove from the heat and let cool. Sift together the cocoa and flour and add the almonds. In a small bowl, combine the vanilla, almond extract, and rum and set aside. In a mixing bowl, beat the egg yolks until light. Gradually add, a tablespoon at a time, 10 tablespoons of the sugar (½ cup plus 2 tablespoons), beating until the sugar is incorporated. The mixture will be pale yellow and thick. Gradually beat the rum mixture into the yolks. At low speed blend the warm chocolate mixture into the yolks and scrape the bowl.

In a clean mixing bowl, beat the egg whites with the cream of tartar and the salt until soft peaks form. Gradually add the remaining 4 tablespoons of sugar and beat until stiff. One third at a time, quickly and lightly fold the cocoa mixture into the yolks. Lightly fold in the beaten egg

*There is always plenty of chocolate in the larder at Rudi's. Their truffles are a subject of frequent press coverage and are reputed to be the only ones in Boston made by hand.*

whites. Do not combine completely. White streaks will show.

Pour the mixture into a 9-inch round cake pan lined with parchment paper and bake on the center rack of a 350° oven for 20 minutes, or until just moist. Remove the cake to a rack and cool completely in the pan.

GLAZE

3½ tablespoons light corn syrup
2 tablespoons unsalted butter
2 tablespoons water
4½ ounces bittersweet or semisweet chocolate
Sliced toasted almonds or chocolate curls
   for garnish

Combine the corn syrup, butter, and 2 tablespoons of water in a saucepan over moderate heat. Stir the mixture as the butter melts, and bring it to a full boil. Remove the pan from the heat and whisk in the chocolate until it is melted and the mixture is smooth. (The glaze is best used warm and can be reheated in a double boiler.)

Invert the cake onto a serving plate. Pour the warm glaze over it, using a spatula to smooth the top and sides of the cake. Decorate the Reine de Saba by pressing sliced almonds or chocolate curls into the glaze. Serve with unsweetened whipped cream or coffee ice cream.

## CHOCOLATE ROLL

*Serves 12 to 16*

7 eggs, separated
1 cup plus 2 tablespoons sugar
¾ teaspoon vanilla
1 cup sifted all-purpose flour
6 tablespoons best-quality unsweetened
    cocoa powder
1 teaspoon baking powder
¾ teaspoon salt
3 tablespoons milk
¾ teaspoon cream of tartar
Sweetened whipped cream for filling (1½ cups
    heavy cream, whipped)
Confectioners' sugar for sprinkling

Beat the egg yolks, 1 cup of the sugar, and the vanilla until the mixture is pale and forms a ribbon when the beaters are lifted. Sift together the flour, cocoa, baking powder, and salt and add to the egg yolk mixture. Add the milk and beat until smooth. Beat the egg whites with the cream of tartar and the remaining 2 tablespoons of sugar until stiff peaks form. Fold the egg whites into the flour mixture.

    Butter a jelly-roll pan (11 by 17 inches) and line it with wax paper, allowing 3 inches of paper to overhang the ends of the pan. Lightly butter and flour the paper. Pour the batter into the pan and level the top with a spatula. Bake the cake at 350° for approximately 10 minutes, or until a wooden pick comes out dry when inserted in the middle of the cake. Let the cake cool slightly in the pan and then turn the pan upside down onto a clean kitchen towel (not terrycloth). Remove the wax paper and roll the cake in the towel the long way (to make a 17-inch log). Let the cake continue to cool in the towel.

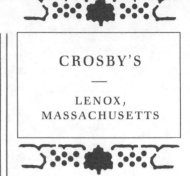

## CROSBY'S

—

### LENOX, MASSACHUSETTS

*Because of the growing popularity of the Berkshires as a resort and retirement area, the catering part of Bobbie Crosby's business has grown tremendously in recent years. Although chocolate roll has been a favorite dessert for generations, this version, by sous-chef Susan Screven, is a frequent choice for local parties.*

When the cake is cool, unroll the towel and spread the cake with a filling of sweetened whipped cream. Roll the cake up. Serve immediately or chill until needed (up to 12 hours). Sprinkle the top with confectioners' sugar just before serving.

NOTE: For a Mexican touch, add 1 teaspoon of cinnamon to the flour.

## CAMPBELL & CO.

—

BOCA RATON, FLORIDA

*When you combine the rich flavor of coffee with the rich flavor of hazelnuts, you are bound to end up with a delectable confection. Please note that one must prepare all but the topping for this grand dessert a day ahead of the special occasion.*

## COFFEE HAZELNUT CAKE

*Serves 10 to 12*

GÉNOISE

5 eggs
1 teaspoon vanilla
⅔ cup sugar
1 tablespoon hot water
1 tablespoon instant coffee powder
1¼ cups sifted all-purpose flour
3 tablespoons clarified butter (see recipe, p. 136)

Using a mixer, beat the eggs, vanilla, and sugar with the whip attachment for 5 to 10 minutes, until the egg-sugar mixture falls from the whip like a ribbon when the whip is lifted from the bowl. Combine the hot water and the instant coffee while the eggs and sugar are beating.

When the egg-sugar mixture is ribbonlike, gently fold in the flour. When it has been incorporated, fold in the butter and coffee. Pour the batter into two greased and floured 8-inch cake pans. Place them in a 350° oven and bake for 30 minutes, or until the top springs back when touched. Remove the pans from the oven and leave the génoise in them for 10 minutes, then turn out onto cooling racks and proceed with the dessert syrup.

DESSERT SYRUP

⅔ cup water
½ cup sugar
1½ tablespoons instant coffee powder

In a saucepan, bring the water and sugar to a boil. Remove the pan from the heat and stir in the instant coffee until it is dissolved. Set the syrup aside to cool while you make the pastry cream.

PASTRY CREAM

3 cups milk
2 teaspoons vanilla
9 egg yolks
1 cup sugar
6 tablespoons cornstarch
1½ tablespoons instant coffee powder
1 cup hazelnuts, roasted and skinned

In a saucepan, scald the milk and vanilla. Using a mixer, combine the egg yolks and sugar and mix with a whip on high speed until the mixture turns a pale yellow. Add the cornstarch and combine well. Gradually add the scalded milk, stirring constantly.

Pour the contents of the mixing bowl into the saucepan and bring them to a boil over high heat, whisking vigorously. Remove the pan from the heat and stir in the instant coffee. Pour the pastry cream into a bowl and spin it over ice until it is cold. Cover and place in the refrigerator.

Remove eight whole hazelnuts from the cup

of hazelnuts and set them aside. Coarsely chop the rest and add them to the pastry cream.

ASSEMBLY

When the génoise has cooled, split each layer in half horizontally. Put one layer on a serving platter and brush it with a fourth of the dessert syrup. Spread a third of the pastry cream on top of that layer and cover with another layer of génoise. Continue until you have four layers of génoise and three layers of pastry cream. (Finish with a layer of génoise brushed with dessert syrup.) Cover and refrigerate overnight.

TOPPING

2 cups heavy cream
¼ cup sugar

The next day, whip the heavy cream, adding the sugar slowly when the cream is half whipped. Continue whipping until the cream is thick.

Remove the cake from the refrigerator and cover the top and sides with the whipped cream. Pipe eight rosettes on top of the outside edge of the cake and place the reserved hazelnuts decoratively on top of the rosettes.

## DATE AND WALNUT CHESS PIE

*Serves 8 to 10*

CRUST

2 cups sifted pastry flour
2 tablespoons sugar
½ teaspoon salt
10 tablespoons butter (1 stick plus 2 tablespoons),
   slightly softened
1 egg yolk
¼ cup cold water
1 tablespoon lemon juice

Sift together the dry ingredients. Cut the butter into small pieces. Combine the egg yolk with the water and stir in the lemon juice. Using two knives or a pastry blender, cut the butter into the flour mixture until it resembles coarse meal. Pour the egg mixture over it and toss together lightly. Cover the dough and refrigerate it for 1 hour.

On a floured surface, roll out the dough to fit a 10-inch tart shell with a removable bottom. The crust will be thicker than most pie crusts. Brush any excess flour off the dough and fit it into the greased shell. Make the crust thickest at the top of the sides. Trim the edges, prick the bottom, and weight it down with dried beans. Bake the crust 5 to 10 minutes in a 350° oven. Remove it from the oven and set it aside to cool slightly.

FILLING

¾ cup (1½ sticks) unsalted butter
1½ cups sugar
3 extra large eggs
1½ teaspoons vanilla
Pinch of salt

METROPOLIS
—
CHICAGO

*Chess pie originated in the South and, it is said, was baked with a latticework crust that made it resemble a chessboard. This modern version of that old-fashioned pie lacks the latticework of the past—its filling makes its own top crust as it bakes—but the old name has been kept all the same.*

1½ cups chopped dates
1 cup chopped walnuts

In the bowl of an electric mixer, cream the butter. Gradually add the sugar while still beating. Add the eggs and beat until incorporated. Mix in the vanilla and salt. Stir in the dates and nuts. Pour the filling into the shell and bake at 350° for 35 to 40 minutes until the filling has set. Cool the pie completely and serve it with whipped cream.

THE CHEF'S
GARDEN AND
TRUFFLES

—

NAPLES,
FLORIDA

## FUDGE WALNUT PIE

*Makes 1 10-inch pie*

3 tablespoons butter
1 pound semisweet chocolate
1⅓ cups light brown sugar
4 eggs
3 tablespoons Sabroso (coffee liqueur)
⅓ cup all-purpose flour
1⅓ cups finely chopped walnuts
½ cup dark corn syrup
1 unbaked 10-inch pie shell

Melt the butter and chocolate in the top of a double boiler over hot water. Cream the sugar and eggs. Add the cooled chocolate mixture to the sugar-egg mixture and add the remaining ingredients, except the pie shell. Pour the mixture into the pie shell and bake at 375° for 50 to 60 minutes.

## PUMPKIN PIE LA TOQUE

*Makes 1 9-inch pie*

PIE

2 large eggs plus 1 yolk
½ cup sugar
2 tablespoons molasses
1 tablespoon ground cardamom
1 teaspoon cinnamon
¼ teaspoon cloves
¼ teaspoon allspice
½ teaspoon nutmeg (omit nutmeg here if you prefer
    freshly grated nutmeg as garnish on the topping)
2 cups cooked, well-drained, and puréed pumpkin
1 cup heavy cream
¼ cup good brandy
¼ cup dark rum
¼ cup Curaçao
1 unbaked 9-inch pie shell, brushed lightly with a
    whipped egg white

Blend the eggs, sugar, molasses, and spices thoroughly. Add the pumpkin, cream, and liquors. Adjust the seasonings. Turn the mixture into the pie shell and bake on the lower shelf of a 450° oven for 10 minutes. Lower the temperature to 400° and continue to bake until a table knife inserted in the middle of the pie comes out clean. Remove the pie from the oven and cool.

TOPPING

1 cup heavy cream
Sugar to taste
1 teaspoon vanilla
A dash each of brandy, dark rum, and Curaçao

Partially whip the cream. Add the sugar, vanilla, and liquors and continue beating till the cream

## THE SPICE CORNER

—

### PHILADELPHIA

*You can hardly turn around in this tiny store, but if you manage to, you will brush against an array of the world's finest seasonings—and five of them are in this pie, along with brandy, dark rum, and Curaçao. For Halloween, Thanksgiving, or Christmas, this is an incomparable pumpkin pie.*

stands in peaks. Smooth the cream on top of the cooled pie and dust, if you like, with freshly grated nutmeg.

## JOHN'S GRAPE PIE

*Serves 6*

PIE

6 tablespoons sugar
2 egg yolks
4 tablespoons unsalted butter, softened
½ to ¾ cup ground pecans
1 baked 8-inch pie crust

Mix the sugar with the egg yolks and beat until light. Beat in the butter. Blend in the nuts. Pour the filling into the baked crust and bake the pie at 350° until it is golden brown and the filling is set, about 10 minutes.

GLAZE

¼ cup rum or Grand Marnier
½ cup apricot preserves
Enough seedless grapes to cover the surface
    of the filling

Combine the liquor and the preserves in a food processor. When the pie comes out of the oven, arrange the grapes, whole or halved lengthwise, as you choose, in a single layer. Work from the outside edge of the pie, going around in circles into the center.

Brush the apricot-liquor mixture over all the grapes and the entire pie filling. Chill the pie in the refrigerator until time to serve it. Incidentally, the pie may look skimpy, but it's very rich.

### ADELAIDE'S CARRY-OUT CUISINE

—

ATLANTA

*The pecans give a crunchiness, the alcohol a headiness to this beautiful creation by John H. Wilson, Jr. It bears only the faintest resemblance to an old-fashioned Southern pecan pie.*

## BRANDIED PEACH AND MACAROON STRUDEL

*Serves 6*

3 large firm peaches
3 tablespoons sugar
3 tablespoons good-quality brandy or Amaretto
8 sheets phyllo dough
½ cup (1 stick) melted butter
Up to ½ cup additional sugar
½ cup dry toasted breadcrumbs
¾ cup crumbled and toasted macaroons

Drop the peaches into almost-boiling water for 30 seconds to loosen the skin. Remove peaches from the water and peel away the skin, using a sharp knife. Slice the peaches. Place the slices in a bowl and sprinkle with the 3 tablespoons of sugar and the brandy or Amaretto. Let stand for at least 30 minutes.

Place the phyllo dough, one sheet at a time, on a dry towel. Put one sheet down and brush with melted butter. Place the next sheet slightly overlapping the first at the edge farthest from you. Sprinkle the sheets with sugar, bread-crumbs, and macaroons. Place two more sheets over the first two, this time joining them vertically. Butter the sheets and again sprinkle with sugar, breadcrumbs, and macaroons. Make two more layers, alternating the horizontal and vertical seams to prevent the juices from seeping out.

Drain the peaches, reserving the juice. Place the slices in a line about 4 inches up from the bottom of the strudel leaves. Sprinkle with the remaining macaroon crumbs and breadcrumbs. Drizzle with any leftover butter and some of the brandied peach juice. Fold the sides over the ends of the peach line to prevent the fruit from falling out during the rolling of the strudel or the baking. Starting at the edge nearest you, roll the

## THE ELEGANT PICNIC

—

### LENOX, MASSACHUSETTS

*This dessert can have endless variations, depending on what fruits are in season. At The Elegant Picnic, the variations begin in early June with strawberry rhubarb strudel. Next come the apricot, nectarine, and cherry strudels of July, this all-time favorite peach version in August, and of course the proverbial apple strudel in September and October. There is a farm near Lenox that provides a Devon-thick cream to go with it. For the rest of us, crème fraîche will taste almost the same.*

strudel away from you. Transfer the strudel to a buttered baking sheet or jelly-roll pan and bake at 350° for 20 to 25 minutes, or until the top is golden brown. The strudel may run a bit, and it will run a great deal if overcooked, so watch carefully. Serve warm, sprinkled with confectioners' sugar. Pass heavy cream or *crème fraîche*.

## THE GOODIE SHOPPE

—

LANCASTER, PENNSYLVANIA

*Ever since The Goodie Shoppe held forth in the living room of former high school home economics teacher Jackie Parker, English Lemon Tarts have been one of the most popular items sold. Though the recipe sounds as if it makes a lot, no one is ever satisfied with just one, and they disappear faster than you can imagine.*

## ENGLISH LEMON TARTS

*Makes 4 to 5 dozen*

PASTRY

2 cups all-purpose flour
½ cup sugar
Grated rind of 1 lemon
¾ cup butter
3 egg yolks (or 4 if the dough seems too dry)

Mix the flour, sugar, and rind in a bowl or food processor. Cut in the butter with two knives, a pastry blender, or the short on-off motions of the food processor. Add the yolks one at a time, mixing until the dough clings together.

Roll the pastry ⅛ inch thick and fit it into greased tart tins or cut it into 2-inch circles and fit it over upside-down cupcake pans to form shallow tart bases. (The shells should be no more than ½ inch deep.) If the pastry tears, press it together to patch it. Bake the shells at 375° for 12 minutes, or until they are lightly browned. Cool.

ENGLISH LEMON CURD

5 eggs
2 cups sugar
½ cup plus 2 tablespoons melted butter
Grated rind and juice of 2 lemons

In the top of a double boiler, beat the eggs well and add the sugar gradually, beating as you add. Add the remaining ingredients and mix well. Cook over hot water, stirring constantly, until thick. Chill.

Using a pastry bag or a spoon, fill the tart shells with the lemon curd. Sift confectioners' sugar over the tops of the tarts, if you like, and garnish with candied violet petals.

## GEORGIA PECAN PEACH TART

*Makes 1 9-inch tart*

CRUST

½ cup (1 stick) chilled butter
3 tablespoons chilled vegetable shortening
2 cups all-purpose flour
1 egg yolk
2 tablespoons sugar
Pinch of salt
4 tablespoons ice water

Blend the butter, vegetable shortening, and flour in a food processor or with two knives or a pastry blender until it resembles cornmeal. Add the egg yolk, sugar, salt, and ice water and blend just until the dough forms a ball. Wrap it in plastic wrap and store in the refrigerator until cool, about 1 hour. Then roll out the dough and lay it in a greased 9-inch tart pan.

FILLING

½ cup apricot jam
4 cups peeled and sliced fresh peaches

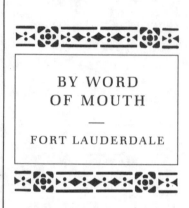

BY WORD
OF MOUTH
—
FORT LAUDERDALE

*What could be more Georgian than succulent peaches and crisp pecans?*

6 tablespoons sugar
1 tablespoon lemon juice

Spread the tart shell with the jam. Then add the peaches, mixed with the sugar and lemon juice. Bake at 400° for 20 to 30 minutes. Baste with the juice from the fruit during the baking.

TOPPING

3 egg yolks
4 tablespoons sugar
4 tablespoons ground pecans
3 tablespoons heavy cream
½ cup chopped pecans

Beat the egg yolks and sugar until the yolks are pale yellow. Add the ground pecans and heavy cream and beat thoroughly. Pour the mixture over the peaches and bake at 350° for about 20 minutes, until the topping is well puffed. Sprinkle the tart with the chopped pecans during the last 5 minutes of baking.

## FRENCH APPLE CUSTARD TART

*Makes 1 12-inch tart*

CRUST

1⅔ cups all-purpose flour
2 tablespoons sugar
½ teaspoon salt
¾ cup (1½ sticks) butter
1 egg
2 teaspoons milk

Place the flour, sugar, and salt in the bowl of a food processor. Add the butter and process until the mixture resembles coarse meal. Add the egg and the milk and process until the mixture forms a ball. Let the dough rest for 1 hour. Roll it out and place it in a 12-inch tart ring. Set aside.

FILLING

¾ cup sugar
3 tablespoons cornstarch
Dash of salt
4 to 5 egg yolks, depending upon size of eggs
2 cups milk
2 tablespoons butter
1 teaspoon vanilla
3 tablespoons apple brandy
½ teaspoon cinnamon
¼ teaspoon nutmeg
6 large Granny Smith apples
Cinnamon sugar
Apricot glaze (see recipe, page 315)

To make the pastry cream, make a paste of the sugar, cornstarch, salt, and egg yolks. Heat the milk until boiling. Add the paste to the milk, stirring constantly. Continue stirring until the mix-

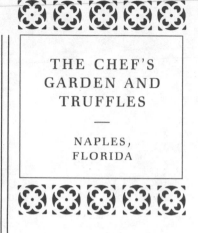

THE CHEF'S
GARDEN AND
TRUFFLES

—

NAPLES,
FLORIDA

*The Chef's Garden is a popular lunch spot in the elegant Third Street shopping area of Naples. For simpler fare and dishes to take home, there is the café upstairs, Truffles.*

ture reaches pudding consistency. Remove from the heat and add the butter, vanilla, apple brandy, cinnamon, and nutmeg. Pour the pastry cream into the tart shell.

Peel and thinly slice the apples. Arrange the slices in concentric circles over the pastry cream and sprinkle them with cinnamon sugar. Bake the tart at 375° for 30 to 45 minutes, or until the top is brown and the apples are tender. Brush with apricot glaze. Serve the tart warm or cool.

## PRUNE PLUM TART

*Serves 6*

½ cup sugar
½ cup (1 stick) unsalted butter
1 egg
1 teaspoon vanilla
1¼ to 1¾ cups all-purpose flour
½ teaspoon baking powder
1½ to 2 pounds prune plums
1 to 3 tablespoons sugar for sprinkling on top

Combine the sugar and butter in a medium-size bowl. Add the egg and vanilla and beat until smooth. Add 1 cup of flour, mixed with the baking powder, and continue adding flour until the dough is no longer sticky to the touch. Press the dough into an 8- or 9-inch springform pan. Cover the pan and refrigerate the dough overnight.

Cut the prune plums in half lengthwise and remove the pits. Make a small slit at each end of each half and place the halves on the crust, skin side up. Press lightly so that the plums lie flat in the crust. Sprinkle the prune plums lightly with the sugar and bake at 350° for 1 to 1¼ hours, until the crust is golden and the plums are soft. Serve at room temperature.

## DANISH PUFF

*Makes 48 pieces*

PASTRY

½ cup (1 stick) butter
1 cup all-purpose flour
2 tablespoons water

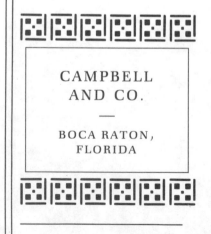

Cut the butter into the flour. Sprinkle with the water and mix, but do not overhandle. Divide the dough in half and pat into two strips, 12 by 2 inches each, on a baking sheet.

### PÂTE À CHOUX

½ cup (1 stick) butter
1 cup water
1 teaspoon almond extract
1 cup all-purpose flour
3 eggs

Bring the butter, water, and almond extract to a rolling boil. Add the flour and stir it until it forms a ball. Remove from the heat and beat in the eggs one at a time. Spread the mixture over the two strips of pastry. Bake at 350° until crisp and browned (about 40 minutes). Cool.

### ALMOND BUTTER CREAM

6 tablespoons butter
2 cups confectioners' sugar
Milk as needed
1½ teaspoons almond extract
½ cup sliced almonds

Cream the butter and the sugar. Add enough milk to obtain an icing of spreading consistency. Add the almond extract and combine until well blended. Frost the top of the cooled *pâte à choux* and sprinkle it with almonds. Cut each strip in half lengthwise and then into 12 pieces crosswise.

## PECAN DACQUOISE WITH BLUEBERRY FOOL

*Serves 8*

PECAN DACQUOISE

**1 cup pecans**
**½ cup sugar**
**¾ cup confectioners' sugar**
**3½ tablespoons milk**
**6 large egg whites, at room temperature**
**¼ teaspoon cream of tartar**
**½ cup plus 2 tablespoons superfine sugar**

Using a 9-inch cake pan as a guide, trace two circles on sheets of parchment paper and place the pieces of paper on buttered baking sheets, with any pencil or pen marks facing down. Smooth out the paper.

In a food processor, chop the pecans until they are fine but not oily. Add the ½ cup sugar and process until the nuts are almost powdered, but again not oily. In a medium-size mixing bowl, combine the nut mixture with the confectioners' sugar and the milk. Beat the egg whites with an electric mixer until they are foamy. Add the cream of tartar and continue beating until the whites are stiff and begin to slide around the edge of the bowl. While beating, gradually add the superfine sugar. Continue beating until the whites are glossy. Mix one large spoonful of egg whites into the nut mixture, then fold the remaining whites into the nuts.

Fill a pastry bag with a #9 plain tip with the meringue mixture and pipe a continuous spiral, starting in the middle of a parchment circle. Repeat with the second circle. Place both baking sheets in a 300° oven and bake for approximately 30 minutes, or until the dacquoise is lightly

THE
KITCHEN DOOR
AT ABIGAIL'S

—

WEST FALMOUTH,
MASSACHUSETTS

*There is no more heavenly dessert than a dacquoise, and the blueberry fool adds a nice New England touch. If you like your meringue layers crisp, assemble the dacquoise just before serving.*

browned. Lower the temperature to 275° and bake until the meringues are completely dry and crisp. (Gently lift off the edge of the parchment paper; if the underside is soft to the touch, the meringues aren't done.) The total baking time will be as long as 2 hours. Remove the meringues from the oven and let cool.

### BLUEBERRY FOOL

**2 pints blueberries**
**Rind and juice of 1 lemon**
**½ cup sugar**
**1½ cups heavy cream**

Rinse and clean the blueberries one pint at a time. The first pint should be placed in a non-reactive pan with the lemon juice, rind, and sugar. Cook until the berries burst. Remove from the heat and cool thoroughly. Whip the cream until it holds a shape. Fold the cooked blueberries into the whipped cream. Then add about half the second pint of blueberries and fold together.

### ASSEMBLY

Place a dab of blueberry fool on a cake plate to anchor the dacquoise. Invert the meringue layers, peel off the parchment paper, place one of the layers on the dab, and press lightly. Place about two thirds of the fool on the meringue and spread it almost to the edges. Cover with the inverted second meringue. Spread the remaining blueberry fool on the top of the dacquoise and garnish with the remaining uncooked blueberries.

## MOUSSES AND PUDDINGS

Hazelnut Chocolate Mousse
White Chocolate Mousse
Peach Mousse
Raspberry Mousse
Candace's Zabaglione with a Twist
Strawberry Sabayon
Amaretto Bread Pudding
Arborio Rice Pudding
Tiramisu
Floating Islands with Fresh Strawberries
Strawberries with Balsamic Vinegar
Orange-Marinated Strawberries
Orange Yogurt
Grapefruit Sorbet

## THE SILVER PALATE

—

### NEW YORK CITY

*In 1977, when The Silver Palate was launched, the shop was a bright spot on a less-than-elegant city street. Columbus Avenue has spruced up considerably since then, and Sheila Lukins and Julee Rosso are still creating gems, such as this winning blend of chocolate and hazelnuts.*

## HAZELNUT CHOCOLATE MOUSSE

*Serves 8*

1½ pounds semisweet chocolate
1 cup Frangelico
4 egg yolks
1 cup chilled heavy cream
¼ cup sugar
8 egg whites
Pinch of salt
1 cup (¼ pound) finely chopped hazelnuts (reserve several whole nuts for garnish)

Melt the chocolate in a heavy saucepan over very low heat. Gradually add the Frangelico. Stir well, remove the pan from the heat, and let the mixture cool to room temperature. When the chocolate is cool, add the egg yolks, one at a time, stirring thoroughly after each addition.

In a chilled bowl, whip the cream until it begins to thicken. Add the sugar and continue to whip until the cream is just stiff. In another bowl beat the egg whites with the salt until stiff peaks form. Fold the egg whites gently into the cream. Fold one third of the cream mixture into the chocolate. Then add the remaining cream mixture to the lightened chocolate base. Gently fold to blend, adding the chopped hazelnuts.

Place the mousse in a serving bowl and refrigerate for at least 2 hours, until set. Garnish the top of the mousse with the whole hazelnuts.

NOTE: The mousse may also be frozen and removed from the freezer a half hour before serving.

## WHITE CHOCOLATE MOUSSE

*Serves 8 to 10*

¾ cup (1½ sticks) unsalted butter
12 ounces white chocolate, grated
5 eggs, separated
½ cup sugar

Melt the butter in a small saucepan. Melt the white chocolate in the top of a double boiler over hot water. Beat the butter and chocolate together with an electric mixer. Add the egg yolks one at a time. The mixture will loosen and separate at first, but continue to beat until it reaches a very thick consistency.

Beat the egg whites in a separate bowl, adding the sugar gradually until the meringue appears soft and glossy peaks form. Fold the meringue into the chocolate. Spoon the mousse into individual *pots de crème* or a large serving dish. Cover and chill. When ready to serve, decorate the mousse with fresh flowers and/or raspberries, or serve with a warm chocolate sauce flavored with Grand Marnier or Framboise.

### TRUFFLES

—

MARBLEHEAD,
MASSACHUSETTS

*White chocolate is a mixture of cocoa butter, sugar, vanillin, and other flavorings, and in its "natural" state it tastes like a mild and sweet milk chocolate. Although technically not really chocolate, since it contains no chocolate liquor, it has become popular for dipping fruits and making cakes and mousses.*

*Situated on Connecticut Avenue near busy Dupont Circle, Suzanne's is popular with the young professionals of the area who pass by—and stop in—on their way to and from work. At Suzanne's they pick up cheeses, pâtés, pastries, pasta dishes, salads, and desserts.*

## PEACH MOUSSE

*Serves 4 to 6*

4 medium peaches, peeled and pitted
¾ cup heavy cream
1 envelope unflavored gelatin
¼ cup light rum
¼ cup sugar
¼ cup cold water
2 egg whites
Peach slices for garnish

Purée the peaches in a blender or food processor. Set aside. Whip the heavy cream until it makes medium-stiff peaks, then refrigerate it.

Place the gelatin in a small bowl with the rum until it has softened. Heat the mixture in the top of a double boiler until it is completely dissolved. Add the gelatin mixture to the peach purée, stirring well.

Mix the sugar and water in a very small saucepan. Cook it over high heat, covered, until it boils. Remove the cover and continue cooking until the mixture reaches 240° on a candy thermometer.

As the sugar is heating, whip the egg whites to a stiff meringue. When the sugar reaches 240°, pour the cooked sugar in a steady stream into the egg whites, whipping the whites at the same time. Fold this mixture into the peach pulp with a whip. Fold in the reserved whipped cream with a rubber spatula. Spoon the mousse into stemmed glasses or chocolate cups. Chill well. Garnish with peach slices.

## RASPBERRY MOUSSE

*Serves 8 to 10*

1 pint fresh raspberries, or 1 10-ounce package
    frozen whole raspberries, without syrup, thawed
1 envelope unflavored gelatin
¼ cup vermouth
¼ cup sugar
2 cups heavy cream, whipped

Purée the raspberries in a blender or food processor until they are smooth. Sprinkle the gelatin
over the vermouth and let it soften and dissolve.
Add the gelatin-vermouth mixture and the sugar
to the raspberries and cook the mixture slowly,
stirring occasionally, until the sugar is dissolved
and the mixture is almost at a boil. Remove the
pot from the heat and set aside until the purée is
completely cool. Then fold in the whipped
cream, place the mixture in a serving bowl, and
refrigerate until set.

## CANDACE'S ZABAGLIONE WITH
## A TWIST

*Serves 8*

10 egg yolks, at room temperature
½ cup sugar
½ cup Marsala wine
2 tablespoons Grand Marnier
½ cup dry white wine
1 pint fresh fruit (peaches and raspberries
    if possible)

Beat the egg yolks and sugar in a bowl with a
wire whisk, or an electric mixer set at high speed,

**CAMARGO
COOKING
COMPANY
AND CAFÉ**

—

CINCINNATI

*If you are looking for an
easy-to-make, attractive
dessert, in or out of
raspberry season, here is
the perfect choice.*

**TRUFFLES**

—

MARBLEHEAD,
MASSACHUSETTS

*The twist in this recipe is
the addition of white wine
and Grand Marnier. The
proportions are different
from those of the classic
version, too.*

for 3 to 5 minutes or until thick and a light lemon color. Add the Marsala, Grand Marnier, and white wine 1 tablespoon at a time, beating well after each addition. Place the bowl over a pan of simmering water and beat until the mixture has doubled in volume and has the consistency of custard. Serve the custard warm or cold over fresh fruit—in a goblet for the best effect.

LEONARDI'S
INTERNATIONAL,
INC.

—

FORT LAUDERDALE

*If you have no strawberries, raspberries will do—or blueberries or peaches—in this refreshing summer dessert.*

## STRAWBERRY SABAYON

*Serves 6*

8 egg yolks
½ cup Amaretto
¼ cup cream sherry
¼ cup dry Marsala wine
½ cup sugar
¾ cup heavy cream
1 quart strawberries

Bring water to a boil in the bottom of a double boiler. Place the egg yolks, liquors, and sugar in the top of the boiler. Over low heat, whip the mixture for 6 to 8 minutes until it is thick and custardy. Remove the pan from the heat.

Whip the heavy cream until it is stiff and soft peaks form. Put both the custard mixture and the whipped cream, in their separate containers, into the refrigerator for 1 hour. Remove them from the refrigerator and fold them together. Put a layer of the sauce in the bottom of each of six champagne glasses. Top with the fruit, then with more of the sauce. Serve cold.

## AMARETTO BREAD PUDDING

*Serves 8 to 10*

1 loaf challah bread with poppy seeds
4 cups half-and-half
3 eggs
1½ cups sugar
2 tablespoons almond extract
¾ cup golden raisins
¾ cup sliced almonds
2 tablespoons unsalted butter, at room temperature

AMARETTO SAUCE

½ cup (1 stick) unsalted butter, at room
    temperature
1 cup confectioners' sugar
1 egg, well beaten
4 tablespoons Amaretto

Break the bread into small pieces and place it in a medium-size bowl. Cover the bread with the half-and-half and let the mixture stand, covered, for an hour. In a small bowl, beat together the eggs, sugar, and almond extract. When the challah is ready, stir the egg mixture into the bread mixture. Gently fold in the raisins and almonds. Pour the mixture into a 9-by-13-inch baking dish buttered with the 2 tablespoons of butter. Set the dish on the middle rack of a 325° oven and bake for 50 minutes, or until the top is golden. Remove the pudding from the oven and let it cool.

Prepare the sauce by first stirring together the butter and sugar in the top of a double boiler set over simmering water. Stir constantly until the mixture has dissolved and is very hot. Remove the pan from the heat. Whisk the egg into the butter mixture. Continue whisking until the sauce has come to room temperature, then add the Amaretto.

THE SILVER
PALATE
—
NEW YORK CITY

*Bread pudding is often associated with the comforts of childhood. Adding golden raisins, sliced almonds, and Amaretto to a challah base puts a spin on this dessert that more sophisticated palates will surely enjoy.*

To serve, cut the pudding into 8 or 10 squares and place them on a decorative ovenproof serving dish. Spoon Amaretto sauce over the squares of pudding and place the dish under the broiler until the sauce bubbles. Serve immediately.

## ARBORIO RICE PUDDING

*Serves 6 to 8*

6 cups milk
½ vanilla bean, broken into 3 pieces
1 cup arborio rice
Zest and juice of 1 orange
¼ cup sugar
3 egg yolks
½ cup half-and-half
⅛ teaspoon nutmeg for garnish

In a heavy nonaluminum pan, bring the milk and vanilla bean to a boil, being careful that the milk does not scorch. Add the rice, return the mixture to a boil, and simmer for 50 minutes, stirring occasionally.

In a bowl, combine the orange zest and juice, sugar, egg yolks, and half-and-half. When the rice is cooked, stir in the orange-egg mixture and heat to a boil, stirring constantly. Remove the vanilla bean and pour the pudding into a bowl. Serve warm or chill for 2 hours. Sprinkle the top with nutmeg before serving.

INDIANA
MARKET &
CATERING

—

NEW YORK CITY

*Arborio is an Italian rice customarily used for risotto, but its starchiness lends a special creamy quality to rice pudding. If it is unavailable, regular white rice may be substituted.*

## TIRAMISU

*Serves 12*

24 ladyfingers, toasted in a 375° oven for 15 minutes
2 cups espresso coffee, cooled
6 eggs, separated
3 to 6 tablespoons sugar, to taste
1 pound *mascarpone*
2 tablespoons Marsala wine
2 tablespoons Triple Sec
2 tablespoons brandy
2 tablespoons orange extract
8 ounces bittersweet chocolate, finely chopped

Arrange the ladyfingers on a plate and lightly soak them with the cooled espresso. Put half of the soaked ladyfingers in one layer in a rectangular serving dish. While the ladyfingers are soaking, beat the egg yolks with the sugar until the yolks turn pale in color. Add the *mascarpone*, the liquors, and the extract, and stir gently.

In a separate bowl, beat the egg whites with a wire whisk until they are stiff. Gently fold the whites into the *mascarpone* mixture.

Use half of this mixture to make a layer on top of the ladyfingers in the serving dish. Sprinkle with half of the chopped chocolate. Repeat the procedure with another layer of soaked ladyfingers, the *mascarpone* mixture, and chocolate. Cover with tin foil and refrigerate for at least 1 hour before serving.

## BALDUCCI'S
—
NEW YORK CITY

Tiramisu *means pick-me-up. This rich, creamy pudding with brandy, Triple Sec, and Marsala surely is that. Its special ingredient, however, is* mascarpone, *a soft, delicate, and perishable white Italian cheese.*

### CARAMELIZED SUGAR

Slowly heat 1 cup of sugar in a heavy saucepan until it turns to a medium-brown syrup. Be careful not to let the sugar burn. Use it while it's hot.

## FLOATING ISLANDS WITH FRESH STRAWBERRIES

*Serves 8*

8 eggs, separated
1½ cups sugar
2 cups milk
2 cups heavy cream
2 tablespoons Triple Sec or Cointreau
1 quart strawberries
1 cup caramelized sugar (see recipe)

Beat the egg whites until foamy, then gradually add 1 cup of the sugar. Beat until very stiff peaks form and set aside.

In a pan of large diameter, slowly heat the milk, cream, liqueur, and the remaining ½ cup sugar. Bring the mixture just to the boiling point and maintain at a "feeble" boil. Spoon portions of the meringue (about the size and shape of a large egg) into the simmering milk mixture, using two spoons. Poach the meringues for about 4 minutes on one side, then turn and poach for another 2 minutes. With a slotted spoon, remove the meringues to a dry cloth and let them drain.

When all the meringues are cooked, strain the milk through cheesecloth or a fine sieve. Beat the egg yolks and gradually add the hot milk, whisking continuously. Stir over low heat until the mixture is custardlike and will coat a wooden spoon. Let cool.

Slice the strawberries into a large serving bowl or into individual serving glasses. Top with the custard and float meringues on top.

Prepare the caramelized sugar and, working quickly, drizzle it over the meringues and custard.

## STRAWBERRIES WITH BALSAMIC VINEGAR

*Serves 4 to 6*

1 quart fresh strawberries
2 tablespoons balsamic vinegar
1 teaspoon freshly ground pepper (ground fine)
1 scant tablespoon sugar

Carefully brush strawberries to remove dirt, and cut away stems. Place the cleaned berries in a serving dish. Sprinkle with vinegar and gently toss. Add the pepper and sugar and gently toss again. Allow the fruit to rest for about half an hour before serving.

## ORANGE-MARINATED STRAWBERRIES

*Serves 6*

1 quart ripe strawberries
¼ cup Cointreau
1 tablespoon minced orange zest
¼ teaspoon cinnamon
1 cup heavy cream
¼ cup grated bittersweet chocolate

Quarter the strawberries, if they are large, and toss them gently with the Cointreau, orange zest, and cinnamon. Let the berries marinate for about 15 minutes. Meanwhile, whip the cream until soft peaks form. Spoon the strawberries into six

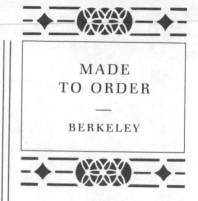

## MADE TO ORDER

—

### BERKELEY

*Silvana La Rocca, owner of Made to Order, comes by this recipe naturally since she was born in Italy, high in the Apennine mountains. Your family and friends are sure to be intrigued by this unusual and refreshing combination of flavors.*

## FROM GRAPES TO NUTS

—

### BAINBRIDGE, OHIO

*Here is an easy dessert that is as satisfying as the most elaborate French pastry, with slightly fewer calories. It looks especially elegant served in champagne glasses.*

dishes or champagne glasses, add a dollop of whipped cream, and top each serving with grated chocolate.

## BAREFOOT CONTESSA
—
### EAST HAMPTON, LONG ISLAND

*Trading a conventional, even high-powered career for nearly round-the-clock duty in the specialty food business is hardly unusual these days. Ina Garten was a White House budget analyst specializing in nuclear energy policy when she spotted an ad for a business for sale on Long Island, drove up from Washington that weekend, and decided to take over Barefoot Contessa.*

## ORANGE YOGURT

*Serves 2 or 3*

2 cups plain yogurt
⅓ cup raisins, plumped in hot water
6 tablespoons honey
1½ teaspoons grated orange rind
Juice of ¼ orange
Scant ¼ teaspoon nutmeg
Scant ½ teaspoon cinnamon
⅓ cup coarsely chopped walnuts

Drain the yogurt in a colander lined with cheese-cloth for 2 hours. Move the yogurt to a medium-size bowl and add the remaining ingredients. Combine well. Chill and serve on its own, or use as a sauce for fresh fruit.

## GRAPEFRUIT SORBET

*Serves 4 to 6*

1¾ ounces sugar cubes (about 20)
3 to 4 large grapefruits, at room temperature
¼ cup sugar
Juice of ½ lemon
½ teaspoon white corn syrup

Rub each side of the sugar cubes on the skin of a grapefruit, to extract some of the oils, rubbing just hard enough to color the cubes. Cut the grapefruits in half and squeeze enough juice to get 2 cups plus 2 tablespoons after the juice has been strained. (The grapefruits will yield more juice at room temperature than if they are chilled.)

Combine the sugar cubes and granulated sugar with the grapefruit and lemon juices and stir well. Set aside until the sugar dissolves. Add the corn syrup. Pour the mixture into an ice cream machine and follow the manufacturer's instructions.

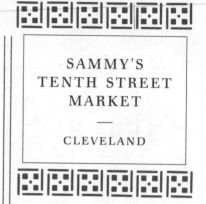

SAMMY'S
TENTH STREET
MARKET
—
CLEVELAND

*The Tenth Street Market is known for its delicious ice creams and sorbets, made completely from scratch and in very small quantities. You can recreate their top quality at home, using one of the many ice cream machines available in every price range. This sorbet works well as a light dessert, or as a "palate cleanser" between courses.*

## THE SHOPS AND THEIR ADDRESSES

Many of these shops operate at more than one location. We have listed only the main address and telephone number for each shop here.

*Adelaide's Carry-Out Cuisine*
(404) 843-3401

3209 Paces Ferry Place
Atlanta, Georgia 30305

*The American Café*
(202) 337-4264

1219 Wisconsin Avenue, N.W.
Washington, D.C. 20007

*An Apple a Day*
(312) 835-2620

691 Vernon Avenue
Glencoe, Illinois 60022

*Balducci's*
(212) 673-2600

424 Avenue of the Americas
New York, New York 10011

*Barefoot Contessa*
(516) 324-0240

46 Newtown Lane
East Hampton, New York 11937

*J. Bildner & Sons*
(617) 267-1040

60 Massachusetts Avenue
Boston, Massachusetts 02115

*Bon Appétit*
(404) 231-3813

2391 Peachtree Road
Atlanta, Georgia 30305

*Bond & Burkhart*
(617) 965-8650

47 Langley Road
Newton Centre, Massachusetts 02159

*brusseau's*
(206) 774-4166

Fifth and Dayton
Edmonds, Washington 98020

*By Word of Mouth*
(305) 564-3663

3200 Northeast 12th Avenue
Fort Lauderdale, Florida 33334

*Café Express*
(713) 963-9222

1415 South Post Oak Lane
Houston, Texas 77056

*Café 21*
(804) 625-4218

742-G West 21st Street
Norfolk, Virginia 23517

*Caffè Quadro*
(415) 398-1777

180 Pacific
San Francisco, California 94111

*Camargo Cooking Company and Café*
(513) 381-5999

49 East Fourth Street
Cincinnati, Ohio 45202

*Campbell and Co.*
(305) 368-2772

3850 Northwest 2nd Avenue
Boca Raton, Florida 33431

| | |
|---|---|
| *The Chef's Garden and Truffles*<br>(813) 262-5500 | 1300 Third Street, S.<br>Naples, Florida 33939 |
| *The Chef's Market*<br>(215) 925-8360 | 231 South Street<br>Philadelphia, Pennsylvania 19147 |
| *Chez Nous Charcuterie*<br>(504) 899-7303 | 5701 Magazine Street<br>New Orleans, Louisiana 70115 |
| *Christin's Charcuterie*<br>(617) 237-6995 | 555 Washington Street<br>Wellesley, Massachusetts 02181 |
| *Convito Italiano*<br>(312) 943-2983 | 11 East Chestnut Street<br>Chicago, Illinois 60611 |
| *The Cookery*<br>(216) 650-1665 | 140 North Main Street<br>Hudson, Ohio 44236 |
| *Cranberry Hill*<br>(201) 746-1331 | 32A Church Street<br>Montclair, New Jersey 07042 |
| *Crosby's*<br>(413) 637-3396 | 62 Church Street<br>Lenox, Massachusetts 01240 |
| *Culinary Capers*<br>(401) 272-0458 | 335 Wickenden Street<br>Providence, Rhode Island 02906 |
| *Culinary Hearts Bakery Café*<br>(201) 753-6961 | 51 Mount Bethel Road<br>Warren, New Jersey 07060 |
| *D'Angelo*<br>(215) 923-5637 | 909 South 9th Street<br>Philadelphia, Pennsylvania 19147 |
| *DDL Foodshow*<br>(213) 859-7741 | 244 North Beverly Drive<br>Beverly Hills, California 90210 |
| *Eichelbaum & Co.*<br>(415) 929-9030 | 2417 California Street<br>San Francisco, California 94115 |
| *The Elegant Picnic*<br>(413) 637-1621 | The Curtis<br>Walker Street<br>Lenox, Massachusetts 01240 |
| *Fernando's International Food Market*<br>(305) 566-3104 | 3045 North Federal Highway<br>Fort Lauderdale, Florida 33306 |
| *Fête Accomplie*<br>(202) 363-9511 | 3714 Macomb Street, N.W.<br>Washington, D.C. 20016 |
| *Fettuccine Bros.*<br>(415) 441-2281 | 2100 Larkin Street<br>San Francisco, California 94109 |
| *Fisher & Levy*<br>(212) 832-3880 | 1026 2nd Avenue<br>New York, New York 10022 |
| *Firehouse No. 4*<br>(304) 345-8080 | 1604 Washington Street, E.<br>Charleston, West Virginia 25311 |

The Shops and Their Addresses

| | |
|---|---|
| *The Fishmonger*<br>(617) 661-4834 | 252 Huron Avenue<br>Cambridge, Massachusetts 02138 |
| *Formaggio Kitchen*<br>(617) 354-4750 | 244 Huron Avenue<br>Cambridge, Massachusetts 02138 |
| *Foodworks*<br>(312) 348-7801 | 1002 West Diversey<br>Chicago, Illinois 60614 |
| *From Grapes to Nuts*<br>(216) 543-3036 | 8300 East Washington Street<br>Chagrin Falls, Ohio 44022 |
| *Gerard's*<br>(215) 238-1226 | 730 South Street<br>Philadelphia, Pennsylvania 19147 |
| *The Goodie Shoppe*<br>(717) 393-3923 | 302 West Chestnut Street<br>Lancaster, Pennsylvania 17603 |
| *Goodies to Go*<br>(617) 863-1704 | 1734 Massachusetts Avenue<br>Lexington, Massachusetts 02173 |
| *Good Taste*<br>(718) 858-0028 | 198 Henry Street<br>Brooklyn, New York 11201 |
| *Gourmet Pasta*<br>(516) 621-0002 | 1 Albertson Avenue<br>Albertson, New York 11507 |
| *Graham Catering Company*<br>(713) 526-0793 | 515 Alabama<br>Houston, Texas 77224 |
| *The Grapevine Wine and Cheese Shop*<br>(305) 475-1357 | 256 South University Drive<br>Fort Lauderdale, Florida 33324 |
| *The Green Grocer*<br>(804) 625-2455 | 723 West 21st Street<br>Norfolk, Virginia 23517 |
| *Gretchen's of Course*<br>(206) 623-8194 | 909 University<br>Seattle, Washington 98101 |
| *The Groaning Board*<br>(202) 337-5084 | 1618 Wisconsin Avenue, N.W.<br>Washington, D.C. 20007 |
| *Indiana Market & Catering*<br>(212) 505-7290 | 80 Second Avenue<br>New York, New York 10003 |
| *Jim Jamail & Sons Food Market*<br>(713) 523-5535 | 3114 Kirby Drive<br>Houston, Texas 77098 |
| *The Kitchen Door at Abigail's*<br>(617) 540-8682 | Route 28A, West Falmouth Square<br>West Falmouth, Massachusetts 02574 |
| *La Prima*<br>(202) 466-4316 | 1050 Connecticut Avenue, N.W.<br>Washington, D.C. 20036 |
| *Leonardi's International, Inc.*<br>(305) 772-3710 | 2861 East Commercial Boulevard<br>Fort Lauderdale, Florida 33308 |

*Le St. Germain to Go*
(213) 859-7778

5955 Melrose Avenue
Los Angeles, California 90038

*Let's Eat*
(415) 388-7800

1 Blackfield Drive
Tiburon, California 94920

*Made to Order*
(415) 524-7552

1576 Hopkins Street
Berkeley, California 94707

*Magazine Cuisine*
(504) 899-9453

3242 Magazine Street
New Orleans, Louisiana 70115

*Marion Cheese*
(717) 392-4237

37 East Orange Street
Lancaster, Pennsylvania 17602

*The Market of the
Commissary*
(215) 568-8055

130 South 17th Street
Philadelphia, Pennsylvania 19103

*Le Marmiton*
(213) 393-7716

1327 Montana Avenue
Santa Monica, California 90403

*Marty's*
(214) 526-4070

3316 Oak Lawn Avenue
Dallas, Texas 75219

*Massimo da Milano*
(214) 351-1426

5519 West Lovers Lane
Dallas, Texas 75209

*Matters of Taste*
(404) 231-3173

3173 Roswell Road, N.E.
Atlanta, Georgia 30305

*Metropolis*
(312) 642-2130

163 West North Avenue
Chicago, Illinois 60610

*Mirabelle*
(214) 528-7589

74 Highland Park Village
Dallas, Texas 75205

*Mitchell Cobey Cuisine*
(312) 944-3411

100 East Walton
Chicago, Illinois 60611

*Monticello Gourmet*
(202) 342-5429

4816 MacArthur Boulevard, N.W.
Washington, D.C. 20007

*Morningside Café*
(713) 527-0398

5555 Morningside Drive
Houston, Texas 77005

*Movable Feast*
(202) 966-1657

5504 Connecticut Avenue, N.W.
Washington, D.C. 20015

*Neiman-Marcus*
(415) 329-3300

400 Stanford Shopping Center
Palo Alto, California 94304

*Neuman & Bogdonoff*
(212) 861-0303

1385 Third Avenue
New York, New York 10021

*Oppenheimer*
(415) 563-0444

2050 Divisadero Street
San Francisco, California 94115

*Ouisie's Table*
(713) 528-2264

1708 Sunset Boulevard
Houston, Texas 77005

| | |
|---|---|
| *The Pantry*<br>(203) 868-0258 | Washington Depot, Connecticut 06794 |
| *Pasta & Co.*<br>(206) 523-8594 | 2640 University Village Mall<br>Seattle, Washington 98105 |
| *Pasta & Company*<br>(804) 428-6700 | 3004 Pacific Avenue<br>Virginia Beach, Virginia 23451 |
| *Pasta Natale*<br>(215) 592-4640 | Reading Terminal Market<br>12th and Arch Streets<br>Philadelphia, Pennsylvania 19107 |
| *Pasta Presto*<br>(816) 756-2000 | #2 Westport Square<br>Kansas City, Missouri 64111 |
| *Petak's*<br>(212) 722-7711 | 1244 Madison Avenue<br>New York, New York 10128 |
| *Le Petit Chef*<br>(612) 926-9331 | 5932 Excelsior Boulevard<br>Minneapolis, Minnesota 55416 |
| *Piret's*<br>(619) 297-2993 | 902 West Washington Street<br>San Diego, California 92103 |
| *Poole's Fish Market*<br>(617) 645-2282 | Menemsha, Massachusetts 02535 |
| *Poulet*<br>(415) 845-5932 | 1685 Shattuck Avenue<br>Berkeley, California 94709 |
| *Provender*<br>(401) 624-8084 | 3883 Main Road<br>Tiverton, Rhode Island 02878 |
| *Que Sera Sarah*<br>(617) 228-1394 | 12 Federal Street<br>Nantucket, Massachusetts 02554 |
| *Rebecca's*<br>(617) 742-9510 | 21 Charles Street<br>Boston, Massachusetts 02114 |
| *Rex's*<br>(206) 624-5738 | 1930 Pike Place<br>Seattle, Washington 98101 |
| *Ribbons*<br>(206) 272-3868 | 1702 Broadway<br>Tacoma, Washington 98402 |
| *Rudi's*<br>(617) 536-8882 | 279 Newbury Street<br>Boston, Massachusetts 02116 |
| *Ryan's*<br>(415) 621-6131 | 4230 18th Street<br>San Francisco, California 94114 |
| *Sammy's Tenth Street<br>Market*<br>(216) 523-1094 | 1400 West 10th Street<br>Cleveland, Ohio 44113 |
| *Sarabeth's Kitchen*<br>(212) 496-6280 | 423 Amsterdam Avenue<br>New York, New York 10024 |
| *Savoir Fare*<br>(617) 627-9864 | Post Office Square<br>Edgartown, Massachusetts 02539 |

| | |
|---|---|
| *Sheer's Simply Delicious*<br>(404) 233-3313 | 3349 Piedmont Road, N.E.<br>Atlanta, Georgia 30305 |
| *Si Bon*<br>(813) 472-3888 | 2244 Periwinkle Way<br>Sanibel, Florida 33957 |
| *The Silver Palate*<br>(212) 799-6340 | 274 Columbus Avenue<br>New York, New York 10023 |
| *Soigne*<br>(617) 627-8489 | Upper Main Street<br>Edgartown, Massachusetts 02539 |
| *Someplace Special*<br>(703) 448-0800 | 1445 Chain Bridge Road<br>McLean, Virginia 22101 |
| *The Spice Corner*<br>(215) 925-1660 | 904 South 9th Street<br>Philadelphia, Pennsylvania 19147 |
| *Suzanne's*<br>(202) 483-4633 | 1735 Connecticut Avenue, N.W.<br>Washington, D.C. 20036 |
| *Take Me Home*<br>(202) 298-6818 | 3213 O Street, N.W.<br>Washington, D.C. 20007 |
| *Taste Unlimited*<br>(804) 625-2098 | 212 East Main Street<br>Norfolk, Virginia 23510 |
| *TooJay's of Palm Beach*<br>(312) 831-1800 | 195 Skokie Valley Road<br>Highland Park, Illinois 60035 |
| *Truffles*<br>(617) 639-1104 | 114 Washington Street<br>Marblehead, Massachusetts 01945 |
| *Val's*<br>(813) 446-6926 | 1736 Drew Street<br>Clearwater, Florida 33515 |
| *Vivande Porta Via*<br>(415) 346-4430 | 2125 Fillmore Street<br>San Francisco, California 94115 |
| *Vivian's Kitchen*<br>(201) 654-6996 | 108 Prospect Street<br>Westfield, New Jersey 07090 |
| *The Watergate Chefs*<br>(202) 298-4444 | 2554 Virginia Avenue, N.W.<br>Washington, D.C. 20037 |
| *Wickford Gourmet Foods*<br>(401) 295-8190 | 21 West Main Street<br>Wickford, Rhode Island 02852 |
| *The Winery*<br>(505) 988-2984 | 202 Galisteo at Water<br>Santa Fe, New Mexico 87501 |
| *Wolferman's Good Things*<br>*to Eat*<br>(913) 432-7130 | 2820 West 53rd Street<br>Fairway, Kansas 66205 |
| *Word of Mouth*<br>(212) 734-9483 | 1012 Lexington Avenue<br>New York, New York 10021 |
| *Zabar's*<br>(212) 787-2000 | 2245 Broadway<br>New York, New York 10024 |

The Shops and Their Addresses

# INDEX